Hey Pup, Fetch It Up!

Hey Pup, Fetch It Up!

The Complete Retriever Training Book

Bill Tarrant

Line drawings by Lou Schifferl

STACKPOLE
BOOKS

Portions of the introduction, plus chapters 4, 5, 13, and 18, first appeared in slightly different form in *Field & Stream,* copyright © 1974, 1975, 1976, 1977, 1979 by CBS Publications, the Consumer Publishing Division of CBS, Inc. Reprinted by permission of the publisher.

Portions of chapter 20 first appeared in slightly different form in *Pure-Bred Dogs, American Kennel Gazette,* copyright © 1977 by the American Kennel Club, Inc. Reprinted by permission of the publisher.

Published by
STACKPOLE BOOKS
5067 Ritter Road
Mechanicsburg, PA 17055

All photographs by the author unless otherwise credited
Line drawings by Lou Shifferl

Printed in the United States of America

10 9 8 7 6 5

Also by Bill Tarrant
Best Way to Train Your Gun Dog
Bill Tarrant's Gun Dog Book: A Treasury of Happy Tails
Problem Gun Dogs
Tarrant Trains Gun Dogs
Training the Hunting Retriever: The New Approach

Library of Congress Cataloging-in-Publication Data

Tarrant, Bill.
   Hey pup, fetch it up! : the complete retriever training book /
Bill Tarrant.
     p.   cm.
   Originally published: Honolulu : Sun Trails Pub., © 1979.
   Includes index.
   ISBN 0-8117-0799-7 : $19.95 ($26.95 Can.)
   1. Retrievers—Training.   I. Title.
[SF429.R4T37   1993]
636.7'52—dc20
                                                         92-39590
                                                              CIP

This book is dedicated to

Margaret Blanche Tarrant and William Walter Tarrant

CONTENTS

Preface

In 1979, I wrote in the first printing of this book, "Just because man no longer understands his place in the universe don't assume all God's creatures have become equally confused and trivial."

I was, of course, speaking of the common sense of dogs. The validity of this statement for humans becomes more apparent to me each passing day.

In 1989, a news report caught my eye that said the National Park Service at the El Tovar Hotel on the lip of the Grand Canyon had just placed mice on the protected species list. Mice, along with deer, elk, bear, and mountain lion, can't be killed there—which means a job may open one day at the El Tovar for a game warden to arrest poaching cats.

Not to be outdone, the city of Tucson, Arizona, stepped into the ridiculous in June 1992. Now get this. A lady has a pond on her property. And the frogs live there to dip and play and croak! Well, you won't believe this, but neighbors called the police and reported the lady because her frogs were "disturbing the peace." And now the punch line: the police wrote the lady a summons.

Now this. In July 1992, it was reported that Denverites wanted prairie dogs humanely removed from their holes. Seems the pope was coming to Colorado to speak, and the planners proposed using a field infested with these earth-destroying vermin. I know nothing more territorial than a prairie dog. Can you imagine all of them vacuumed together in a barrel or whatever? You talk about a melee.

Now the reason I mention all this is quite evident. Modern man has lost his mind. But not in this book. This book keeps faith with nature and good reason and humanity. Also, this was the first retriever book written solely for the hunter—not the field trialer—and it brought about, then, the concept of the hunting retriever clubs in America, where dogs would not be asked to trip over their own instincts to pass some mechanical field trial test. Instead, they would be tested only on how well they did the very thing God planned for them: hunt.

Another important development since this book was first published was the creation of the National Bird Dog Museum and Field Trial Hall of Fame in Grand Junction, Tennessee. You'll note on page 488 that we had all met in Oklahoma City in those days to produce this reality, but it came to pass elsewhere. And this was essentially because of the efforts of my good friends Wilson Dunn and Gary Lockee.

Also, it has been John McAssey (see page 41) who interested the association of retriever clubs in the Hall of Fame. They are now forwarding money to build their own wing.

So here's to you and Pup—a guy (or gal) with a dog who both know what God really had in mind when He put you on earth. Something that's a far cry from what too many modern men, who are now divorced from nature, think today.

Bill Tarrant
September 1992

Introduction

W. C. Fields said, "I never met a drink I didn't like." Will Rogers said the same thing about men. I say the same thing about dogs. The way I feel, God proved His love of man when He gave him the dog.

I've been spun around by my fellow man, forsaken by loved ones, used and discarded by friends. Man has a way of playing a game called, "You play ball with me and I'll ram the bat up your nose." I've never met a dog similarly disposed.

I've walked cross-country in deep snow late at night and had the company of a dog I didn't ask to come along.

I've sat alone in a sad house and cursed my fortune while the dog curled at my feet had a faith in tomorrow I could not find.

I've been hours late getting out a dog's feed pan and never heard a complaint.

I've yelled in rage to clear a room of man and beast only to see a few minutes later one black nose and two bright eyes poke around the doorjamb to sense the spell of the room. I but shifted in my chair and the rascal was in my lap. The men who cleared the room? They may never come back.

I've picked up dogs with broken bones and taken them to a vet. No pain could make the dog cry out to his benefactor.

Milk-drips on the kitchen floor.

I've seen children calmed at night with a dog on their pillow. There could be no better pacifier, no finer protector. I might sleep through whatever befell the child, or shy from an intruder. The dog would do neither.

I've seen dogs break ice to retrieve a duck, stand on point with a thorn in a pad, go down a 70 per cent grade to head a sheep, chase a car cross-town to be part of a family outing, sniff out a warehouse while a policeman crouched outside with drawn pistol, lick a sick man's feet, kiss a crying child's cheek, stare beseechingly at a mother's worried face, raise an arm of a dead-tired man who'd worked too hard to make ends meet.

I've seen men bury their dogs and not be able to stand up to leave the grave. And I've seldom known a man to mention a dog's parting.

Milk-Drips on the Kitchen Floor

A while back most of us read in the newspaper about a woman who died and left $14 million to her 150 dogs.

I can hear em now. "That's stupid," the disgruntled said. "Lots of people could have put that money to good use." And likely among that group of worthy recipients would be—themselves.

But I ask the critics of this woman's will to consider this:

Remember that time you came by a pup? All the doubts? Puddles on the carpet. Gnawed shoelaces. Milk-drips on the kitchen floor. But for reasons of your own the pup moved in.

And how did he come through the door?

Did he say, "Hi," so you could understand? I mean, was he fluent in the American language? Did he come bearing gifts? It's always good to see those types. Did he represent a social coup? Had he done things? Been places? No?

Well, if he didn't have any of these things going for him then surely he was pedigreed. They're worth money, you know. Oh, you say you gave $2 for him at the dog pound. Well, was he pretty to look at, then? "No, kind of rangy," you say, "and wobble-kneed and pinched nosed." Well then was he strong or fearless? Could he do some work, help protect the place? What's that? "How strong and fearless can a pup be at ten weeks?" I see your point.

Then let's face it. That pup came into your home absolutely worthless and a total foreigner. I ask you, how many of those types you taken in lately?

And when this improbable guest got through the door, what did he do? I see. He puddled on the carpet, gnawed shoestrings, dripped milk.

So you threw him out, right?

Nope, wrong.

Why was this?

Well, when that pup came through the door he had three things going for him: a wagging tail; a rough, wet tongue; and an eagerness to say hello to everyone in sight.

It was like just meeting you made his day. He quivered with excitement. Rolled over in submission. Nuzzled up so's the warmth of his body came soothing to your heart through the skin of your ankle. So you picked him up. That's the way with love. It's contagious.

And you stood there holding this pup close to your cheek, smelling that last-night's-ice-cream-carton-smell of him, your fingers sunken into his soft belly, woven through his silken fur, when across your face goes that rough, wet tongue.

Your fingers sunken into his soft belly.

What you had in your hands was absolute, non-diluted, ever-growing, non-demanding, can't live-without-you, take-me-wherever-you-go, hurry-back-if-you've-got-to-leave love.

And I ask you this question:

Who do you have in mind, like this, to leave your money to?

And I Do Not Walk Alone

But, most of us outlive our dogs, God giving them about 12 years and us close to 70. So it's the dog who leaves a legacy to us, not the other way around.

How many of us go in memory now where in step we went before: toe-to-tail to freedom's call, the call of gentle wildness, us out walking with our dog?

Whenever I think this way, I always remember Rene. I trailed that dog so many years to so many places. We hunted, sure. But we did so much more. We once looked down a hand-mortared flintstone well together. My voice drummed about in there and Rene tilted his head,

4

cocked his ears. As men are but boys grown tall, Rene was always a puppy.

We poked about in old barns, scurrying rats, making feral cats skitter, spooking great horned owls to wing.

Remember the time I thought I shot him? The flushed bird was skimming the grass, but far enough ahead when I fired. I didn't notice the great gash across Rene's chest till later. God, the shock when I did. I dropped the gun, the bird, and both my knees. Sweeping Rene up I raced to the pickup and into a strange town to a strange vet.

The man lectured me while he sewed up the dog. Guilty, I endured the rebuke about a city man—but I lived on a farm—shooting his dog. Then I noticed, there were two strange vertical rips in the skin, one above the other. That's it! Rene hit the barbwire fence abandoned in the tall grass. Why I stumbled over it.

I told the vet to go to hell, paid him, picked up my sewed-up dog, and cried with joy all the way home. But then I had to drive back to the field—to get my gun and bird.

Remember? Remember when the dog played ball with me and the boy? I'd pitch, the boy would hit, the dog would field and fetch the ball to the pitcher's mound and I'd race to first base to tag the boy.

We had to stop that game. Rene turned pro. He started playing so close to the batter's box to get a jump on the ball I was afraid he'd get hit with the bat.

And then the day the boy, the dog, and I were walking out back by the dam. A great bull snake was sunning himself on the concrete shelf. Startled by our arrival, the snake fell into the pond. This dog Rene—Wasatch Renegade, sire of two field champions—was a Labrador retriever, and things that splashed were things to fetch. Off the dam Rene leaped, grasping the great snake, making for shore, the snake wrapping itself around and around Rene's neck, biting his right cheek. A bite, incidentally, containing no poison and amounting to no consequence.

Rapidly I started walking toward the house. The boy sprinting to stay beside me. Huffingly he asked, "Why are we going so fast, daddy? Why, daddy?"

I told the lad, "I've got to go to the toilet."

Inside the house, after flushing a stool I never used, I stood at the kitchen window, looking out at the Lab holding the great bull snake, and lectured the lad, strongly, saying, "Don't ever be afraid of snakes, son."

5

Rene loved kids, farm ponds, and anyone who'd throw anything for him to fetch.

But Rene with the laughing eyes, and his way of walking on his hind legs to better look me square in the face, and the ever-waving flag of his tail, and the low gutteral whine he'd make when he was trying to tell me something—Rene died. And then I carried him the last time. Carried him and buried him. Mixed prairie grass grows on his grave so no one can recognize the place. But I do.

I go in memory now where in step I went before. They are strong, sure steps.

And I do not walk alone.

All men who are dog men walk a similar trail. The butter-ball pup angling off to one side, or the seasoned field worker hired on for the gun, or the gimpy, stoved-up senior canine citizen who can't hear, can't see, can't run—they all walk to side one time or another in a dog man's life.

The memory companions are set down front and back, absent in presence but not in mind. They are so often the reason the dog man chooses this spot in the marsh for his blind, or goes out of his way in the field to check that thicket, or makes sure to probe around the hole

The butter-ball pup angling off to one side.

Pepe hunted his entire life, and on occasion would win you a field trial.

For seven years Pepe and the author never missed a morning in the duck blind — a record he treasures above all others.

Scoop is a big, bold dog who handles water like a landing barge and land like a Caterpillar tractor.

by the cottonwood out back. Some dog, some time, showed the dog man this is where the action is, this is where we harvest.

So, Rene trails with me evermore. And other dogs will join him. Can you imagine the string I'll put down when I'm old? But I know one thing— The string can be no match for yours. We're all like that about our dogs—and our memories.

If a Dog Owned Me

A new memory coming for me will be named Pepe. He's an old dog, Pepe. Peppy no longer is he.

For reasons of sentiment I take Pepe with me to the fields—though I must dally a lot to wait him out. Pepe walks at heel, reluctant to strike out and sniff.

In man years Pepe—AFC Renegade Pepe—is 105. He's arthritic with eyes pop-bottle opaque. Pepe wheezes a lot as he locomotes, grunts when he scratches. If Walter Brennan had been a dog, I think he'd have been a lot like Pepe.

Scoop the master harvester!

Pepe's young kennel mate is a dog named Scoop. Scooper he is. Taking long draws on the wind, casting himself in big loops, scooping up all feather that's idling in grass clump or thicket.

Scoop moves like John Wayne did when John was younger—or Robert Mitchum. Like his hips were double-jointed. It's a swagger of competence. Scoop is 42.

I've learned a lot about life from Scoop and Pepe. Pepe likes to hold up and lounge under a tree, thinking long deep thoughts.

Scoop has no patience for that. "Let's activate, not meditate," says he. "What's over the next hill, or in the gully by the dump, or the plum thicket by the pond?"

But I remember when Pepe, too, was a seeker. No idler under trees, then. Off and running he was. As a hunting companion and a field champion—the only work he knew—he was one of the best. I'll never forget the trial he won at Colorado Springs. The water blind was planted behind three beaver dams, each one a little higher and sharper and meaner than the one before. Pepe lined that blind. And it was all run at an angle to the world.

Scoop coveted ducks even when hanging from game bag.

So, what if I'd forsaken Pepe in his old age? Let's say I decreed since Pepe could no longer work, he no longer had value. I could have put Pepe to sleep. Or if I kept him on I could have been exasperating. Yelling things like, "Can't you do nothing to earn your keep?" Or I could have given Pepe to some farmer who wanted a dog to ride in the bed of his pickup.

BUT I REMEMBERED WHAT A DOG WOULD HAVE DONE IF HE'D OWNED ME AND I MET MY OBLIGATIONS

I said, "Pepe, old boy, you taught me love and tolerance and humility. Taught me all those things God said man should have but only dogs do."

Yes, that's what I said, said it to a dog. Said it to so many, now. For I've been doggy since I was a pup. Wild dog, tame dog, big dog, small dog, tough dog, soft dog, lap dog, bold dog, shy dog, herd dog, guard dog, bird dog, sled dog, sick dog, bright dog—they've all entered my life to take me on as a hand. And I've not always learned well.

But if you think I'm without wit, you ought to see some people I've met.

13

Two paths crossed in the woods and we, we took the one that was hard to see.

West Slope Realists

I could have anticipated the comments overheard on the trail the other day when one of my Labs and I—each with back packs—climbed up, over, and down the Continental Divide.

I've lived close to this dog for five years. I can honestly say I've never seen him happier. He fairly laughed on that trail. The pack? He didn't even know he had it on, except when his saddlebags got wedged in the rocks where the trail narrowed and I had to grapple him through.

But the ding-a-ling comments of passersby were: "Isn't that too heavy for that dog? Aren't those straps choking him? What's the matter, can't you carry the gear yourself? What'd you give him, the heavy stuff? Boy, I'll bet he'll be glad to get out of that."

Now, these were comments from day hikers, summer strollers, those who mince-footed up the gradual, smooth-worn east slope of Pawnee Pass, some 30 miles northwest of Boulder, Colorado.

Dropping over the divide and coming down a steep grade. Leaving behind the forest foreigners. The comments changed to, "That's really great. Where could I get a dog-pack like that? He's really having fun, isn't he? Do you think I could train my dog to do that?''

The west slope climbers were people who knew enough to hazard the grade, who desired to escape the human condition, who sensed the natural order of the universe—that man and beast alike were both put here to work.

It was these west slope realists who petted the dog, instead of scolding the master. It was they who invited the dog to share their jerky and freeze dried dinners. Incidentally, never once did the do-gooders on the east slope reach out to console the dog. They just gave lip service, not a helping hand.

Modern man, you bewilder me.

You bewilder me when you don't know the nature of things. Like the ad we've all seen, a rubber suit for retrievers. Can you believe it! So the water dog *won't get wet* if it's raining.

How's the dog going to fetch the ducks? Walk on water?

Just because man no longer understands his place in the universe, don't let him assume all God's creatures have become equally confused and trivial.

In this book we won't.

1/The Nature Of Things

Most everyone thinks they can train a dog. Like it was some God-given reflex. Same as eating, excreting, or blowing your nose. Well, it ain't so. Matter of fact, the only men or women I've ever met who could train a dog were those first trained by dogs.

My Okie trail and training buddy, Delmar Smith, the guy with the snoose manner, ticky-tack grammar, and dung-boot etiquette, my candidate for PhD—professor of hunting dog—says, "To train like a pro, you've got to think like a dog."

Delmar's right. To train a dog you've got to know more than the dog. Few humans do.

Why? Because we've divorced ourselves from the nature of things. Some 98 per cent of all Americans live on 2 per cent of the land. We live in cities. What's natural is out past the sewage disposal plant.

Consider! A bear is capable of taking a clean bite out of a walnut rifle stock. Capable of bending a .300 magnum Weatherby rifle barrel into a V. And yet, people have their kids handing bears cookies for the camera. Only thing about these people that's natural is they're naturally dumb.

It's hard to be an outdoorsman anymore. We have out-of-car-doors-men, out-of-hi-rise-doors-men, out-of-cabin-cruiser-doors-men, out-of-Beech-Bonanza-doors-men. But we don't have many outdoorsmen. We're just not outdoors.

And if we don't know nature, how we gonna know nature's residents: the animals?

To modern man an animal is a foreign language. Yet, you can read em like a book. Take a dog— If you've got one in a stress situation, trying to teach him something, let's say. He'll not take the lesson till he gives in. And how does a dog tell you he's given in? Well, his shoulder and leg muscles will relax, but you may miss seeing this. So watch for a swallow. For a dog to swallow is for a dog to sigh.

Sigh? Yes. What do you do when you resign yourself to your fate? That's right, you sigh. Every animal does. Take a horse. He sighs by smacking his lips while wetting them with his tongue. You just gotta know how to read em. And that's hard to learn living 50 stories up in concrete and steel.

Now you can force a dog to do something before he's accepted you—or what you want him to do—and this dog will grudge you, fight you, be a resentful worker. Or you can read him, see when he's ready to take the lesson, get done what you want, and have a happy worker.

Sure, there's lots you've got to learn. But there's something else more important than gaining dog knowledge. That's your dog attitude. So you can't go to Pup knowing it all. But you can at least go to him admitting just this! You're dumb. Pup's dumb. Start together. Respect each other. Take it easy. Have some fun. And that's what this book is all about.

Now, I'm the writer and you're the reader not cause I think I'm smarter than you, but because I admitted long ago I was dumber than you think you are. Lord, was I dumber than I thought I was. And everyone was calling a dog a dumb animal. Yet, I was finding dogs smart. The more I learned about dogs the smarter they got. And the only dumb animal I was dealing with—was me.

I want to save you all that. I want to get you started right. Not only to train your dog, but to know how to use him after you've got him trained. Now, many training books you read aren't going to do either: they're taking the dog afield with misguided notions, not proven fact. Why is this? Maybe they're written by men who still think they're smart?

The best dog training book I ever read was written by Tom Fairfax, an Englishman, in 1689. That's 300 years ago. And I've always wondered, if Tom had all that smart then, what's happened to it, now?

Here, I'll show you—

Outsmarting Ourselves

WHY SHOULD MODERN MAN SAY A DOG OUTSIDE A DUCK BLIND SPOOKS DUCKS? Can't you hear em now? "Get that dog down. Throw grass over that dog. My God, can't you get that dog out of the water?" All this whining when Tom Baker, the decoyman of Nacton, England, tells me he's lured 200,000 ducks to market, from 1919 to 1967, by *promenading a dog outside a duck blind*. Then he produces the estate ledgers to prove it. Now I like this, for opinions die but records live.

WHY DO SOME MEN SWEAR YOU CAN'T HUNT A FIELD TRIAL DOG?

River Oaks Corky, the only retriever to achieve 506½ combined open and amateur field trial points; Buddwing, the winningest red setter ever; Sandringham Sidney, the Queen's yellow Lab, the only retriever to ever win the game fair three times; Pacolet Cheyenne Sam, the Brittany who won all the nationals, both afield and on the bench—all these champions were mighty good meat dogs that stood for a barrage of harvest guns.

D. L. Walters perches black Lab before blind. Why not? See chapter 19.

It was the last hunt for Corky and Flannery. Author wrote it up and Field & Stream *called it, "The Sun Also Sets."*

WHY IN AMERICA DO WE USE GIMMICKS AND WEIRD TOOLS AND INSTRUMENTS OF TORTURE TO TRAIN A DOG WHEN DOGS ARE BROUGHT ALONG IN GREAT BRITAIN—AND IN AMERICA BY TRAINERS WHO KNOW WHAT THEY'RE DOING—WITH LITTLE MORE THAN AN OCCASIONAL CHUGGING OR A GLARE?

I've seen dogs shot with guns, somersaulted in water while a handler held the button on an electric collar transmitter, be drug across a pond with a cable tied to a Jeep, have their front leg broken by a man trying to teach force retrieve, be whipped with a BB loaded whip, be used to drive cattle to market then abandoned in the town, be run down with horses, be told to sit and then had their back leg ground into concrete by the heel of a boot. The atrocities I've seen committed in the name of dog training, in the name of dog handling, in the name of dog caring.

Such people should train gorillas. And let the gorillas be equally motivated and equally armed.

The pinch collar: chapter 9 tells you how to use it.

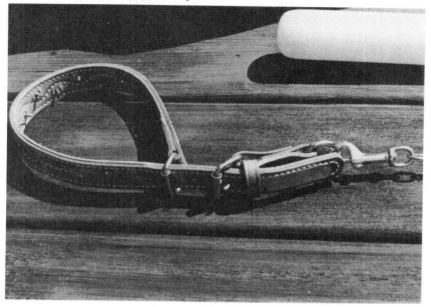

Bill Meldrum wins 1st place ribbon at game fair wearing Jayhawk insignia that adorns dust jacket of this book. Author gave Bill the lapel pin, Bill gave ribbon to author.

WHY AMONG OUR TRAINING GADGETS DO WE CHOOSE SOME THAT ARE FLAT INJURIOUS—YET CLAIM THEY AREN'T? Like the choke collar. Want a dog that can sound like he has throat cancer? Then use it. Yet, the pinch collar, which may be the most humane and most effective training collar ever perfected, is considered barbarous by Americans and actually outlawed by the English kennel club.

WHY, ALL OVER THE WORLD, HAS FIELD TRIALING SEEMINGLY DIVORCED ITSELF FROM EACH RESPECTIVE KENNEL CLUB'S STATED PURPOSE FOR A FIELD TRIAL'S EXISTENCE?

Look at your rule book. The Standard Procedure for Non-Slip Retriever Trials states, *"The purpose of a Non-Slip Retriever trial is to determine the relative merits of Retrievers in the field. Retriever field trials should, therefore, simulate as nearly as possible the conditions met in an ordinary day's shoot."*

An ordinary day's shoot!

When we get more into this in later pages you'll see why I submit, if men shot like this, and trained dogs to hunt like this, they'd both be on food stamps.

Think not?

Then tell me, why in America do we cast a dog on a blind when there's been no shot fired? If we haven't shot anything, what's out there for the dog to retrieve? We want some duck left over from the day before?

When on a day's shoot would we force a retriever down a channel blind? Would we not walk the bank, get beside the downed bird, then cast our dog to fetch?

WHY HAVE STEWARDS OF FIELD TRIALS AROUND THE WORLD SEEMINGLY CONDONED A GAME THAT DESTROYS THE NATURAL INSTINCTS NEEDED IN A GUN DOG FOR A DAY'S HUNT?

The sole and express purpose of field trials is to improve the breed. Through the process of selection and elimination to create a better dog than we had before. Yet, field trials today are altering the conformation of gun dogs even more than any bench fanciest ever thought of undertaking.

Think not? What about a Lab's nose? In America the dog that wins is the dog that marks. I mean, button-hooks the bird. The dog sees the

Michael Paterno casts '71 national amateur champion Dee's Dandy Dude for channel blind with drastic angle water entry at '73 national amateur. Dude won again.

An ordinary day's shoot: a relaxed and treasured thing. This boy and dog are opportunity's nomads, walking a road for dove.

*John Olin, sippin' and talkin' at his
Albany plantation, prompts Lab to
openly wonder, "Anything in that
cup for me?"*

bird down, he doesn't smell it out. What use is the nose?

And on a line, the dog that wins is the one that runs over the planted bird. He doesn't smell his way to the bird, he's cast from the line like a rifle bullet. No sidewinding path, no hunting, no nose.

DO OUR LABS LOOK LIKE ANGUS BULLS ANY MORE? Cobby, great heart girth, heavy shoulder muscles, cape of clumped muscle draped over the neck, broad nosed, broad heads. No.

John Olin, chief of all locks, stocks, and barrels at Winchester Arms tells me at his Nilo kennels, Alton, Illinois, "Bill, these Labs today resemble greyhounds: pinched nosed, thin legged, long eared, spider waisted . . . and that infernal spitz tail arced over their back."

The field trial game made them this way. Dogs that win at the game are sought out to sire the next generation's contenders. It all perpetuates itself. The game demands speed as it's played today, not stamina. Judges like to see gravel thrown from the line, water left in a whitecapped V.

But on a day's hunt? The hunter needs a dog that paces itself. A dog capable of staying afield, and working afield, all day. No brilliant bursts, instead, a long sustained pull.

Nearly 40 years ago the great Chesapeake retriever, Dilwyne Montauk Pilot, was cast into Great South Bay for a shot duck. The duck proved a cripple: it swam to sea.

Pilot followed till the sight of him disappeared. This was during a field trial; the judges went to a land series. Still later, they came back to water to test the remaining dogs.

In the middle of this third series here comes Pilot, swimming back through the new water test, a mallard drake stuffed in his mouth.

The judges threw Pilot out of the trial and the gallery told the judges they'd not leave with their lives if the trial weren't stopped, right then and there, and Pilot given first place. Pilot won the trial.

Pilot was bred for stamina, not speed. The field trial game was in its infancy. Pilot was as different from the average retriever of today as an arctic tern who migrates 20,000 miles a year is from a Gambel's quail who may never fly more than 200 yards a launch.

Scoop's hyped-up to leave sizzle trail once the casting hand slices upwards.
Like a rifle bullet he'll pierce whatever stands in his way.

There's tons of knowledge gained by studying trainers of other breeds...

Another thing—

WHY DO SO FEW RETRIEVER TRAINERS AVAIL THEMSELVES OF THE AMAZING TECHNIQUES EMPLOYED BY BIRD DOG TRAINERS? Or continental gun dog trainers. Or more to the point, sheep dog trainers? Since it was the shepherd who gave us the whistle and hand signal.

But there's another point to be made. Why do so many sheep dog trainers, continental gun dog trainers, and bird dog trainers know so little about retriever training techniques?

If we knew what the other guy was doing we'd shake off a lot of ignorance and get a new insight, as well as a new challenge.

For example, why do we assume a retriever can only hear a whistle, say, 300 yards, when at Chatsworth Park, England, at the International Sheep Dog Trial, I saw border collies answer the whistle, before a loud 10,000 spectator gallery, in a high wind, in excess of 800 yards.

Spending a week outside Hallbankgate, England, at Tarn House, the home of English shepherd Ray MacPherson—the man who won the world sheep dog championship twice in a row—it came to pass one day Ray had to whistle a dog down on a high ridge. Ray peeped his

. . . whether seeking sheep, quail, or duck: all these men can teach us something.

27

whistle, I don't mean blast, and the dog stopped like he'd been shot through the brain. How far away was the dog? One mile.

Yet the gripes we've all fielded while judging retriever trials when the dog is 100 yards out and he's turned off his handler and the handler is charging, "He can't hear. The gallery is too loud. Those kids are yelling. A motorcycle must be over the hill. That jet is drowning out my whistle." Ho Hum.

I've been with Bill Meldrum when he handled the Queen's dogs at the British Game Fair before 35,000 spectators. The noise level on that field was about the same as inside a diesel power plant. Not one British handler griped about the noise. Not one dog failed to hear a whistle.

WHY CAN'T MODERN MAN UNDERSTAND HE USUALLY GETS THE BEST PERFORMANCE FROM A GUN DOG THAT'S ALSO A HOUSE PET? Why must it be assumed a gun dog performs better if he lives the life of a San Quentin convict?

My puzzlement goes on and on. But I conclude with this reality, with one answer to all these questions—we are tunnel blind. We know

Ray MacPherson cast a dog to the mountain rim
above this house one day to gather a pod of sheep. Distance? One mile.
The dog answered all whistles.

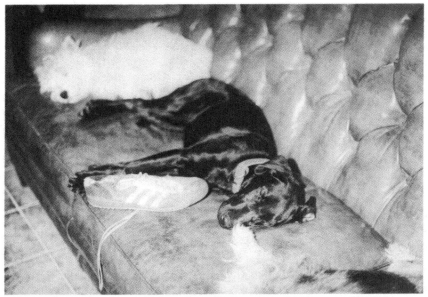

A happy home is where all dogs share living room, kitchen, and holidays.

little of what's happening in other nations, and we know less of what's happening with other breeds.

One staggering revelation to me is this. In all my travels to many of the recognized gun dog nations of the world—26 of em so far—and with the hundreds of top trainers I've gone to field with, I've only met two men who made up champions in more than one breed.

A multi-national, multi-breed approach will broaden our horizons in retriever training.

And if you think I'm too critical— Well, the basis of this book is positive, not negative. From now on we don't deal with what's wrong but what's right.

We can do a better job of training our retrievers than we have until now.

And we can use our retrievers in the field more fully, and more wisely, than heretofore.

But let's say we don't. Let's say we go on just like we are going. No matter. Whatever the game may be this book will tell you how to train your dog to win it.

A cocker fetches missed blue rock. A German shorthair pointer learns to follow a blood trail. Two coon dogs say, "Let's get goin." Welshman Talbot Radcliffe, English springer spaniel breeder whose dogs have won many American nationals, casts a pup from a rock dam. President of Germany's griffon club, Franz Kroninger, points to sign which declares, "Swimming forbidden." All these dogs and all these people can teach you something about training retrievers.

Her T-shirt says, "The More I Know Men . . . The Better I Like My Dog!" Little wonder, since God gave dogs all those virtues He said man should have.

The Duchess of Devonshire presents team shield at international sheep dog trial while flop-eared mutt looks on. This is that rare event at a field trial where a person has papers and the dog doesn't.

I summed up how I feel in a cameo I did for *Field & Stream* when I wrote, ''Should the day come when the modern retriever is tested on how well he dodges turnpike traffic to arrive at a grocery and fetch up a dressed turkey from a deep freeze, dibby up at the cashier, and make it home to deliver to hand—I'll be training and vying to get my dog there and back to win.''

In other words, should the world divorce itself totally from nature, should all field trial grounds be layered with concrete, should all game birds be driven from the earth by agribusiness, still, by reading and following the principles in this book you can win whatever game remains. You can harvest whatever bird's left out there to grace your table.

But more important you can have the friendship of a dog: a gift God made for his love of man.

2/If You Were a Pup Would You Pick You?

There was hill fog when we left Kilsyth but it burned off in route and we followed the hip-high lane that sides the mountain moors to corkscrew down and through and on past the village of Comrie with its kilt museum and surrounding hills of obelisk war monuments.

We've got a good Lab down, name is Ben, and we've been moving partridge in a beet field for two hours. Ron Montgomery, secretary of the Labrador Club of Scotland, brings Ben to heel, motions me to a stand of hawthorn, pulls a thermos from his kit bag, pours tea.

We hunker down and sip, watching sheep graze and wood pigeons flap past. There's nothing like a day afield, it makes me feel like gold.

A half-mile to the south is a highway. A great line of cars move both ways. Then we hear the whine of a British motorcycle—and Ron starts laughing. Ron is a serious man. I say, "Funny huh?" showing surprise in my voice.

The man's eyes dance. They are dark, if not black. And like a black Lab's coat they only glisten when wet, or light hits em just right. Now they dance. He says, "It's a joke ... about motorcycles." He points to the road.

"Well, let's hear it."

"You want a joke?" he asks. "I thought you only wanted to talk about birds and books and dogs."

"A lot of books are dogs," I tell him, "others are for the birds. Let's hear the joke."

"Well," he begins, "there were these two men riding piggy-back ... in the highlands of Scotland ... on a motorcycle.

"Eventually they got cold so they decided to take off their jackets, put them on backwards, and zip each other up. That way the cold air couldn't enter the cloth strip down each side of the zipper."

I nod, remembering bass fishing in Kansas in March. Cold air can enter a zipper in a high wind.

"All went well," Ron says, "and they were carrying on when they hit a bumpy road in a wee village. The driver didn't notice at first ... but he blooming well bounced his rider off.

"Turning back to trace his trail, he came upon a small crowd gathered in the street. Leaping from his cycle he ran forward, asking, 'Is that my friend. Is he alright?'

"And one of the villagers told him, 'Well I can't tell now. A queer thing you know? When we first got here the lad was sitting up, just laughing and carrying on ... but since we turned his head round right he seems to have taken a turn for the worse.'"

Got Your Head On Straight?

I know a prince of a man who loves to hunt. But the guy's an elitist, a little bit antiseptic. He has a duck blind with a sidehouse built for his retriever. There the dog sits all during the shoot—never sent to fetch.

Why?

Two reasons I've been told: one, the dog may shake water on the hunters, and two, the wind will blow all the ducks to one bank of the little pond, anyway, and they can be picked up when the shoot is over.

THE GUY'S GOT HIS HEAD ON BACKWARDS, WHAT VALUE THE RETRIEVER?

I know another man who's All-American. Know what that means? In order to do anything the average American's got to have a machine.

This man has machines to skim him on top the duck marsh, plow him through it, roll him beside it, take him to and from it. He has a duck plucker that hurls feathers like an explosion in a mattress factory.

And his dog? Well there's no machine to train it, so it's not trained. Matter of fact, I've never known it to be taken to a duck blind—or anywhere else.

THE GUY'S GOT HIS HEAD ON BACKWARDS, WHAT VALUE THE RETRIEVER?

Sometimes coming from town I see a camper full of out-of-truck-doors-men heading down the interstate, poker cards on the flop-down

Ben retrieves red leg partridge . . .

. . . then waits for wood pigeon decoy set to be spread.

Jim Culbertson with sons Rocky and Wade: the family that trains together stays together —and makes mighty happy mutts.

table, Old Stump Remover at elbow—heading for the pheasant fields. It's opening weekend and this will be the only hunt for this crew—and their dog—this year.

THESE GUYS HAVE GOT THEIR HEADS ON BACKWARDS, WHAT VALUE THE RETRIEVER?

Jim Culbertson, Wichita, Kansas, high school coach and former junior college All-American football guard, takes his field trial Labs to run traplines, root out quail, walk up prairie chicken, play Frizbee, ride to the grocery, pull the kid's sled, jump on the trampoline, den rabbits, loan to a teenager who's got personal problems for the therapy of love, chase coons, serve as team mascot—

And yet, Jim's never had a dog break at a field trial. But I've seen his dogs leap from the boat at the click of the safety. Jim Culbertson makes great Labs, happy Labs. JIM'S GOT HIS HEAD ON STRAIGHT, HE LIVES WITH HIS DOGS.

John McAssey, Boise, Idaho, does the same. John's one of two men in America to judge over 100 AKC retriever trials and he's presently secretary of the Labrador retriever club.

John likes to tell you about Mainliner Mike. This Lab was one of the greats, one of the early double headers. A double header is a dog that wins both an open and an amateur back-to-back at a licensed retriever trial on the same weekend.

Know what Mac and Mike did during the summer? Went trout fishing. Mac would fish with barbless hooks, get a trout to rise and bite, then tell Mike, who's been waiting on the bank, "Fetch it up." Mike was the most novel dip net since the invention of aluminum tubing. YES, MAC HAS HIS HEAD ON STRAIGHT. HE LIVES WITH HIS DOGS.

Dick Cook, the miniature wildfowl carver of Stingray Point, Virginia, takes his field trial champion Lab out on Chesapeake Bay for clam digging. No, the dog doesn't dive for clams, he eats em.

Joe Wooster, world premier decoy carver, takes his Lab for spring glassing of the northern flights near Ashley, Ohio. Joe wants to get those nuptial colors right on his wood counterfeits.

JIM, MAC, DICK, AND JOE HAVE THEIR HEADS ON STRAIGHT. THEY LIVE WITH THEIR DOGS.

If it's not your intent to live with yours then don't take one on. Pups and dogs demand total commitment. And that's what they give back.

Pups are like a bucket; you can only pour out what you've poured in. If you've not got the need nor inclination to pour a lot of time and thought and effort into Pup then let him pass. Otherwise, I can predict, you'll just end up kicking the bucket.

Looking Up From the Pup's Viewpoint

Before you adopt a pup you need seven things: 1) the right temperament, 2) sufficient time, 3) a place in your house Pup can call his own, 4) a private yard, 5) a car to get Pup about, 6) some old clothes for yourself, and 7) a stretch of country to let Pup out.

Temperament

When picking a pup the average guy wonders, "Does this one have the stuff? Will he do a good job for me?" These are good questions to ask yourself. If you were a pup would you pick you?

What's your nature? Are you easy going, reserved, quiet, reflective, slow to anger, soft voiced, methodical, patient, sweet dispositioned, in other words, good natured? If so, Pup picks you. If not—

Say you just landed on a strange planet. In other words, you're just like Pup coming through your front door for the first time.

Now you're walking through the place and there's alternating black and white squares. You haven't noticed but you've been stepping on the white ones. Oops! You just stepped on a black one.

Into and down the hall comes an 18-foot monster (that's about how much bigger than you, you are bigger than Pup) all frothing at the mouth, eyes bulged, face purple, arms flailing, voice booming like a howitzer. And this monster grabs you and swings you in the air where he cracks you across the butt with his open palm and dangling you by the scruff of your neck races you to a door and throws you into a yard.

Now, as a pup, do you ever hope to see this guy again? How long will it be before you trust him? What's that? You say you're too busy trying to dig out of this yard to talk to me now?

Well, before you dig out, tell me this. What did you do wrong back there? Oh, you say you don't know. Well, welcome to the world of the pup in the house of a madman.

Now, you remain the pup, and let's enter the house again. Only this time when you step on a black square a man appears who walks forward slowly—the man's smiling—he kneels down, coos to you, picks you up, rubs you, holds you in the hollow of his neck, saying, "Oh what a great pup you are, what a grand fellow, what a clever dog you'll be some day."

Joe Wooster casts Happy through timber tangle for downed wood duck.

Dick Cook offers Lab one more clam.

The guy or gal with easy manner can bring a pup along ...

Happy lad entertains litter.

Talbot Radcliffe takes a break to feed exotic birds.

New York Yankee, Jim "Catfish" Hunter,
holds paw of red setter.

Author's wife cuddles coyote pup.

You want to see this guy again? You say you never want to leave?

But are you wondering? I know I am. What's this thing about black squares—and this guy not caring? Either it makes no difference to him, or lessons in black squares can wait, or maybe, he's put some kind of black square on the floor that just doesn't matter.

Hey Pup, Welcome Home

If you're worried about the carpet or the sofa or the doo-dads, and you turn purple and scream and run like you had the scours everytime Pup walks through, or stands up, or squats down, you don't have a house for Pup, you have a minefield.

All that pick, pick, pick, will wear Pup spiritless. And one maniacal act will destroy him forever. That's right. One heavy hand is identical to one atom bomb. You will destroy the enemy but there'll be nothing left to conquer. One hand, or one bomb, will do it.

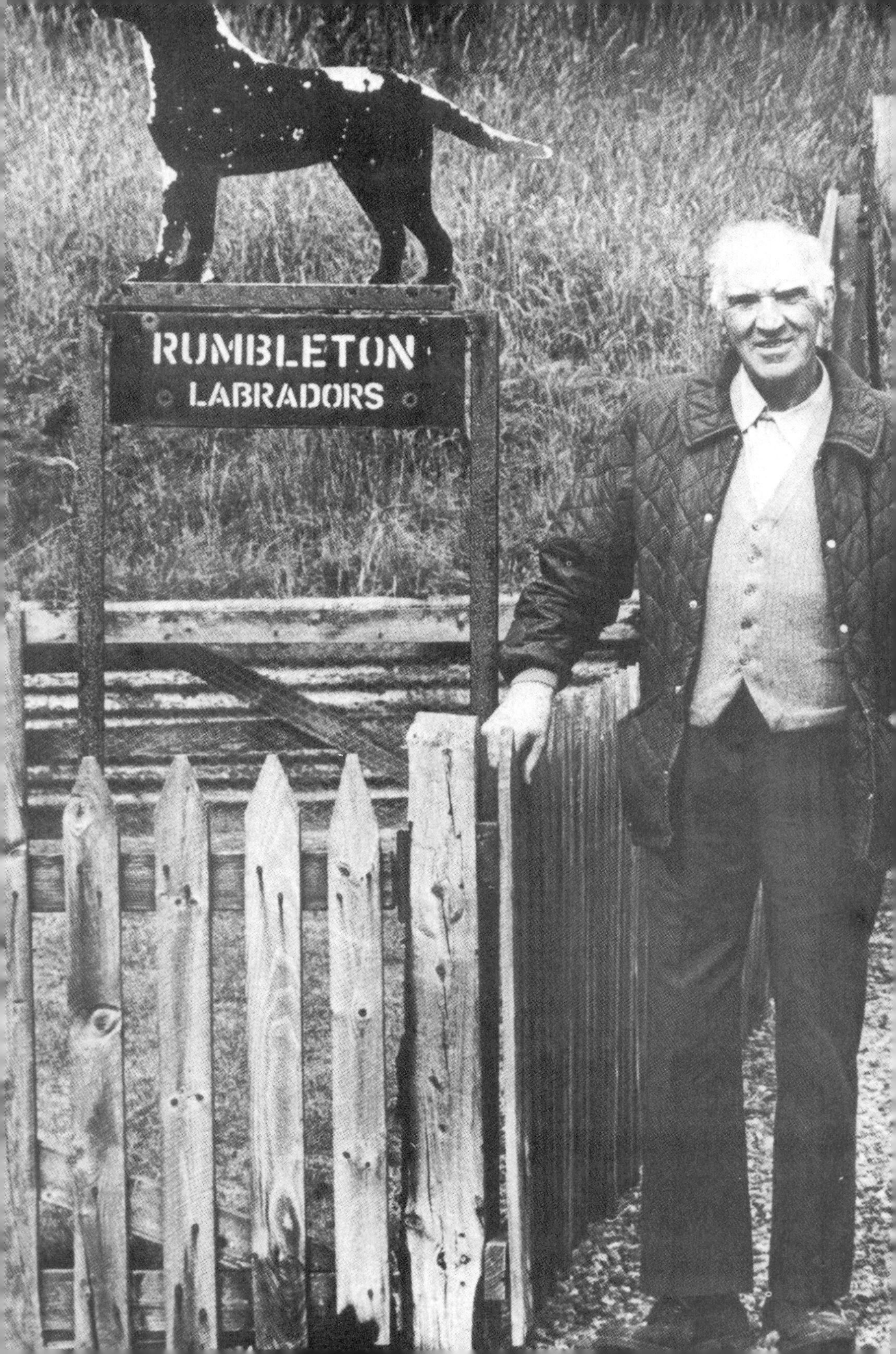
RUMBLETON
LABRADORS

So with your temperament right, let's get your house in order.

Pick a room for Pup that has no carpet. Something that's hard wood, or linoleum, or tile. Now if a buddy misses the spittoon or a pup doesn't get you to the back door in time—you can mop it all up. It makes for good friends, and good gun dog prospects.

Whatever's adangle, store it. Whatever's breakable, put it away. Whatever's chewable, move it to another room. Pup-proof the place, remove all temptations, all attractions that will cause Pup to displease you. Pup will hear, "No," too often in his life: reserve your, "No," to bring him along, not to protect your property. Build a room where seldom a discouraging word is heard.

Why? Because this is the most important place, at the most important time, in Pup's whole life. Here's where Pup learns every nuance of your voice, your facial expressions, your body movements—every quirk in the beast that is you, the man—and you learn the same about Pup.

This is where you deal with Pup in whisper. Read that sentence again. Alright I will. **THIS IS WHERE YOU DEAL WITH PUP IN WHISPER.** That, pardner, is the most important sentence in this book. For we're going to train Pup by voice. We're going to work with a small jeweler's hammer when everyone else, for the most part, uses an 8-pound sledge.

When we lower our hammer we drive Pup into the ground, maybe one inch. The other guy? One drop of the sledge and he drives Pup flat to earth. Consequently this trainer has no reserve. The voice having been used up, he must resort to a whip, a boot toe, a rock—to make an impression.

Us, we can raise our voice one notch and drive Pup down a little further. But just as important, we change that voice and we pump Pup up. By living with Pup we can string him along with our voice just like he was a yo-yo. Shoot him out, put him down, pick him up, toss him high, make him hum, make him go.

No way can this be done with us sunk in the overstuffed and Pup out back in a kennel. In training Pup there is no substitute for constant contact.

Cricket selects toy to chew and heads for private spot.

Dogs like something over them; makes 'em feel safe.

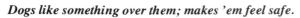

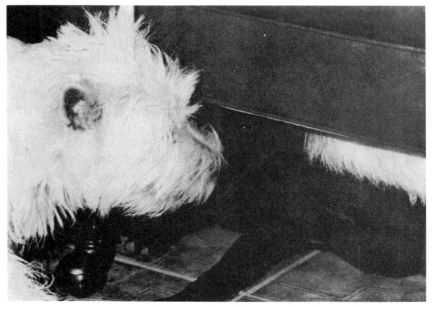

Tug, the terrier, decides to try Cricket's tennis shoe and sweeps it from toy chair.

Mike Espile, a Basque shepherd whose family owns a 100-year operation in sheep and land, took me along one day while he was loading ewes for market at Litchfield Park, Arizona. The bitch he used was 10 months old, a mongrel, a gift pup. What this gal could do was unbelievable. She loaded sheep, sure, but while doing so I noticed she knew sheep, she knew corrals, she knew trucks, she knew Mike, she knew the other shepherds, and she had a vocabulary of something like 50 words.

I asked Mike, "How on earth did you train her so young?"

"I'm no dog trainer," he answered, laughing, "I just take her everywhere I go in the back of the pickup."

Jack Knox, the Scottish sheep dog trainer living near Montello, Wisconsin, winner of both the Canadian and American nationals this year, says, "It's in the house the basic training starts. The dog comes to you because maybe you give him affection. He stays because you brag on him."

Jack adds, "If you start to force a thing into a pup he'll always resent it. But if it goes in freely and he's wanting it to happen then it's just part of his life."

49

And Jack concludes, "In Scotland I'd take a pup to the hills with me each day and he'd learn by doing. He'd learn naturally. But in America there's not that much work to do. Here, the trainer has to make work to train the dog, so using the house is part of making up for so little work about."

Jack's right. If your days were spent afield, the dog always at side, he'd learn everything in the natural unfolding of your mutual pursuits. But you can't take Pup to the plant, to the office, to the store. We live in a world set apart from nature and we must innovate to train a pup.

That's why we can't hazard the chance of putting Pup in a backyard kennel. Too much chance he'll be forgotten out there. Yet, he must be kept there during the day, and possibly during the night. It's just up to you to spring him when you get home and bring him into the house.

For dog training starts just like the Bible: In the beginning there was the word and the word was good.

And as Christ said, "My father prepares a house for you."

You prepare one for Pup. One conducive to puppyhood and training. Not one filled with mystery and taboo. A house designed to protect and showcase Pup, not your belongings.

The Kennel Blind Pup

Every time your life touches Pup you're teaching him something. Also, everything else that touches Pup is teaching him, too. It can be disastrous, absolutely disastrous, when a kennel run is the teacher, or the alley, or even the fields. Pup left alone out there can learn things you would never teach.

I've kept and trained as many as 32 personal dogs at one time— that's right, in those days none of the pups entered the house. I've had pups go from the umbilical cord to the grave that never set foot inside my door. Around the old place they were second class boarders, and I might add, second class gun dogs.

I still use my kennel, but it's for specific purposes and always of short duration. I'll tell you why:

Years ago I began noticing strange things developing in a kennel run—and all bad—so I decided to experiment. I was raising coyotes at the time. Was there anything a wild dog could teach us about training?

I purposely kept one litter of coyote pups for four months just like they'd been sentenced to solitary. There was no kind word, nor helping

Pups love their crates: will hang around 'em even when loose.

Jack Knox asks Craig, twice American and once Canadian national champion, to pen sheep.

hand, nor friendship nor sympathy nor love nor Sunday visitors nor yard privileges. That's right, never once were they out of the kennel. Never once did their paws touch grass or dirt.

All these coyote pups knew was a straight 24 foot run of concrete, two side and two end panels, one water bucket, one gravity flow feeder, and a dog house.

The day of the experiment arrived. I threw open the kennel gate and let em bolt. Bolt? They froze in the back. I had to walk in and shoo em out.

I'll never forget what happened. Each of them went tail over chin when they hit a terrace that crossed the hill half-way between the kennel and the creek. When they hit a second terrace, they flipped again.

Hard to imagine isn't it, what a momma coyote and a bunch of litter mates can teach a coyote pup out in the wild in four months. Coyotes make the most adaptable wild dogs in America today. Yet, divorced from the true nature of real life, these pups couldn't even handle a mound of dirt.

Days later I met one of these little guys on the road heading north from the farm. This road had a shallow ditch on each side, and each ditch was clogged with five-foot high weeds.

The pup saw my car and started running straight up the road. Now think of this. He could see straight ahead for a half-mile. He knew the car was gaining on him. Plus, he'd been living in the wild for three weeks so he knew there was an open plowed field to each side of those weed stands.

Yet, FOR THE LIFE OF HIM, he couldn't, or wouldn't, leap sideways and crash through that heavy weed cover.

Here, the most adaptable wild dog in dogdom couldn't cope, couldn't adapt.

In field trial terms I'd developed a lining coyote. A coyote so conditioned to running straight in a kennel run he couldn't leap sideways even if his life depended on it.

When the pup reached the railroad tracks and there was daylight, he whipped to the right and started running a straight line down the tracks.

I stopped the car and tried to grasp what I'd seen, sat there and thought and watched the coyote maintain a line alongside the steel rails. I'd proven again what we all know: deprivation, isolation, neglect, destroys pups.

But more than that. I've been leary of kennels ever since.

Bonnie and her brood.

And if you think I learned something else, forget it. I can just hear the cogs in your head, "He developed a lining coyote." Sure, the coyote would line, but what good would it do? He wouldn't break cover, he wouldn't quarter to hunt, and he couldn't use his head—even to save his life.

Got the Time?

Remember the tune, "I can't give you anything but love, baby?" Well, Pup needs that, but he needs more, too. He needs time.

There's few men whose lives don't grant them time to train a pup, bring him along, humanize him, sensitize him, and turn him into a gun dog.

The bare minimum required is, say five minutes in the morning to toss a dummy, rub Pup's ears, scratch his belly, and freshen his water.

When you get home from work at night, toss the dummy again.

After supper, take Pup out for five minutes of yard training.

Just before going to bed at night, have another go with the dummy.

That's 20 minutes, split into four segments, and that's more than ample to start a pup.

Five minutes at a time is ample for early puppy training. Here Pup is loved, molded into sit position, and cast for sock.

Pups let to their own druthers will fetch. Here a one-year-old brings in box turtle while tyke fetches stick.

But that's only one kind of time. That's the time a pilot, for example, is actually taking off or landing the plane. What about all the cruise time?

While reading your paper you can dangle an arm and scratch Pup's ears. Put a bare foot on him while you're having your supper—sure he's under the table! Take time during TV commercials to get a tidbit and tell Pup, "Sit." When he's complied, give him the reward, tell him, "Good Boy," and go back to the tube.

Snatch-a-minute-training is great for several reasons.

One, Pup has a very short attention span. Five minutes is more than ample for training sessions until Pup is six months old.

Two, let's hope the trainer doesn't get frustrated in five minutes.

Three, Pup's not going to be a stellar performer every time out. If he's off his game, put him away.

Four, training different times of day gives Pup a different look at the dummy. The shadows change. The earth dries up. The wind starts to blow. But at night— That's when you and Pup can have fun. You stand in the light and toss the dummy into the dark. Launching into the black unknown will help Pup build confidence. He'll also learn he has a nose. And without making an issue of it, you've started Pup on blind retrieves. Admittedly he's going for something he may have seen thrown, but he sure never saw it fall.

Five, retrievers are working dogs, the instinct being bred into them just as sure as God put spots on brown trout. Training sessions are work-substitutes. Sure, we know they're play sessions. But to Pup's mind, work is play.

If you can't find work for a working dog then don't put him on relief in your back yard. An idle dog that's bred for work is nervous misery. Such a dog eats metal buckets, he eats his own feces, he chews down the dog house, he fence fights, he digs great holes, he sulks and gives you mean looks, he runs a half-mile straight out of a kennel gate when finally released just for the sheer joy of feeling a muscle move.

He dives in lakes in search of sticks to fetch. He brings you dead toads, box turtles, hedge balls, cattle dung, tree limbs, anything, just to be doing what God put him on earth to do.

Have a heart. Take a Pup to fetch. Turn time on your hands, or time on your rear end, into a gun dog.

" . . . a small yard outside your back door . . . " makes this Brit fetching happy.

To shovel it up is part of the deal.

58

A Piece of Land Pup Can Call His Own

You can't do Pup justice without a parcel of land outside your back door. Private land. Your land. Whenever you train a pup you can't have any distractions. A public park won't work. One, Pup can't concentrate there, not with kids squealing and sandwiches spread on the ground and joggers who apparently need chasing. Two, you have neither the time nor the inclination nor the patience to both train Pup and explain to some city-type that you're not mistreating the animal.

However, a public park is great for exercising Pup on lead. Just today I was putting the dogs away after walking a park when a guy came past, asking, "Did you get the wiggles out of em?" And I felt warm and good and my faith in urban man renewed. The guy was being friendly and Lo and Behold, he made sense. That's exactly what I did: I took the wiggles out of em.

Having a small yard outside your back door gives Pup, one, a place to upchuck or stool on a moment's notice; two, a kindergarten where he'll learn to heel, sit, stay, and fetch; three, a playground where he can chase sparrows, bury bones, tear up an old tennis shoe; and four, a sanctuary where he can sit alone and think.

You don't need a lot of space. Just 20 × 75 feet is ample for starting Pup on single retrieves.

Now mind you, this yard must be Pup-proofed the same as your house. No need putting Pup someplace it's inevitable he'll be yelled at. If you've got exotic plants out there you don't want eaten or drug out by the roots or tinkled on or rolled in—then move em.

This yard is also Pup's toilet. If you can't grant him that, and you handle the shovel, then forget about taking on Pup.

Also, if you don't want to rake up chewed leaves, or bits of garden hose, or blankets that have been drug from the dog house and ripped to pieces, then do Pup a favor. Never bring him home.

And one more thing. This yard is where Pup barks. His kingdom. His territory. He's king of the mountain and will permit no encroachment. There are ways we can keep the noise down, but not the feeling of territoriality. Pup may want to put the meter man on the roof. Be prepared.

Wheels

If you own some velvet upholstered gobble-up-8 then forget about Pup. What Pup needs is transportation fit for a dog. An old pickup with the paint faded off and the fenders knocked in, where the wind

" . . . *transportation fit for a dog* . . . "

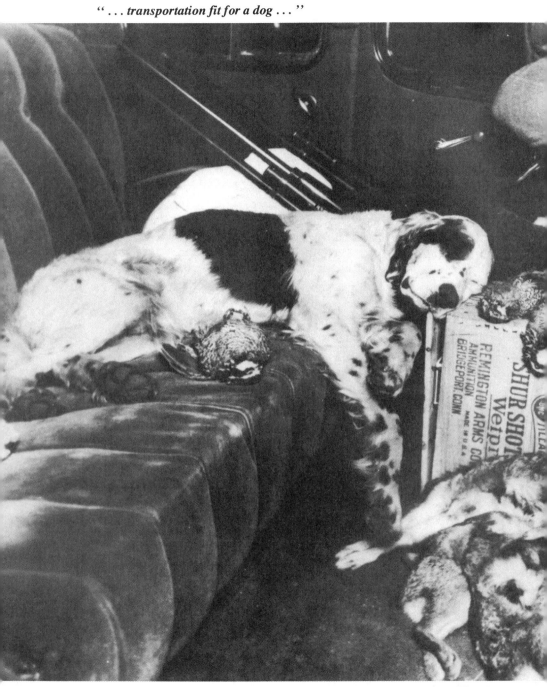

Jeans and patches make proper duds for dog training.

whips about the cab and tickles Pup's nose. Or an old station wagon with the ceiling ripped out and the floor mat splotched with mud leavings. For this rig takes you and Pup training. And your mind's on Pup, not wheels.

Once again, you want to keep Pup in a fussless environment. When Pup gets to be a dog things can be different. You can kennel him on the floorboards of your Mercedes and take him to the bank. But while Pup's a baby he requires a world where you never have to say, "No."

Dudes Aren't Trainers

Same with your clothing. Pups can't tell the difference between your tattered canvas field pants and your green Tux with the beaver cuffs and leopard lapels. Yet, how many times I've seen hunters encourage their gun dogs to leap up for a pat of love or encouragement only to go into the motel, change into their 'see-me-duds', then knock Pup's head off because he leaps to greet when he's taken from the car to dump.

Either train Pup never to leap or leave him stashed while you're gussied up.

"The good earth," makes for good pups, ...

Two pups lead each other to water.

The Good Earth

You can't shoot guns in the city limits and Pup's a gun dog. You must find Pup some country. He needs a place where he can meet and learn to manage varmints, ditches, ice, puddles, sticks, toads, stink birds, gulleys, cactus, bluffs, logs, sandburs, butterflies, skunks, hedge balls, fallen apples, cows, box turtles— Pup must learn the territory. He must assure himself there's nothing out there that's going to hurt him. Plus, he must learn to handle land and water.

You can have a lot of fun, a lot of memorable moments for both yourself and Pup, in the parlor or out the door in your back yard. But in the country is where Pup will have the time of his life. Especially if he's got another pup, or pups, to lead him on. That's the ideal. Pup'll break cover because he's being pulled on by one of his own kind, not because he's being pushed by you. He'll take to water to be part of the gang, not to be launched alone and fearful into the dark and unknown.

This is where it helps to join a dog club, where you can go with

A litter of Brits takes their first field walk.

Three Lab pups claim right to a gunnysack.

Brit pauses to leap for butterflies.

Five Labs and a Brit churn water for a stick, . . .

... then run it all off.

others of like interest and animals of similar capability to romper-room in the day. But one word of caution. You're there for training dogs, not politics. It's easy to get them confused. Just ask yourself this question, what's being proposed? Does it further the breed or improve the lot of the dog? If not, then stay out of the discussion. Most dog club arguments are not about dogs.

Or not being close to a dog club you can gather up the neighbor's pups. Note, I didn't say dogs. Dogs can intimidate and overlord. Make it pups. Or make it kids. Your neighborhood kids come right next to pups as the best thing to be following that pup of yours. Or leading him.

Pup will need this free reign to knock holes in the skyline for nearly a year. No instructions, just hide and go seek, touch and go, bump and run, jerking the socks off butterflies, diving for clam shells, chasing a squirrel up a tree, leaping to catch a meadow lark, limping back to you with a thorn in a pad, running sideways upon meeting a horse, finally dropping the fish skeleton he's carried a half-mile waiting for you to take.

Should you have only one dog, and no country, you can still train in the city. Here, Bob Feffer and his Lab, Babe, invade a swanky country club — no, he didn't seek permission — tooting his whistle while paying customer tries to putt; . . .

... and tosses dummy into a borrow pit.

And I'll grant you this— Maybe a year's too long. But for other pups, not long enough. You know your charge. And you're in charge. Do as you see fit.

So these are the imperatives, the seven musts: temperament, time, yard, country, clothes, car, and a place in your home Pup can call his own. You got these? Then go get your pup. Telling you how to pick him comes up next.

3/That Special Pup

Each December a bunch of the boys hole up at Delmar's diggins for a week. Down by Oklahoma City. And we take in every go-round of the National Finals Rodeo and chew Levi Garrett and leave rally stripes down the sides of our pickups and stop for nachos and enchiladas on the way home every night and train dogs every day, or go horse lookin.

There's Dan Opie who propped up his ranch on the east Oregon desert, foaled a stud, produced five world champion halter mares out of him, then sold Sir Quincy Dan for a half-million.

B. J. Pierce is there. He was '52, '53, and '55 world class calf roper. Got a farm now, and a ranch, and a ropin arena, and serves as a school principal.

Plus, there's Orren Mixer, world's greatest quarter horse painter. No, he don't paint horses. He paints pictures of horses.

And Delmar with his 10 national gun dog championships—

It's a big trophy group.

Yet to see these guys all sittin there, soppin up runny eggs and white gravy with their biscuits—a morning ritual at the Holiday Inn out north on the highway—you'd think, "There's a crew that's seen hard times . . . and their outlook don't look no better."

It'd be a natural notion. We go by what we see, or what we think we see, or what we're told we see. Notions-in-our-heads, that's what it is. And such notions can be dead wrong, especially when it comes to pickin a pup.

Your retriever can be any breed of dog...

German wirehair pointer slurps duck from pond, German shorthair pointer retrieves battered mallard, weimeraner winds her way through tules, Australian shepherd keeps stick away from Lab pup...

The Retriever

This pup we're pickin for you. It doesn't have to be a recognized retriever, you know? That is, a breed designated by AKC for retriever field trial competition. There are six of these. Chesapeake Bay, curly-coat, flat-coat, golden, Labrador, and Irish water spaniel.

Your retriever can be any breed of dog. They all retrieve. How else do you suppose their ancestors toted dinner home, moved their young from nest to nest, or carried those bones they buried for a gameless day?

If you fancy a Gordon setter, let's say—that's the dog you always wanted—then go ahead and get him. Whatever notion you have in your head, we'll teach to fetch.

The only drawback to taking a Gordon, or Brittany, or English setter, or cocker spaniel, or German short hair, or any of the other pointing or flushing dogs to a duck blind is they just don't have the coat nor the constitution for cold water.

That's not to say they won't try. They'll give it their teeth-chattering best. But like a carp, their best will come in warm water. The good

retrievers are like a grayling or a trout. Throw in a block of ice and they start to cavort.

I've made retrievers of such unlikely candidates as Australian cattle dogs, border collies, peekapoos, west highland white terriers, great Pyrenees, coonhounds, boxers, Manchester terriers, St. Bernards, miniature schnauzers, fox hounds, bulldogs, and many a mutt. Some of them were hard mouthed, others were gun shy, and all of them didn't love cold water, but they retrieved game.

Most dogs still have some hunt left in them. And there's fetch left in them all. Maybe for nothing more than your house slippers, but that's fetching.

You'll hear talk, "Well if you want a dog that can find you game, you shoot it, and they fetch it up ... then get a springer." Or a pointer. Or a setter. Or any of the continental versatile hunting dogs.

Others will tell you, "Now if you're a duck and pheasant hunter; you can decoy a duck, or walk up a pheasant. You don't need a dog for that. What you need is a dog to find and bring you the bird once you've shot it."

Always the assumption is a retriever either won't hunt, or shouldn't be permitted to. They're called non-slip retrievers. That means you don't slip the collar from their neck till you send them to fetch.

Yet, I've seldom had a Lab that wouldn't do it all. Pepe would point. Thunder would bring so many live quail to hand I had to quit taking him. Who wants a limit of bobwhite and he's never popped a cap?

Rene and Scoop would tell me where the bird was and when it was coming up by the cock of their ears, the angle of their neck, the set of their haunches, and the action of their tail.

Happy, a Lab sent to me by Bill Meldrum, the Queen's trainer, was the best rabbit dog I've ever owned.

God didn't make retriever specialists: man did. The dog God sent hunted his meal, stalked it, jumped it, caught it, and ate it.

No ancestor of any Lab ever lived who hunted non-slip. This game of holding a dog back just for a retrieve was contrived by man.

So I let my Labs do it all. That's why I wouldn't own a field trial Lab I couldn't take hunting. And that's why I've owned many a hunting Lab that could never trial. After all, the purpose of a trial is to simulate a day's hunt: not the other way around. The hunt is the thing. That's the ultimate. That's what it's all about.

. . . English setter shares honors with Lab, Welsh springer spaniel proves too much for yellow Lab pup . . .

. . . English springer spaniel gives up chukar, American water spaniel commands bow of boat, English setter heads home . . .

...Griffon awaits reward of love for bringing in mallard, English springer spaniel stands for duck, and border collie races to catch Frizbee.

The Big 6. Chesie pup accompanies Ann Walters to line ...

What's the Breed For Me?

We've come to that part in the book where writers tell you the relative merits of a Lab, a golden, a Chesie, and the rest. They write, "Let's pick the dog for you. What kind of hunting do you do? What disposition do you like in a dog?"

In the real world: that is to say in the duck marsh, the tidal flats, the stagnant swamp, the Canadian prairies, the piney woods of Dixie, the steep slopes of the Rockies, the flooded timber along the Mississippi, the hedge-rows of mid-America, the salt cedar arroyas of mesa country, the timber tangle of New England, the pot holes around the Great Lakes, the hills of live oak in west Texas, and all the rest that's huntin-country-America, any retriever will do.

Sure the Chesie may have been a big sea waterfowl specialist. And the Lab and golden developed in Britain for grouse and partridge. But Chesies will get your pheasant, and the Lab and golden will take to water for any duck you shoot.

The curly-coat, the flat-coat, and the Irish water spaniel were the foundation stock for the Lab and golden. They combined to build a

... Lab pup rockets from water ...

better product at the turn of this century and haven't really been heard from since.

Therefore, retrieverdom involves the Big-3 and each of them has become all purpose, all country, all handler, all bird and all dog.

So pick a pup from the Big-3 like you picked your spouse: whatever turns you on. Just grab hold one and go.

Not So Fast There Buddy

"But just a minute," you say. And I answer, "What's the matter?" And you challenge, "What of disposition? These dogs all have different temperaments."

"As a breed?" I pipe. "Yes," you insist. And here we go again.

I don't know how long it'll be with us. This prejudice we have about retrievers. The assumption Labs are tractable, goldens are soft, and Chesies are hard-headed as whales. We're aware of the advice given by some writers to train Labs with a whip, goldens with a willow stick, and Chesies with a two-by-four.

The fact is: dogs, not breeds, have dispositions. And to strike a dog with anything is to admit you're the one that's whipped.

There is this— Mean parents can throw mean pups. This has nothing to do with breed. And I've seen spookiness, hard mouth, sulkiness, whining, and piggishness thrown by a sire and dam. It could be the dam teaches these things in the nest. I grant that. But I've seen sires have these faults and they've shown up in the pup—and the sire was never near the nest.

The sire and dam give the pup a predisposition to act. Good or bad. But man can change this. That is, man can change it in a pup. With a dog that can be a different matter.

I've seen cowboys fly out of a corral like quail in a coveybust. Escaping a young mustang that's all hooves and eyeballs. Delmar can enter the corral, walk straight to the horse, look it in the eye, say something to it, offer up his hand for the horse to smell, turn his back to the thing, walk away, and the horse will follow him like a pup. Total time taken? Less than two minutes.

Delmar knows a kicking horse can sire a kicking colt. But he also knows the right handler can take the kick out of the get. He knows the same thing about pups.

So disposition— Believe what you want. Go the traditional breed way if you want. But I'll tell you this. The pup you get is going to act the way you teach it, be he Lab, Chesie, or golden.

And I repeat. I'm talking pup, not dog.

It can be hard, or nigh on impossible, to alter the nature of a dog. A dog is never too old to train, but if he's got something stuck in his head, you may never get it dislodged.

Scoop was an 18-month-old wonder when I bought him. I saw him win a big derby at Kansas City and had to have him. The check was written. The next weekend he won a bigger derby at St. Louis.

But Scoop could never make it as an open dog. He refused to sit anywhere his testicles could get cold or wet. He'd soak em all day swimming in the lake, trying to catch barnswallows that flew under a low door of a derelict boat house where I did my writing. He'd emerge after nine hours with his scrotum shrunk and wrinkled to resemble a brace of prunes. But he'd never lower his butt to touch those jewels on the cold, wet ground. You can't win an open with a dog *standing* at heel.

If you tried to make Scoop sit— He'd go right up your arm like he was eating a roasting ear. Scoop made a fine hunting dog.

... Irish water spaniel poses ...

Facts and Figures

Pure-Bred Dogs American Kennel Gazette is the official publication of the American Kennel Club. It's issued monthly and each volume is a library of data. You can subscribe by writing: 51 Madison Avenue, New York, N. Y., 10010, U.S.A.

By analyzing figures offered by the *Gazette* for the last possible reporting year we learn that among all dogs registered there were 41,275 Labs, 30,263 goldens, 2,906 Chesies, 156 flat-coats, 142 Irishmen, and 45 curly-coats. That's how the nation picked them.

Putting the retrievers up against all breeds registered, the Lab emerges 6th most popular dog in America for that year. The golden is 10th, the Chesie 45th, the flat-coat 104th, the Irishman 106th, and the curly-coat 117th. Total breeds registered: 122. Total number of retrievers, 74,787.

As I assemble this chapter, Jim Crowley, manager, show-field trial plans department, AKC, writes to tell me there were 29,115 starters in 184 licensed trials this past year. While 20 years ago 8,742 dogs started in 100 trials.

80

DOROTHY CARTER

...and all five retrievers settle for this photo which appeared on the first cover of Retriever International. *They are counter-clockwise, starting at 6:00, curly-coat, Chesie, golden, Lab, and flat-coat.*

This means two things: the game has exploded, and its's harder to win. Starters have nearly quadrupled in 20 years, but the number of trials hasn't even doubled.

Turning back to the *Gazette* we discover there has been a decline of 10.2 per cent in individual dog registrations from 1971's high of 1,129,200 to the present total of 1,013,650. On the other hand, since 1971, dogs in competition have climbed from 721,753 to 1,084,689, a 50.3 per cent increase.

These figures include dogs in all sorts of competition: bench, retrieving, pointing, tracking, flushing, obedience, and so forth.

It all adds up to this: the number of dogs in America is dwindling. The quality of those remaining has been, and is being, upgraded. Less but better has become dogdom's reality.

Retriever Field Trial News—voice, conscience, archives, of the retriever world—is a publication issued 10 times each year. Get yours by writing: 4213 So. Howell Avenue, Milwaukee, Wisconsin, 53207, U.S.A.

A review of the *News* tells us there were 9,149 dogs started in 164 open stakes during the last reportable year. An average of 55.8 entries per trial. Twenty years ago there were 92 trials offering an open stake for 2,939 starters. An average of 32 dogs per outing.

Amateur stake data for the last reportable year is: 163 trials, 7,258 starters, and an average of 44.5 dogs per trial. The figures for 20 years ago are: 83, 1,968, 23.7.

Analysis of the *News* reveals there were 44 retrievers elevated to field trial champion during the last reportable year, and 37 in the amateur. Since there were 75,000 retrievers registered during the last reportable period, it would indicate one retriever out of every 1,704 wins an open championship, and one out of every 2,030 ever becomes an amateur champion.

Yet, during the last reportable year there were 9,000 starters in the open and only 7,000 in the amateur. Consequently, the odds for making up one of these 44 open dogs is 205-to-one, based on starters. And for the amateur the percentage drops to 189-to-one.

Within this group of dogs earning an open field trial championship during the year, 40 were Labs, three were goldens, and one was a Chesie. This lot includes 33 males and 11 females.

In the amateur stake there were 34 Labs, two goldens, and one Chesie, divided into 25 males and 12 females.

Totals for both stakes are 74 Labs, five goldens, and two Chesies, among which 58 were males and 23 were females.

Therefore, the chances of making a field champion of a Lab are 15 times better than with a golden, and 37 times better than with a Chesie. And the chances of winning the national open? The last time a golden won was 1951, and a Chesie has never done it. Also, no breed of retriever but the Lab has ever won the national amateur.

In Great Britain the figures run about the same.

The International Gun Dog League held the first retriever trial in history in 1899. It was won by a flat-coat named Painter in a field of six flat-coats, one curly-coat, one Irish water spaniel, two cumbers, and one field spaniel.

The first Lab to compete in the society's trials appeared in 1904, the first golden in 1913. The first retriever championship—for those breeds recognized today, minus the Chesie which is an American dog—was run in January, 1909, and won by the Duchess of Hamilton's Labrador, Dungavel Phoebe.

There are 40 recognized field trial clubs in Great Britain, today, that

British game fair where bird boy casts decoy to water then retrieves across retriever's path as dog's cast for duck. Spectators gather about score board which shows results of each test for each dog.

The grass-colored retrievers: golden

conduct trials two months each year. In the last British national open there were 25 dogs qualified, which included 21 Labs and four goldens—eight bitches and 17 dogs.

At the last national open in America there were 67 Labradors, five goldens, and two Chesies qualified to run. The field included 49 males and 25 females. Since the inception of the national open, 33 Labs and four goldens have won it. No Chesie has ever garnered silver. Among the winners, 30 were males and seven were females.

But Liars Can Figure
and Figures Can Lie

Therefore, based on field trial data, the evidence overwhelmingly indicates the dog most likely to win the game is a male Lab. And since the game is supposed to simulate a day's hunt in the field, that's what you should pick to take hunting.

But there are other considerations.

Some people just prefer the looks of a golden or a Chesie. Then there's tradition: what's been favored in your part of the country? And what of color? Most people want a black Lab, saying a yellow one represents negative pigmentation. And they say this like it's bad! I don't know. In England the yellows seem the most popular. And they win at trials. In America it's the other way around.

Chesapeake

yellow Lab

Some hunters want a yellow Lab or a golden or a Chesie for they insist, "These dogs are less likely to spook ducks at a blind. They're already camouflaged the color of grass." But I've said before, regardless of coat color, all dogs attract ducks. And none repel them. The proof is in chapter 19.

Other hunters want a black Lab for upland game. Less chance, they say, of shooting the dog by accident. He can be seen in heavy cover.

Then there's the group that wants a chocolate Lab. Such dogs are rare and scarcity is valued by some people.

There have been dog men reject a Lab with his short coat and featherless legs, saying, he's more subject to kennel callouses on his elbows. The Chesie and golden, they argue, have built-in knee pads; not like the basketball players wear em, but turned around.

But the Lab seems dripless when coming from water and clingfree when coursing upland cover, so others forgive the callouses.

There are those who object to the odor of a Chesie's coat when it's wet. I've never noticed. But then, unlike a retriever, I've never been heralded for my nose. The only dog that really got through to my senses when wet was the great Pyrenees.

A golden's coat, it is argued by some, can catch a lot of debris when the dog's questing for upland game. For those not prone to coat grooming, this is reason enough to reject him.

But for cold water— Through selective breeding the Big-3 have

*FC & AFC Keg of Black Powder, third from left, heels trembling until cast
for group fetch.*

*Of course, some people have their minds made up regarding retrievers and
that's that.*

anti-freeze in their blood and styrofoam in their coat. This is not to say one litter, or one dog, won't be more cold-blooded than another. But retrievers have now been winterized for the job better than any other breed of gun dog.

To own either a Lab, a golden, or a Chesie is a privilege. It's a proud and grateful man who has any one of the Big-3 quest and fetch for his gun.

And I keep thinking, if a dog did the choosing, would he be as harsh and picky with us? The way it is now, any man who picks one is good enough for the dog. He just jumps in the crate and goes.

Other Choices To Be Made

There's hardly a waking moment in a dog's life he can't be diverted by sex. And if he's asleep, he'll wake up.

Yet, a female only comes into season twice a year. And a spayed female — never.

The trouble-free retriever is a spayed female. But she's inclined to put on weight and spayed bitches can sometimes seem moody.

But even that can be preferred by a city dweller who tires of the male forever lifting a leg and throwing sod in departure.

Males are generally more hard headed to train. Females more inclined to please. Males require constant intimidation for they're always trying to test you. Why shouldn't the dog be the leader of this man/dog pack?

A female works for affection. A stroke down her back and some sweet talk will generally keep her bright-eyed and fetching. That's not to say she'll never turn you off. But you can click her back on with a gruff voice and a scowl. She can't stand detachment. She's got to be close and wanted and praised.

There are apartment dwellers who want a small Lab; this usually means a female. Others avoid such dogs for they're handicapped, they say, as field trial contenders. Some just can't see over tall grass.

I've never found this a hardship. All my dogs will leap to see what's going on. And Jim Culbertson's FC & AFC Keg of Black Powder was one of the finest Labs I've ever hunted, ever campaigned, ever known. She could do it all and she couldn't have weighed more than 45 pounds.

Jim and I sent Powder where big dogs would have trouble going:

Hunting rabbits at Balmoral castle, Bill Meldrum cuts off pass with Meddler, the cocker, while his kennel boy drives rabbits with black Lab.

under multiflora rose to root out quail, for example. And yes, Powder had to stand like a praying mantis on line to see the marks down. But with such enthusiasm no judge ever marked her down.

When she was in tall cover she'd leap to get her bearings—leap and hover and look around and her ears would stand straight up—and I never knew her to come back without the bird she was to fetch.

Just last month Bill Meldrum and I were hunting rabbits at Balmoral, Scotland; the Queen's autumn retreat. We had the Queen's cocker, Meddler, and an English springer spaniel, and a Lab down. Meddler did most of the retrieving, and those rabbits were every bit as big as she. Plus, Meddler had to bluff her way to hand with the hare: the big dogs trying to take it from her. Meddler got the job done. Tiny females can do it all.

Eeny, Meeny, Miny, Moe

"Okay," you say, "Enough of this computer business and all this hair splitting . . . how do I pick a pup?"

Functional confirmation: that's what matters. Retriever men want dogs built for work. Look at drastic arch in dog's back as he hits water.

Note Lab protect face by smothering water with slap of legs and paws: holding head high.

And I repeat, "I've already told you, just grab one and go."

But you can't let this stand, asking incredulously, "But which one?"

And I say, "A wise man never picks a pup, he picks a sire and dam. It's the litter you look for, not the pup that's in it."

Look at the parents—not at pedigree, not at papers—but at performance. Only the parents are a known fact. The pups are unknown. Their performance lies in the future. But it may be in the seed.

What do the parents do? Do they hunt for the gun? Every day or just some time. Do either of them compete in trials? How do they do? Will they hit cold water, crash through briar, stay afield all day? Are they birdy? Crazy birdy? Gun shy? Timid?

If you go to see the litter, ask the breeder to show you the dam work. He can't object to this unless she's ill. I saw FC & AFC Nodrog Penny, the great wee bitch of Gordy Olinger, win an open in ice water and suckle her litter between series.

If you know where the sire is located and you can get there, ask to see him run, too. If he's kenneled in Mongolia, have someone you know in that country jump on a camel and go take a look.

If you conclude neither the sire nor dam can do what you want, then why do you think their beget could? Reject them. But if both sire and dam please you don't think their pups will be carbon copies. Dogs don't always throw true.

In this regard you want to know if the sire and dam have been bred before? What did they produce? Were they bred to each other? What came of it?

We've noted before, the national champion is always singled out for volume stud service. But these dogs are not always prepotent. Super Chief and River Oaks Corky were. They competed against their sons and daughters in many a national championship. But I've known other national champions that never produced a contender.

That's why breeding to news clippings won't work. Just because a dog's got the ink on him doesn't mean he's got the seed in him. You must choose a litter from performers. And not just performers in the field: but in producing good babies, as well.

I'm convinced God sends a great dog down whenever the mood strikes him. To be the one who gets God's gift it makes more sense to me to spend my time praying, instead of picking.

Congenital Defects

In analyzing parents we assure ourselves they're both free of hip dysplasia, progressive retinal atrophy, heart worm, and other defects that can be passed on through seed or womb. But there again, we look to parents, not pups.

Just a minute— We must pause here for benefit of the veterinary profession. You must know that hip dysplasia—which oversimplified, is misfitting of the ball and socket joint of the hip and usually accompanied by osteoarthritis of the affected joint—does not follow the rules of simple Mendelian genetics. It is possible for dogs deemed to have dysplasia to not have the genes to pass it on.

It is also possible for a dog with normal hips to pass the genes and the beget suffer dysplasia. Still, I recommend you buy your pup from dysplasia-free parents.

And you must also know—no matter what anyone else tells you—a dam can carry immature heart worms in her muscles through three gestations. That's three pregnancies after she last showed positive.

If the dam is presently a carrier of immature heart worms, these can cross the placenta membrane and infest the pups in the embryo. The mature heartworm will not develop in the pup for nine to 12 months.

Okay, back to picking a pup.

We want the sire and dam to have high toenails so they won't be inclined to strike the ground and break, pronounced bone balconies over the eyes to knock away stubble, heavy hind quarters for launching, a dark iris so they won't gather too much light, a loose skin so it will roll and self-release when snagged, and a heavy tail for a rudder.

We want the sire and dam to carry a high tail. This will assure us of a longer pelvic drive muscle. We also want a deep heart girth so the offspring can have room to breathe when he gets hot—like out for dove. Or when he becomes stressed—like out for a diver that's not shot dead.

We want a big domed head in mom and dad that can hold lots of brains. We also want short ears. Those palm-frond ears muffle out distant whistle and voice commands. We want a tight foot so it won't be inclined to get sore: won't splat when put down, or pick up debris between toes. We want the teeth right, not over- or under-shot. And a nose that knows it all.

And then, we want this set of parents to have a history of tractability and trainability. In other words, they're quick to learn and easy to get along with.

Plus, the parents must have desire, a compulsion to fetch, that matches a salmon's need to spawn. "Come hell or highwater," I once wrote, "let the whole world totter. Have John boats shipped by the water he slipped. Let masts be torn by the gale he'd born. The old Lab was fetching, no matter the wretching."

Let em have that.

Pick of the Litter

If you really want to look silly and waste a lot of your time, and the breeder's time, then go to a kennel, get with a litter and act like most everyone else: clap your hands, roll a ball, toss out a pigeon, dangle a strip of cloth, walk a duck by, clank the dinner pan, sit and see who comes to you, note the one who always stays in the corner, watch the bully that's got all the others down, find the one eyeing the duck pen when all the rest are eating.

How many great Labs were left after all this nonsense was undertaken and finished?

Just off the top of my head I know two that are immortals.

Two immortals: Corky in master's trophy room...

King Buck. He won the national twice. He was the last pup left. All the experts came and made their scientific selection and left King Buck. I mean that's like watching all the kids throw a ball and leaving Jim "Catfish" Hunter.

What about River Oaks Corky? He only won the derby dog of the year, three national amateur championships, and two national Canadian opens, plus he became the highest open point dog of all time.

Corky was the dreg of the litter. Why the breeder couldn't even find a home for him. Like King Buck, Corky wasn't sold till he was three or four months old. Then a woman bought him, sight unseen, as a gift for her husband.

So you want to pick a pup? Then don't pick him. Ask the breeder to do it for you. Call him, tell him you want a male or female, big or small, and have him send it.

But picking the breeder—

Join your local retriever field trial club. Go out and work with the members. See what their dogs are doing. Attend the field trials when the big-leaguers come through. Look at them run. Which one do you like?

... King Buck on open lawn.

Subscribe to *Retriever Field Trial News*. Keep track of who's getting the job done.

Pick a pro. Ask him what he has in his string that's good. What does he have coming up for breeding?

If all this is denied you, then sound out someone who's already hip-high in retrieverdom and ask him to intervene for you. Have him direct you to a litter, close your eyes, stick in your hand, and make your fateful draw.

"But," you ask, "what about the men and women who win all the time? They always have a contender. How do they pick their pups?"

That's a good question and the answer is—they don't.

Big time dogs are made up by some guy, like yourself. And sold to somebody else, like Mr. Moneyfeller. There are exceptions. But mighty few.

The field trial game is a money game and don't you forget it. Many a good dog has been buried by money. Let me explain. Jim Culbertson, as a high school football coach, was offered $1,000 more for Powder than he earned in a whole year.

Jim wouldn't sell his dog. But he couldn't campaign her more than four times a year. Powder may have been the greatest bitch that ever lived. We'll never know. A lack of money buried her.

On the other hand, many dogs have been made by money. Not great dogs, but marginal dogs.

Let's face it, you got time and money to campaign your dog 20 times a year? Can you drive up to 1,000 miles every weekend, pay $100 for a motel, another $50 for gas, $20 a day for meals?

Can you take Thursday and Friday off, every week?

Can you afford $70 each week for entry fees in the amateur and open?

Can you shoot $8 pheasants over your dog before each trial. I mean crates of pheasants, if that's what it takes.

It takes money, big money, to campaign a champion. So the moneyed man usually picks the proven winner, or the young dog that shows he's going to have it all. The moneyed man seldom picks a pup from the nest with hopes of winning the national. Why the odds are 75,000-to-one against him.

That's why finished retrievers have now sold for $30,000. The man who made the purchase knew what he was buying and paid for what he got. He paid to skirt the odds. He did. He won the national.

And just another minute— Let me explain something. The dog game is for the dogs, not for man. What's good for the dog is what matters. What improves the breed. Far as I'm concerned Mr. Moneyfeller gave the $30,000 dog a chance to try. The dog did—and won. It matters not who owned him. Great dogs are owned by everyone. They honor themselves, their breed, and dogdom.

A Tip of the Hat to Mr. Moneyfeller

Should you curse the money-man, you're mighty short-sighted and just a little bit dumb.

Do you think your neighbor's going to put off the kid's dentist, the wife's deep freeze, his new car—to make pup a champ? Not if he knows the odds.

You going to England to look for new blood?

You hiring the pros to develop new training techniques?

You picking up the bill when the field trial club goes into the red? You buying the trophies? You paying your own airfare and hotel meals to chair the national committees?

You putting out maybe $250,000 per dog in land, kennels, help, birds, vets, and all the rest to make a winner that stands at stud for $500?

When you put a pencil to it, I don't care what you pay for a pup, its's a bargain.

And when you win, don't just say, "Old Pard did it all," or "I thank my wife for seeing me through this ... and throwing bumpers," or "Without the help of all the pros this could never have come to pass."

Sure, all you say is true and needs said, but you should add, "And thank God for every man and woman who smokes ready-mades instead of chewing Red Man, drinks from a glass instead of a can, eats fish eggs instead of beans ... for picking up the bill that paid my way here today."

4/The Fit Pup

So you followed my advice, and totally unseen, your pup was picked by a breeder. He arrives at the airport this afternoon. Great! Now what do you do? Throw him a bumper? Buy him a duck of his own?

Nope. First thing, right off the reel, take the pup to a vet. You told the breeder you would do this when you made your purchase. The sale is subject to a clean bill of health; you paying freight both ways.

So, to the clinic you go.

The Four Maladies

He's sitting there. Reared back. Smoking his pipe. Legs crossed so the ankle of one perches on the knee of the other. He has that bright, scrubbed, compact, orderly look of eggs in a crate.

He says, "Bill, people buy pups that get sick and they don't always know it. They don't always know what to look for and the sickness gets worse. It's imperative they check this in the bud ... they must always take a new pup to a vet."

So saying, the vet rests the stem of his pipe on the sole of the suspended K-mart tennis shoe. Then he adds, "They come into my clinic with some real messes ... because they delayed." He shakes his head, saying, "What a shame."

The man speaking is Dr. Dick Royse, premier vet who practices in Wichita, Kansas. A scholar, mind you, who nevertheless speaks in three and four letter words. Doc wants to be understood, not stood in awe.

He's one of a vanishing breed. A vet raised on a farm. A vet who can mix good old horse sense with new college smart. I'll never forget the time he told me one of my field trial Labs had Monday morning sickness. Turned out to be something he remembered seeing in work horses. Worked hard and left to rest on Sunday, the horses were stoved up come Monday. I'd worked this dog hard, and sure enough, he'd rested in the crate during a trial. Doc put his finger on it. He knew. And I've gone with him ever since. Never to find him wrong.

Now his car is parked in my farm drive on a Sunday afternoon and Doc's sitting at my kitchen table—to answer questions you may have about your pup's health.

"It's not always a breeder's fault a pup gets sick," he says. "Matter of fact, a high percentage of ailing pups are really not the result of breeding, nor litter care.

"By their nature, chewing on everything, always curious and poking their noses in everything, having little discrimination in what they eat, and maybe, having a weak resistance that permits disease to find an easy host . . . these are the reasons pups get sick."

Doc's left hand polishes the pipe bowl apple bright. He lets the smoke spill out with his words, "Now Bill, seventy-five per cent of the so-called puppy illnesses . . . seventy-five per cent or more of the sick pups to show up in my clinic . . . have distemper, manges, parasites, and/or diarrhea. So your retriever pup owner should know what these are. What causes em. What to look for in symptoms. What to do about it.

Distemper

"Take distemper . . . this is a viral disease, highly contagious from dog to dog, especially in the young, though no age is necessarily immune.

"It's transmitted by direct contact. But in all probability the transfer is airborne. Distemper is an all-encompassing disease. The pup is simply sick all over. I mean he's not like a pup with tonsillitis, let's say. This pup is sick in every inch of his body.

"What's a typical case? A guy goes out and buys a pup. He's excited about getting this little guy. The pup's cute, he's warm, he cuddles up. The guy sees the pup grown up and the two of them off after birds. The guy forgets to ask about shots.

"Maybe the pup's had em, maybe not. Or, the guy's told the pup's

Dr. Dick Royse has that rare mixture of book knowledge and field smarts. He'd make a brilliant professor but could never take those committee meetings.

had his shots but will need a booster at such a time. The guy takes the pup home and gets busy. He forgets about the booster.

"Alright, the pup's exposed to distemper virus. Maybe a dog down the street has it, a waft of breeze blows virus right into the pup's nose. For about ten days the owner won't know there's anything wrong with his pup, for that's the incubation stage. The pup stays his fat, roly-poly, romping self. Then wham!

"Or let's say the pup didn't get a shot at six weeks when he should have and the guy buys him, takes him to a vet, gets the shot. Could be the pup's already carrying the disease. And the shot won't help. There's not enough time for it to work. There's just no instant immunity to distemper.

"Or distemper can sneak in the back door. Maybe the pup gets a bacterial infection, say tonsillitis, and he's sick. While his resistance is down distemper can make its entree.

"So, first off, with the purchase of any pup ... it's just good insurance ... get a distemper shot if he's not had one, or a booster when it's needed. Now, it so happens some geographical areas see more distemper than others. Your vet will know what's needed for the place you live.

"And keep up with the boosters, even for an old dog. After all, a retriever in the field comes into contact with coyotes, skunks, racoons ... and all can be carriers of distemper virus.

"And yes, contrary to popular belief, distemper can be cured. A rascal to be sure, but cure can sometimes be made. Depends on the stage the vet gets the pup, the pup's natural resistance, and his response to treatment.

"Now there's a lot of confusion about distemper shots. A puppy shot is a serum and it'll last the pup about two-and-a-half weeks. Whereas a permanent shot is a vaccine that can give the dog lifetime immunity, though most vets like to tighten this defense up with an annual booster.

"And what are the symptoms? People will lift their pup up and he'll upchuck. 'Distemper,' they'll say. Hardly. Pups vomit easily, what with their scavenging habits and their voracious eating. A pup'll upchuck like a baby, Bingo!

"What you got to look for is lethargy; runny, pussy eyes; snotty nose; quite often a dry short hacking cough; usually a loss of body weight; a poor appetite or no appetite at all. A very sick pup."

Diarrhea

Doc pulls a Sir Walter Raleigh pouch from his jumpsuit breast pocket and packs the pipe. Midst puffs that bellow the fire on the match he continues, "Diarrhea. This can be very serious." Doc must stop to puff. "If a pup has an irritated gut wall, that gut wall is reacting with inflammation," puff, puff, puff, "and it's thickening, so this interferes with the absorption of food materials into the pup's system, and often, particularly if it is a bacterial type infection, some bacterias release toxins."

The pipe's going now, Doc says around the stem of it, "And toxins are immediately absorbed through the irritated gut wall. I mean fast. Thus, the pup can become toxic. In a sense he's poisoned, though it's not all as radical as actual poisoning.

"Prolonged diarrhea can produce enough thickness in the colon that it can result in colitis. And colitis as a disease entity is very difficult to handle. Some colitises can never be cured.

"And what is colitis? That involves a very thick colon wall, particularly the interior wall. The colon, or large bowel and colon, is responsible for absorbing fluid into the system.

"That is, as the digestive process goes on, the content enters the large bowel and colon, and these organs pull essential fluids for body use before the bowel is emptied.

"And if all this doesn't function properly, then that essential fluid goes out in profuse diarrhea. Over a period of time that thickened colon lining can't function, and it just goes on and on, even to the point of dehydration.

"Consider this— The intestinal wall is made up of literally millions of tiny villi. These are very small projections that produce a lot of surface for fluids to be absorbed. But as these are coated over, as they are thickened, they don't function well.

"You end up with fluids going right through the pup like a garden hose. The colon is smooth, there's nothing to cause friction, to catch the food material and absorb the liquids back into the system, to make the bowel firm.

"Now you've got pancake stools, or liquid stools. And what we want to see is firm stools, well formed, segmented. Liken them to a cigar, the diameter of a cigar with tapered end. Also, stools with a lot of mucous in them show evidence of irritation in the bowels, whether or not the pup has diarrhea he's got irritation.

"Feces may be the dog owner's most helpful insight into his pup's health. That's why he should clean the kennel every day—not put it off, nor leave the job to someone else. Is the stool firm? The dog man will learn this when he goes to shovel. Is there pus in it? Blood? Worms? Nondigested food? What's its color?

"Now if a pup has diarrhea for one day, but he's happy, and he's eating good, then fine. But should that diarrhea continue, get to a vet. Never try to home treat. Do, and you'll get in trouble. Particularly if the diarrhea is being caused by parasites.

"Let's say you find worms in the stool and you give the pup a home remedy to kill them. Well, most oral worm medicines have purgatives in them . . . the pup's got diarrhea along with the worms and you just gave him a laxative."

Doc jams a fingertip in the pipe to compress the black tobacco. This smoking is a Sunday pastime. I never see the pipe at the clinic. He makes a lot of puffing it and says, "So, what are the causes of diarrhea? Well, obviously, worms. Parasites irritating to the gut wall, such as coccidiosis, hook worm, and whip worm. These can all cause diarrhea.

"Then there's milk or milk by-products, bacterial infection, viral infection, a sudden change in diet, or a dog running loose.

"A garbage-can scavenger can honestly eat, and will eat, anything from meat wrappers to chicken bones that are tainted. Then there's accidental ingestion such as a dish of peanut brittle on the patio table.

"Or the dog can drink an irritant. Dogs can literally drink anything from paint thinner to kerosene. Also, retrievers worked in a stagnant pond can pick up algae responsible for diarrhea. And diarrhea can appear as a symptom of many diseases such as distemper, hepatitis, nephritis . . . almost any disease that attacks the dog as a whole.

"Now, since parasites are so closely related to diarrhea, let's take a look at them. Just the common ones: round worms, hook worms, coccidiosis, and occasionally you'll see whip worms and tape worms in a pup.

Parasites

"The most damaging are hook worms for they are blood suckers. They attach themselves to the gut wall and not only do they irritate the gut wall and cause diarrhea, they actually suck blood and deprive the dog of nutrients.

"Whip worms locate themselves in the cecum which is similar, kind of, to the appendix in a man. They require a vet's care, as does everything showing up in sustained diarrhea.

"Coccidiosis is a protozoan parasite. It imbeds itself in the intestinal wall, irritates the wall, and in its reproductive cycle it tends to burst out, irritate the wall, and you'll see intermittent diarrhea. Coccidiosis stems from poultry and birds. Retriever trainers should always be on the lookout for this one.

"Round worms also irritate the gut wall but they are not the blood suckers that hook worms are. Often they'll migrate into the stomach and the dog will chuck em up. Thus the owner becomes aware his pup has worms and ladies who see this can be nauseated.

"Tape worms live off the intestinal content. They attach themselves to the animal but take nothing directly from him.

"In all cases there is no home diagnosis for worms.

"Pups are more susceptible to worms because of their habits. They scavenge, they lick, they chew anything, even the feces of other dogs. Or when still suckling, the dam can go out and lay in the yard, pick up worm eggs on her udders, the puppies nurse, swallow an egg, and away goes the cycle.

"It doesn't mean you've got an unhealthy pup just because he has worms. It's like you wrote in your gun dog book, Bill, 'It's no shame to have em, it's a shame to keep em.'

"Now there's a difference between having worms and having worm disease. If a pup has hook worms to the point he's anemic, and he has a profuse bloody diarrhea, and he's depressed, and he's not eating ... he has hook worm disease.

"But if he's got a little diarrhea and he's a fat, roly-poly pup and he's eating good and the vet diagnoses hook worm in him and the pup's treated and he gets well ... he just had hook worms, not hook worm disease.

"Whenever a pup shows prolonged diarrhea it's imperative the owner take a stool to a vet for analysis. There is no other way to diagnose worms. And home cures? Home cures may knock one type of worm, let's say, but what if the pup is host to five different kinds ... all at the same time?

"Have a microscopic analysis of the stool made, let the vet treat specifically for each specific parasite he discovers.

"Same goes for external parasites, fleas, ticks, mites. Now fleas and ticks can be a problem ... but they're things people usually can see. Look at the pup's belly. You'll probably see the fleas make a break for it.

"The tick? Rub the pelt. You'll find em if they're there. But an odd one can go down an ear. Then it takes a vet to dig him out.

"For fleas and ticks the vet can recommend a dip or a powder. You can get these pests checked.

"But ear mites— These you can't see. And they can create serious problems if left unchecked. They are especially prevalent in hunting dogs because of the big-floppy ears. And you can tell if your pup has em. He'll dig at his ears, shake his head, slap his ears against his skull so hard you can hear him in the next room.

"If you don't have a vet take care of ear mites the condition may end up in an ulcerated ear. Never use a home remedy. The oil in such things will soothe the pup but who's to say what you're using has the specific insecticide to kill the specific parasite living in your pup's ear? Also, don't expect ear drops the vet sends home with you to knock mites overnight. This can be a long-time, ongoing fight."

Mange and Fungus

Doc gives up on the pipe, lays it on the kitchen table, asks if I've got any coffee. I'm pouring when he launches off, saying, "Other common problems in pups are mange and fungus. People will buy a pup knowing there's a spot on his skin, but they'll assume he lost that by scraping against the kennel or tumbling about with his litter mates.

"But anytime a pup has hair loss of any kind, particularly if there's itching associated with it, you need a specific diagnosis such as derived from a skin scraping or a culture to identify what's wrong. And the treatment for sarcoptic mange, demodectic mange, and fungal infections are each specific. And they all differ from each other.

"So if you home treat, how do you diagnose the problem? Demodectic mange usually leaves a rather vague, non-descript area of hair loss and often that's all. Sometimes pups don't even itch.

"Sarcoptic mange, depending on its stage, quite often will leave a little scaliness around the rim of the ears, sometimes around the neck and usually on the feet. It scales off like dandruff. And these puppies are itchy.

"Fungal infections don't always manifest themselves with a nice round circle that's characteristic of ring worm. They can take on a lot of different appearances. The most common symptom is a kind of dry encrustation, a scabby look, with loss of hair.

106

"But don't trust any symptom. Don't think you can figure it out. Let the vet check it."

Doc decides to give the pipe another chance. He reaches for it, checks its innards, pokes it about, sticks it in his mouth and lights up again. Through it all, he's saying, "There's other problems a vet sees too often with pups such as pyoderma, hernias, retained testicals, cleft palates, blindness, deafness—but the four we've discussed make up most of the vet's case load. Distemper, diarrhea, parasites, and manges.

"To keep a puppy in good health the owner must monitor the little guy, know when he's ill, don't let something progress till it becomes serious.

"Never try to home treat. Always go to a vet. Not cause we need the money. That's not the point. But because we trained ourselves to know what to look for, to identify what we find, and to treat the condition with specific medicines or techniques.

"Your pup's welfare means more to us than our take home pay.

"And that's about it," concludes Doc, as he knocks out the pipe on the ashtray and pokes it in his breast pocket, "We want to help this guy have a buddy, not a bed case."

5/Housebreaking Pup

So the vet told you Pup was fit—and now she's yours. The deal is made. What next? It's a matter of getting a handle on what Pup leaves behind.

Hope springs eternal! If not, it grudgingly stands up. For the ultimate woman. Innovative as Samantha, sultry as Marlene, cheerful as Pollyanna, provocative as Liz, cool as Princess Grace.

And more— One to tie flies, paddle the canoe, load shells, clean birds, work the plug knocker, scoop kennels, quote Frost, carve decoys, set up fly camp— Alas!

Hope sits down. Mine does. Last season's collapse came over a flirt named Cindy. Maybe I was over my head? Too much fire and too much class: disposed to neon, not boondock.

She arrived wearing a fur coat like those lookers in Black Velvet ads. More than this, she had a beard and eyebrows and ear liners and four stockings of silver. She clicked her toenails, strutted lock-kneed, wiggled her petite butt.

I admit to being dazzled. And you're right: she couldn't carve decoys. Matter of fact, in the out-of-doors she was reputed to be good only as a ratter.

But I was hooked. She would snuggle. And when she perked those silver eyebrows and gazed with those gun-blue eyes! I even overlooked her independence. Of course that's our era: women who don't need men. But even to include female miniature schnauzers?

Anyway, Cindy's moved in. No nylons entangle me from shower rod, my razor stays intact, and the bank hasn't called about overdraws, but there are signs of concern underfoot. And I endure, slipping about, padding with layers of paper towels, pouring salt and vinegar and

Cindy, the everywhere schnauzer, asks a hi-style pointer what he's doing; sails midst an English springer spaniel, Welsh springer spaniel, and Brittany; kisses Lab; then taunts Happy to give up his tennis ball.

realizing, again, it takes a composite chemist, psychologist, Job, and nine-flat dash man to housebreak a pup.

And I was doing alright. Cindy was coming along. Honest she was. But she became a critic. Every time I left my typewriter she'd leap on the table and shred the manuscript. Right out of the machine. I mean rip it out and chew it up and strew it about. Well a stained carpet I can take—

Cindy began spending her days in the kennel. To be replaced by Spunk. Now this gal came through the door an angel, those white ears a halo. And what a face. Soft as cotton candy. And her touch— She stands and reaches out and the weight of her paw is less than a breeze.

And two rolls of paper towels later, here comes Cricket. So named for the knees of her back legs stick out like a cricket's and she's forever with song. If you can call whining a song. And when she plops on my lap it's like a Budweiser Clydesdale. And she plops all the time for she's jealous of Spunk who's laying there with her belly bared, me stroking it.

Spunk and Cricket take the sun on top their dog house while Tug leaps off.

So it goes, a man with his women— At least with gals who'll never be housekeepers, but must be housebroke.

Which is simple, really. What goes in must come out. Right? So we merely control intake and designate outgo.

Now anyone can do this, even if Pup's giving you that don't-pay-attention-to-me-till-I-ask-you look. That was Cindy's specialty. Just like a critic.

Spunk believes I'm her pet, not the other way around. And it's me she's training.

Cricket? She knows in the end she'll win. She's seen my house resembles a hunting lodge and the blood of the hunt stirs in her veins. It's a waiting game she plays—as do all women—knowing she'll come into her own, and own me.

The Four Ts

Toilet training will make or break both you and Pup. This is where it all begins. And the way it all ends can be predicted from the way this goes.

112

This is when Pup learns her first command, "No."

And learns her name, for her name is given as a command second only to, "No."

This is where Pup is first touched by you in exasperation: and she knows it's exasperation, you running with her stuck out front, racing toward the door. You notice I didn't say, "... through the door." Cricket's legs stick out too far.

This is where Pup first feels a collar and leash.

This is also where Pup first hears praise from you for a job well done.

This, then, is the single most important training situation in Pup's entire life. And in yours.

This is when you put into practice the absolute imperatives of good dog training: touch, timing, temperament, and transfer. The FOUR Ts. They'll be with us the rest of this book and with you the rest of Pup's life.

TOUCH: You can't teach Pup anything unless you make and maintain contact. With Pup we use a collar. With a horse we use a bit. With an elephant we use a pole and hook. When the pup and horse and elephant are trained, our only contact is the vibration of our voice touching their ear drums.

This is why Pup must live-in with you: must become sensitized to your voice. Your voice is the ultimate contact: especially at long distance.

TIMING: To teach Pup anything you've got to repeat the same thing, the same way, the same place, at the same time ... time and time again. Pup loves sequence and routine. Build on this. Don't depart. Don't innovate. Get channeled and stick.

TEMPERAMENT: You never get mad. If you do, it's all over. You're finished. Pup's finished. And that's that. There is no more.

TRANSFER: Pup advances her learning by transfer. She learns to transfer your command to her act.

The FOUR Ts will be with us from beginning to end. We'll teach Pup nothing without them. Now, we'll teach potty training.

And let's get this said and stuck right now: never, never, never, rub Pup's nose in her accidental leavings. One, you've grabbed her and that can't be. Two, you've forced her head down and that's none of her business—even though it is her business. What do I mean? Well tell me, what on earth's the principle in sticking Pup's nose in her mess—and by this act, stop her from messing again? You know? I sure don't.

I'm sure the practice came about by dog trainers who weren't on the job. Who weren't present when Pup made her mistake. And it is a law of dog training, you know, that you can only correct Pup when she's caught in the act. That's the only way Pup knows why you're upset. If you wait to correct her while she's lounging in the corner—but you just saw the pile she left—then Pup realizes you're upset because she was lounging in the corner. Hardly! So sleep-at-the-switch dog trainers return Pup to the scene of the crime and rub her nose in it. By their very act they admit they goofed. Stay on the job. When you can't monitor Pup, put her out.

And even more imperative, never strike Pup with anything when you're angry. Be it rolled-up newspaper, flyswatter, or worst of all, your hand. Yet, these devices can help you maintain control. That's why you swat Pup at play. She feels the sting—discovers the power of you—but you've not put her down. Your face and your manner show Pup you're not upset. Thus, another reason why Pup must live-in. To learn your every facial expression, your every move.

But, when you are upset, just *show* Pup the flyswatter and she'll cower. She'll know she did wrong. You will have intimidated her, you will have pointed her away from some bad act—without ever lowering a hand.

IN ALL PUP'S LIFE NOTHING BAD IS EVER GOING TO HAPPEN TO HER SHE CAN ASSOCIATE WITH YOU. NO MATTER HOW STRINGENT YOU MUST GET, YOU CAN NEVER BE VIEWED BY PUP AS THE CULPRIT.

You've got to use your head, not your hand, to train Pup. That's why I said up front, you've got to be smarter than the dog.

Pup must always view you as her benefactor, her saviour, her one true friend. It'll always be you who rescues Pup from the pain and injustice of life. Always you who brings joy and happiness.

Only once will there ever be an exception to this. That's when Pup knows what to do, yet refuses to do it. That's when Pup meets her maker. And that won't come during potty training.

Self Feeding

We use some aids in housebreaking Pup. One of these is dry food: that plain rough stuff in your kennel that comes in 50 pound bags. That's right, the coarse feed that drives a 70-pound field hand is perfect for a seven-pound what-not pup like a schnauzer or a terrier, or a seven-pound Lab pup.

Jack Knox totes away puppy food prize at Alabama sheep dog trial. It's that hard, rough stuff so good for feeding young 'uns.

The only exception to this is a sick pup that needs a prescription diet to get back on her feet.

When Pup first arrives, say she's six to ten weeks old, we pour out a portion of dry food in a pan and put it on the floor along with all the fresh water she wants. We note how much Pup eats. We give her this amount about four times a day, each time putting down and picking up the pan. But always leave the water.

Once Pup's settled in and we've determined just how much she eats in a day, we start filling her pan, putting it on the floor, and letting Pup self-feed. Pup will eat only what she wants, leave it, and come back when she's hungry.

There are many benefits to self-feeding. It frees you from tending the pan, it appeases pup, she always knows there's food on hand, and it keeps Pup's weight down. That's right, a self-fed dog eats less than one who's portion fed.

As always there are exceptions and they must be noted. I've seen dogs, not pups, but dogs who would try to eat 50 pounds of food if it were left out. A week with a gravity flow feeder and they usually stop gorging. But during that week you've got to lock the feeder shut, to be opened only when you're cleaning kennels.

You'll want to work out a routine with Pup. Say you keep her in a kennel crate on the back porch over night. When you get up in the morning, release her to dump, then give her the pan in the house, in the yard, or in the kennel. Wherever she is going to spend the day.

About five o'clock in the evening, store Pup's pan. By storing the pan you give Pup five hours before bedtime to clean out. Now you have some hope of getting through the night with no morning surprises.

By the time Pup is 16 weeks old, you can leave the pan filled, and on the floor, all through night and day. Pup's learned to control herself overnight, especially if she's locked in a small nest she doesn't want to foul.

If you prefer moist dog food, or semi-moist dog food, or people-food, then feed it. It's your pup, your house, and your mess.

By serving hard kibbles, however, you avoid greasy pans and spoons and carpet stains where food's carried and dropped. You also provide gum stimulation, jaw exercise, puppy tooth satisfaction, tooth cleaning, perfect nutrition, a healthy dog, a slim figure, and a firm stool.

And folks, a firm stool is what it's all about. Pup's going to have accidents. Better we be picking up what looks to be those little cigars Doc Royse talked about, than splots of chewing tobacco. Dry food produces a firm stool since the ingredients are bland and compact well. Kibbles also take Pup longer to chew and that aids good digestion.

You're In This Thing Together

Each time Pup drinks or eats or wakes up she must be rushed outdoors. Also, apart from postmeal or postsleep needs, Pup'll be telling you when she's got to go by showing restlessness, suddenly taking off and leaving the room, circling an area with nose down. Watch her.

You can't train a dog unless you can read her. Pup'll never do anything she doesn't tell you beforehand she's going to do. And she'll never lie to you; only man will do that. So watch Pup, learn to understand what she's telling you, believe her, and act fast.

When Pup tells you she's got to go, swoop her up and run. I say

Lad trains during feeding asking yawning pup to "Stay," while concerned momma looks on.

swoop, not grab. We never make a fast move toward Pup. Starts her to ducking. Make your approach smooth, cheery, and gentle. Make her think you're taking her to a party, not to her execution.

From the time you get Pup till the time she dies, she'll be wearing a plain leather collar—built for stout—with a welded D ring. You'll not be able to find one short enough for Pup. Get any good hunting dog collar and cut off the end. Try to save that long end and she'll just chew it, or one of her buddies will.

Now don't go buy some five-and-dime import collar of genuine plastic with a crimped D ring. Get a real dog collar at a real hunting dog outlet made of real leather and real steel. Pup's going to test this collar, severely, and it's got to be built to hold. Have the supplier stamp Pup's name, your name, your address, and your phone number on the collar's brass nameplate. If you lose Pup this I.D. may help get her back. Of course your best assurance for recovering a lost dog is a tatoo in the ear.

The reason we don't use a chain collar is three-fold: one, retriever

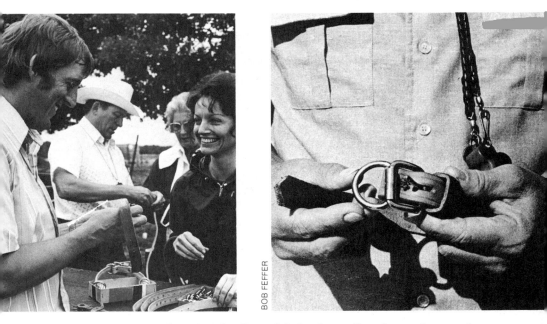

BOB FEFFER

Rick and Delmar Smith adjust plain leather collars for seminar students. Author displays good, stout, plain leather collar with welded D ring and roller buckle. When collar is fitted properly you can just get two fingers inserted to the first knuckle.

trainers sometime use it to choke Pup, or to whip Pup. Then to intimidate Pup on line at a field trial some trainers have the chain collar in their pocket which they jingle; to let Pup know it's there. You'll never be tempted to strike nor choke Pup with a chain collar if you don't have one.

Also it should be noted, there have been trainers intimidate performance by burning dogs with cigarettes then tossing the butt down on the casting line so the dog keeps it in mind.

Others have shot their dogs with BB guns. A small number of these have carried a metal container of rattling BBs in their pocket to the line so the dog'll think the handler's armed.

We're going to train Pup to run out of joy, not fear. And trainers who don't? Let em read Gandhi. He said, nonviolence is the technique of the very strong. I say people who must be brutal to get a dog to perform must either enjoy it, or they're tunnel blind, or they've just got mighty little gray matter.

But back to the chain collar.

The second reason for avoiding the chain collar is it can severely choke a lunging dog, even if the trainer is not being brutal. We just want a collar to hold Pup, not gag her.

And three, a chain collar can get hung up in a kennel, or afield, and choke Pup to death. We put our leather collar on Pup so we can just squeeze two finger tips between leather and fur. Only the most freakish accident can happen with a collar cinched this snug. But you must check the collar often; Pup's growing.

Traditionally, retrievers are worked on marsh and field without a collar. Not Pup. She'll wear it quartering for upland game and swimming after ducks in the marsh. The only time she'll not have it on is at a field trial. AKC rules require a dog work in her birthday suit.

Okay, when we sweep up Pup she's already wearing her collar. We bundle her in hand, go through the door, walk to a specific place in the yard, put her down, and attach our leash.

Why walk her out? Because, if we don't carry her she may tinkle in route.

Why to a special spot? Well, Pup's picked this spot when we've let her run loose in the yard. She's marked it. Here lies her scent post. So we always come back. By doing so, we trigger a response in Pup to tinkle, we decrease distractions—Pup's mind doesn't wander so much, she's already investigated everything here the last time she was brought to stool and the time before and the time before—and we put Pup down with all her old friendly smells.

But know this about spots of ground in a Pup's world. If anything bad ever happens here, she'll associate the pain with the place. And incidentally, with whom she was with. And she'll never want to go there again. She may not even want to be with you again. This is one of the few laws of dogdom.

Now we've got to attach our leash. Why? So Pup can't wander. And sometimes, getting one of these things snapped is a chore. Some you can't work. Some you can't get in hand. And it's even harder to do in the dark. So we don't use a snap-on lead. Instead, we just have a ⅜th-inch nylon cord that we thread through the D ring and we stand there holding both loose ends.

And why are we standing out here? How else are we going to know if Pup dumps? Especially if other dogs are using the area and we've not scooped up. And, how else are we going to check the stool for blood, pus, worms, etc. But most important, how else are we going to command, "Stool," and get the job done? We can't do that with us inside and Pup out.

So that's what we do, we stand there, holding two ends of a nylon cord, maybe late at night, and we're encouraging, "Stool."

If "No," is the first negative command taught Pup, then "Stool," is the first positive one. Teach it. Pup can learn it. In the beginning, wait till Pup squats then give the command. Like her having to go was your idea. Keep this up. By transfer, she'll eventually go when you say, "Stool."

This is a valuable command to teach. It gets Pup in and out of the rain quickly, let's her clean out before going to the line at a trial, or before getting in a duck boat, or before entering a motel room.

Now you may go out doors four times before Pup goes once. Endure. Be kind. Maybe your mother didn't have diaper service. This can be a payback.

These backyard runs also provide an excellent opportunity to teach Pup several voice commands. In four weeks Cindy-the-schnauzer learned, No, Cindy, outside, come on, good girl, and sometimes I think, hurry up!

When Pup dumps give with the praise. I mean this is the most important thing to happen since you fired your gun with mud in the barrel and it didn't explode.

Salt and Vinegar

But if you can't read Pup and she starts dumping in the house and you come on like Attila the Hun—remember the monster, he was 18 feet tall and you stepped on the black square?—then the first thing you'll know is all the piles and puddles will disappear.

But your nose and your stocking feet will find them. That's right, what Pup can't do in the open she'll do in discreet corners, behind furniture, under the bed, or wherever she can go in peace without you going berserk.

Now you've got a real problem. You've not been fair with Pup so she's not going to be open with you. It may be you'll have to put her in the kennel when you can't be watching her.

But a kennel-kept-pup develops another problem. They're concrete, or hard-surfaced, oriented. This means they naturally want to dump on the foyer slate, the kitchen linoleum, the utility room tile. That's good in a way, it saves the carpet. But it's bad, too. If you don't convert Pup to grass she'll dump on drives and sidewalks which may be tracked inside cars and homes.

When accidents do happen, clean up the mess and hold down call-back odors as follows:

Tinkling: Blot up urine with paper towels, sprinkle area with table salt, let dry, vacuum, pour vinegar on area, scrub with old cloth towel, and let dry.

Dumping: Pick up firm feces with paper towel, or scrape up pancake feces with cardboard, sprinkle area with table salt, let dry. If soil remains, then use any commercial rug cleaner bought at any grocery store to remove the spot. Last of all, vacuum.

"But why not train on paper?" you ask, "I've heard this is good." Do so if you wish. But eventually that paper must be taken outdoors to train Pup to tinkle somewhere other than in the house. I don't want Pup making off for Nebraska or Oklahoma. That's where papers blow in a Kansas wind.

Besides, residents in tight quarters don't want last night's news stuck on this morning's yard. Space is minimal for condominium, apartment, and mobile home dwellers. They want their yards and access-ways slipless and sightless.

Paper, either flat or rolled into a swatter, just doesn't figure with me in good toilet training.

Now there's another thing— Pup needs her own room.

On first arrival she'll protest being locked away—either in a room, or in a kennel crate in a room. She may whine and scratch. Don't give back voice. Let her cry it out. As for claw marks on the door, install a face plate—that's good for kicking open when you're carrying groceries—or keep Pup in her shipping kennel.

Whether cardboard box or airlines crate, it's home sweet home for Pup. To save doors from scratching pups, install kick plate.

As Pup grows older, this room, or kennel, or orange crate, or whatever, is going to become her sanctuary. That's where she'll go when she wants to be alone. Incidentally, all dogs feel more comfortable with something over them. That's why you find them asleep under a coffee table, or beneath a bush. Don't put Pup in a bare room where there's nothing to crawl under. Like a forward air observer during combat, she'll feel uneasy exposed.

Eventually Pup will become possessive of her domain. And she'll be content there. Got to leave for the evening? Don't want a howling Pup? Then put Pup in her special place. Want to take Pup on the road? Don't want the motel manager evicting you in the dark of the night? Take Pup's special place with you. It'll be her home away from home. A home-sweet-home with no puddles, no piles, and no protest.

Problem Pup

But what if you've flat got a problem pup? One that just refuses to tell you she's got to go out and tinkle?

This gal will have to be shut up in her kennel crate. She'll strain hard not to foul her nest. Keep her there till you've decided it's time for her to dump, then take her to the yard. When she goes, give with the high praise.

When you bring her back in, put her back in her crate.

If she whines in there, say, "No." If she persists, then put a sound-burst bark collar on her (more about this later).

At no time will you hit Pup with anything, but she'll show intimidation. Her ears will lay flat to her skull, her eyes will be but slits, her tail will go under, her leg joints will protrude above her back, what with all that slinking about.

But Pup will eventually give up her exile to be with you, with you and a dry floor.

For there's no limit to the good effects we can achieve in training— with our voice, our body language, our facial expressions, and contrivances such as a kennel crate.

If you strike, beat, kick, or pick up and throw Pup for pottying, you're going to lose her for life.

You're going to take the spirit out of her and you'll never be able to put it back in. It's like Humpty Dumpty—not even with all the king's men.

Spunk tells Cricket, "Babe . . . you ain't seen nothin' yet."

You're going to make Pup fear you and she'll never trust you as long as she lives.

Your relationship is finished—and you've not even gotten started.

On the other hand, give Pup the benefit of the doubt, let her have a mistake or two, keep everything low voiced, low keyed, and never raise a hand—you'll get the job done and you'll have started building a lasting friendship with a gal who'll be your eager buddy for the rest of her life.

Just last night, Cricket, the Lab pup, edged through the kitchen door, made it down the hall, and dumped on the living room shag carpet. If I'd seen her in the act I'd given her an act of my own—for she knows better. But she got away with it and when I discovered what she'd done, there was absolutely nothing I could do with her about it.

I did heel her in there and got her looking at the feces and told her, "No," and she went down like a punctured tire. But she's yet to learn how to tell me she wants out the back door. That's my fault. And that's my responsibility.

But is this fault sufficient enough for me to punish myself? Hardly. Well, Cricket's my equal—she can't be punished either.

But Cricket will eventually learn. I've just got to think more of her than a shag carpet. And I do.

She's 22 weeks old and yesterday afternoon she made her first double retrieve. You think I'm going to destroy all that for two hard cigars on a shag rug?

And Spunk, the white terrier— You think she's given up, you think she's going to let Cricket get her man? Hardly. She's going for single retrieves so hard when she hits the dummy she flips completely over. On her return to hand she looks over at Cricket as if to say, "There's nothing to it," and I also note her indicating, "Babe, you ain't seen nothing yet."

6/The First Trainer

Wild dogs hunt, locate, stalk, point, flush, chase, kill, and fetch game.

There never lived a wild dog who wasn't a retriever.

And who's the trainer?

Momma.

That's right, momma-dog. Little wonder, then, female-humans make the second best puppy trainers; momma-dog being first. Women and girls have that soft touch, that soft voice, that instinctual patience and genius required to bring a babe along.

But among some breeds of wild dogs, momma has help. Maybe dad and a sister. Or even a brother. And among all wild breeds there's the assistant trainers: the pups themselves. The proctors who take over when momma leaves the nest. Her junior enforcers when she's home but weary.

Yet, no matter who may be giving a hand, momma's the top dog. It's *her* litter that has to be prepared for the world and she makes sure they're ready.

And how does momma train her pups? By providing shelter, food,

Momma rules the roost: here she enters whelping bin to learn what's going on.

warmth, housekeeping, touch, and love.

Where she provides a cave, we offer a crate. Where momma bundles about her pups, we hold them in our lap or bed them down in cedar chips to get through a cold night. Some of us have even been known to take them to our own bed.

Where momma swallows and digests Pup's leavings the first three weeks of his life, then goes distant from her nest to dump so predators won't know where she lives, so we shovel up after Pup for as long as we have him.

Where momma touches Pup, we do too.

And as she loves, so do we.

And as she feeds, we do likewise.

But this isn't training, you might say. Yet in a way it is. Momma is creating an environment where training can be absorbed by Pup, plus, she's gaining his affection so he'll be inclined to pay attention, do well, and please her.

That's why Britons say, "You can't train any dog unless he loves you."

But I've heard too many Americans claim, "You can't train any dog unless he fears you."

Well, Momma's pups both love and fear her. She gives and she takes away. She permits or she denies. She is the giver of life and the executioner—note her shoving the pup aside when it's body temperature drops below normal. She is God on earth. Or she is the instrument of God on earth. And so are we.

Now I don't care how angry momma gets, nor God, I've never known either to grab up a pup, nor human, and beat him, throw him, kick him, slam him into a wall, slap him with a water hose, choke him with a rope—

Momma trains with reward and punishment. If Pup does what she wants he gets loved; a lick in the face. If he doesn't he gets growled at; maybe slightly pinched by momma's front teeth.

That must seem amazing to those Americans who think training must be brutal.

How I wish they could spend a day with momma.

Watch her! She's standing in the whelping bin. Boy, she's mad. Her jaw's stuck out, a low roll of thunder comes from her throat, her ears are flat to her skull, her eyes but slits, and the hackle stands up all down her back. Look at those bare canine teeth.

BUT IT'S ALL CONTROLLED THREAT, MOCK RAGE. A DISPLAY OF VIOLENCE. NEVER AN ACT OF IT.

Yet, should that be mandatory, there's just no alternative, the strike comes fast. And it's a marshmallow shot from a cannon. The pup thinks he's been killed. For momma is a great actor. And her bark is worse than her bite.

Important to all this, there's no pick, pick, pick. God save Pup, and us, from the nagging trainer.

So that's momma's punishment to achieve desired behavior: an actor of voilence, never an act of it.

She rewards the same way. A lot of display. She's content and feels good toward her brood so she lays on the floor of the whelping bin and gurgles in her throat. Her stomach and throat are bared. She tucks her legs in fetal position. Her eyes are half-closed. The pups literally run all over her.

Let's compare these two postures: one of threat, the other of submission.

In threat, momma-dog stands tall and moves directly over the errant pup. She looks down on him and breathes the hot fire of her rage right into his face. Her face is contorted in anger.

In submission, momma-dog lies lower than even her pups, she rolls on her back she bares her vital parts, she closes her eyes so she has no defense. Her face is placid.

Hey, there's a new kid on the block. Let's follow him and see where he goes. Oh heck, he got away. Brothers and sisters can be enforcers, so can older pups. But be careful, they can also intimidate, robbing a pup of spirit.

Remember this. The postures of threat and submission are mighty important to the dog trainer. As are the sounds, the facial expressions, and the gestures made for each.

The Basics

And what does momma-dog teach her pup? What does she know they must learn for survival? Well, you may be surprised to discover—

First off, she teaches, "No Noise." A wild pup can't whimper, can't bark. If he did, the litter might be discovered and eaten by a predator or routed out and killed by man. So that's what we also teach—just carry on from momma—"No Noise."

If the first demand for survival is a tight lip, the second is to stay where you're put. Momma must leave her pups to hunt their meal. She can't have them tumbling out of the nest, romping about in daylight, or worse yet, wandering off.

So she teaches them to stay where she puts them. There is no more valuable lesson for Pup in his whole life. We will continue to teach the same thing. And require it of Pup, forever.

But the experienced retriever trainer will protest, "That can't be. If you force a pup to stay before he's learned to retrieve you may take the hunt out of him, rob him of his spirit."

And our answer is, "That's right. If you use the methods nearly everyone's used till now. But we're training different."

What else does momma teach?

She teaches Pup to stay down. Not to jump on her. Nor to bite her. Nor to bother her when she's not in the mood. We certainly teach the same.

Momma teaches Pup how to hunt, stalk, leap, catch, kill and fetch. We'll continue with momma's lessons right up to the killing. Pup'll do none of this. Since all his fetching will be for us.

Momma further teaches Pup when to eat, exercise, play, work, and sleep. We will, too. It's downright amazing what a clock a dog has in it. I mean to the minute.

And most important, momma teaches Pup she's the boss. No ifs, ands, or buts. And always the Pup tests her. And always he's put in his

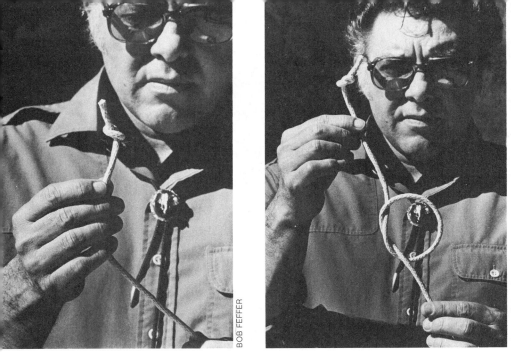

To make a litter box check cord, tie an overhand knot in one end of cord. Tie another knot nine inches down. Leave it open. Insert first knot through open second knot. Snub up and pull tight with big loop about pup's neck.

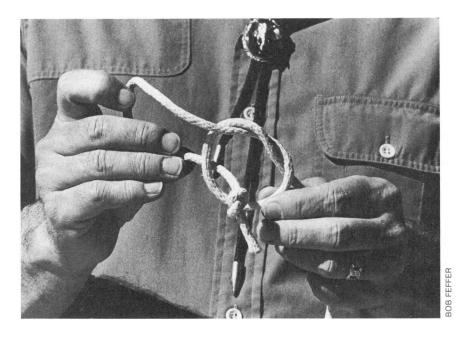

132

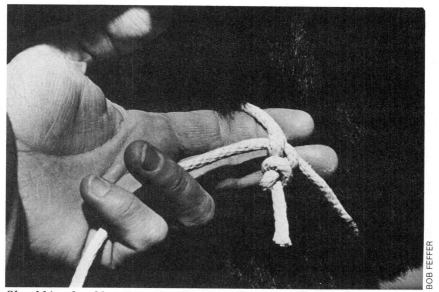

Should just be able to insert two fingers to first knuckle. Check often: pups grow fast.

place: the rank of an underling. There can only be one leader in a pack. And when Pup leaves momma, the pack leader will be you.

But once again, remember, momma stays in charge with a growl, a grimace, and a false threat. A show of force with no teeth. We'll continue with her winning ways.

Stay

Always with dogs I'm repeatedly amazed with the many miracles of God. And with the knowledge, "God does work in strange ways."

Nowhere is this more true than momma teaching Pup to stay. For, momma's teaching more than just stay. Much more is happening to Pup than him just sitting there.

Think of it—

What do we do in society to try and achieve compliance from someone who just won't heel, sit, stay, fetch, down, come, or leave it? We may put him in prison. Put him in prison and tell him, "Stay."

133

Coyote pups with litter box check cords huddle in corner when trainer arrives. Here the lot reluctantly heels. But alone, they step right out.

Well, is our purpose just to place this guy in storage? Or is it to give him an opportunity to think things over? To sort out other alternatives? To provide the solitary, vacant, leisure for perspective that all seekers require to find new ways?

What did your mother do when you were bad? Did she tell you to sit in the corner? If so, and while there, did you get into any more mischief? Did you enjoy your stay? Did you vow to mend your ways?

When an athlete's in training the coach puts him in a jock-strap barracks and says, "Stay." When a Marine is in basic training the drill instructor puts him in a squad room and orders, "Stay." When a devout person wants to be closer to God he is asked to go on retreat and "Stay."

Always when preparing for a new life, or changing an old one, or girding one's loins for stress, or cramming for a breakthrough in knowledge, the person must hole up and "Stay."

And when he emerges— He comes forth bold, confident, dedicated.

It is this reality we use to train dogs.

Welcome to the world of the litter box check cord, the chain gang, and the short-tied pup.

The Litter Box Check Cord

Pup's ten days to three weeks old. He opens his eyes. Imagine his amazement. What a great world out there. A world of more than finding momma's nipple, bundling with his litter mates, waddling off to stool on shaky knees.

Pup can see, and the retriever blood in him decrees, "Don't just sit there, fetch something."

What better time to start training?

Especially with our methods: where Pup bears no grudge, no balk, no opposition. And he never associates anything bad that happens to him with a human being.

Well Pup was born free. We all are. But soon comes the fetters. All life's freedom is short-lived. And do we protest? You bet we do. So Pup's going to raise King Cane the first time we tie anything on him. For our sake we don't want his protest directed against us.

So we enlist the aid of momma's little helpers. Pup's litter mates who all along have been helping momma. We'll use a litter box check cord.

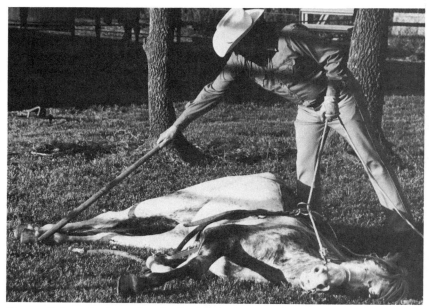

Serpentining check cords take the boogeries out of a pup just like Delmar does for a horse by touching him everywhere with a pole.

A litter box what?

A check cord. Remember? We can't train Pup unless we've got ahold of him. It's one of the FOUR Ts: Touch.

So we buy a bundle of ⅜- or ¼-inch nylon cord and cut off enough two foot sections to make each pup a lead. Tie an overhand knot in one end of the cord. Pull it tight. About nine inches down, tie another overhand knot—only leave this knot open. Open and loose enough we can slip the first tight knot through it (see photos).

Now place this big loop around Pup's neck—just slide it over his head—and with two fingers between cord and fur, tighten up the second overhand knot. No way can this knot slip to either come loose or tighten and choke Pup. Rig all Pup's littermates with such a cord and let em go, trailing about 18 inches of line behind them.

What happens? A pup ambles past dragging his cord. Another pup sees the cord edging along. "What's that?" he wonders. He reaches out and slaps the cord with a paw. It keeps going. He leaps and grabs it in his mouth. But it keeps sliding. He clamps down. Now, the pup dragging the cord comes to a halt. The first halt in his life. And he sits

136

Pups like litter box check cords: encourages them to rough house.

down, thinks but a split-second, then goes berserk. He lunges, he leaps sideways, he falls backwards. Something's got him and it won't let go and, just maybe, his world has come to an end.

Once more he gives it everything he's got and jerks loose. Free at last, he wonders—What on earth was that?

Later, he's stopped again. Or he's stopping some other pup. And after a few days of this it's all a game. And everyone's playing it. And cords are wrapped all about and tangled up and chewed and now— when Pup's cord is grabbed he just goes with it. He's learned to give to the lead. And that bears repeating. PUP'S LEARNED TO GIVE TO THE LEAD. Pup's neck has been sensitized to give to the collar: our primary contact for controlling Pup in early training. And it's all been done without our laying a hand on Pup, without Pup bearing a grudge against man.

Go ahead, walk in. Reach down. Pick up the end of a trailing litter box check cord, give it a pull, heel Pup away.

Is there any comparison between using this method, or waiting till Pup's ten weeks old—then outfitting him with a collar, snapping on a lead, and ordering, "Heel," as you step off and expect Pup to follow?

You bet your training whistle there is.

With pups training pups all their resentment and all their fight is directed against each other—and forgotten.

With you training Pup all his resentment and all his fight can be directed against you—and maybe, never forgotten.

Using Our Head

So that's how we're going to train retrievers. By using other dogs to do it or by positioning Pup to train himself. We're going to use our head, not our hand. We're *making* retrievers, not *breaking* them.

But there comes a day when the litter box check cord—or any other training device—can no longer be used. The litter box check cord is finished when all the pups have sharp teeth and they chew the cords off. But by then you've made your point and it's time to move on to another training aid; the snubbing post.

But let's pause a moment to note:

It's strange how many things that really get the job done in dog training, with the dog not associating anything bad that happens to him with the handler—it's strange how many naive onlookers think the trainer's being inhumane. You'll find more than one critic who has his head on backwards.

Then for other trainers, humane training is beating a dog *lightly*. Such trainers will be hardput to see the significance of what we do. For one thing, we're not being physical and they don't see how we can ever expect compliance. Plus, we're not using sorcery. So this turns another group off. They think training is voodoo. And the last group we lose are the dogooders, for we're not training with cookies.

Ron Montgomery, secretary of the Labrador Club of Scotland, is probably the finest puppy training man—there is a woman—in Great Britain. He's thought it all out.

He's reasoned if he leans over, gets down on one knee to feed his pups. And if he does the same to love them. Then when they're coming back from a retrieve, if he gets down there they'll associate that with joy and come all the faster.

They do. Many trainers on this side of the Atlantic have used this technique before. But not on the east side. Over there a handler stays erect. What on earth would a gentleman be doing on the ground?

But seeing Ron's success, some of the British handlers now get

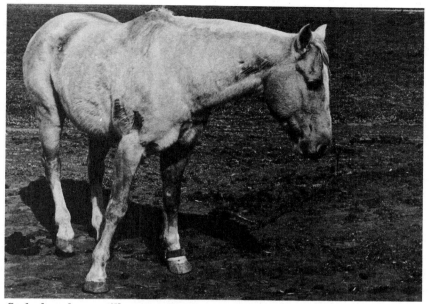

Staked out horse will eventually let his milk down . . .

down on one knee at a derby—and Pup, seeing this for the first time, wonders what on earth is awaiting him. Has he done something wrong?

Ron's asked his colleagues why they do this. They say, "Because you do." Ron further asks, "And you don't know the reason?" And they reply, "Yes, because it seems to work for you."

It works for Ron for more reasons than his bending over to feed or give some loving. It works because Ron is no longer 18 feet tall. Plus, remember Momma's position of threat? She stood over the pups and looked down. And her position of submission? She got below or equal to the pups, down on the ground.

Another thing—

In those years I've been gun dog editor for *Field & Stream* magazine, I've learned to fear the one-sentence letter. The letter that asks the editor, "My Lab refuses water, how do I get him to enter?" Or, "My springer eats the bird, how do I stop him?" Or, "My pointer runs to the car when I fire a gun, how can I make him stay at my side?"

. . . same result can be predicted for a renegade dog. Dogs can be short-tied outdoors or inside. Collie suckles her pups while chained to a tree. Her attention is neither on chain nor pups, but on sheep being worked to front.

140

Short-tied pups grow self reliant, bold up, start looking forward to training sessions.

What you can ask in six words, "How do I get to Heaven?" takes a Bible of 843 pages—that's just the Old Testament—to start the routing.

Whatever happens with a dog, people feel the solution has to be simple. After all, it's a dumb beast, right? Wrong! Some of the smartest associates I've ever had were dogs. And some of the dumbest were people.

Many such people assume correcting a dog's problem is like replacing a washer on a leaky faucet. It may be they'll need to replumb the house. But they don't know this, can't imagine this.

Such people *know* dog training is simple. Just common sense, anybody-can-do-it-simple. Simple it is, that is granted. But you don't correct one problem without creating another. And you don't correct one problem without changing the dog's thoughts and habits in a whole lot of ways.

Dog training is like chain wrestling: it's compounding and progressive. One hold introduces another until you get your pin. And that in itself is amazing to people. It doesn't take strength to be a champion

Cricket is short-tied, alone, to fence post two hours at a time. Or, she's chained with her buddies on a three-chain lead and the lot of them take their grudge out on each other.

wrestler: it takes fulcrum, balance, and conditioning.

People are prone to look for the wrong things. Like a man I know, who when a boy, thought he'd seen the circus when he merely watched the parade between the spur track and the big tent.

When it comes to dog training, too many people are standing on some corner thinking they've seen the real thing go by. What they saw was either a pariah on the prowl, or a promenading poodle.

I swear, I've met more than one of these guys who caught one of these dogs and took him hunting. When the guy got home he wrote me a one-sentence letter.

The Snubbing Post

The snubbing post is our gift from the horse trainer. One who must handle a rank mount. I mean a real outlaw. This is a horse that'll kill you. And this is a trainer who makes horses, not breaks em.

The horse is taken to a vacant field, a big one, a lonely one. A steel stake is driven into the ground; the horse tied on a short lead. Get him tied for stout and leave him. Leave that horse day and night, making certain he'll not suffer from exposure. And have that chain no more than nine feet long.

Now you come back the next morning and offer some food, a pail of water. You shovel up the 18 foot circle and go. Never once looking at the horse. Never once speaking. The horse has just been snubbed.

Back you come the next day to do the same.

And the third day.

About the fourth day, Ol' Man Killer will be looking for you. Why? Well, for three days you're the only nice thing that's happened to him. Ol' Man Killer has concluded you're the only one who cares. And rather than stay out there forever, he'd rather go with you. Halter him, snap a lead, and see if he doesn't walk away. I don't mean on his hind legs with his front hooves flashing. I mean he walks away like a real gentleman.

You just got yourself a horse to start training. And the horse has a purposeful, enjoyable life before him—instead of being executed in a soap factory.

Therefore, nothing better can happen to Pup than be short-tied.

But not on a round-the-clock basis. Just a couple of hours a day will keep him biddable.

Each Pup requires a schedule that fits the master's life—and the dog's disposition.

Here's a typical day around my place. I awaken at six, release the pups from their kennel crates on the back porch, let them air, feed them.

Following a 15-minute romp in the backyard I put them in their kennel run. Except, one of them will be taken off by himself and short-tied. Which one? The one that's bulling up on me, the one showing resentment to training.

Since I work at home I can go outdoors and release this short-tied pup in about two hours. Now he goes into the kennel with his buddies.

During the afternoon all the pups and I will take a Happy Time walk. That's when Pup does what he wants. We're in some wilderness and he's learning the territory. Or we're in a park, exercising on lead. Or we have a formal training session.

That night, all pups come into the house. At ten o'clock they're put out for airing, then back into their porch crates.

But everyone doesn't work at home. Which means Pup will either be short-tied all during the day the master's gone, or he can be short-tied at night when the master's home. Either way works fine. But

Tug earns himself a session with the bark collar.

remember, you can't leave Pup tied too long. Leave him as long as you think necessary.

Jack Knox, winner of the American and Canadian sheep dog championships, keeps his border collies snubbed tight all day, every day.

There's a good reason for this.

Let my buddy, Delmar, tell you why. Delmar says, "When you get to any trainer that's successful, he's got those boogers tied up out there. This teaches em obedience. Teaches a dog to stay where he's put. Makes him self reliant. Gets him to know you are the only way out. And you never abandon him. You always come.

"The dog gets to looking for you."

About here, Delmar usually adjusts his Copenhagen, rolls down the pickup window, spits, goes on to say, "Those dogs ain't runnin loose out there, they're tied short, and the only freedom they know is when you give it to em. They're wanting to see you. And if all you do is train ... then you've got a dog that'd rather train than anything else. Training to them is being free."

144

Delmar spits again and says, "And every time that dog's turned loose, he means business. But the common ones that are just running loose ... going up and down some kennel run ... their mind's not on their jobs ... being let loose to them is just being able to throw a bigger loop.

"The business ones are tied up."

Yes, nothing better can happen to Pup than be short-tied. It cures all problems. Many you didn't even know you could get rid of with a hank of rope and a post knocked into the ground.

If Pup's timid this'll bold him up. If he's rank this'll stick a flower down his gun barrel. If he's a sulker this'll bring a wag to his tail. If he's a day dreamer this'll get him tense.

What Pup learns short-tied is: one, no matter where you leave him he must stay there, two, he won't get hurt, and three, you'll always be back. The result is, Pup discovers he's self sufficient, nothing bad is ever going to get him, and he can depend on you.

And all the while, mind you, Pup's continuing—right from the litter box check cord—to give to the lead.

Cricket and the terriers take their first walk on three-chain lead. Fifteen minutes later, Cricket heels right at the seam of my pants leg —off lead *(see page 148)**.*

BOB FEFFER

It's a strange thing about dogs. They'll let you position them to be trained with no grudge. Like just now— Those two white terriers are barking out there. I had to leave the typewriter and go buckle the sound-blast bark collars on each of em. Now they won't bark anymore. The collar's telling them, ''No.'' If I go out again, they'll run to me for affection. But if I'd gone out there and yelled, ''No,'' or worse yet, given em a swat, they'd not look forward to seeing me. They're being told ''No,'' and they're not barking, but they hold no grudge against me.

So it goes with a short-tied dog. You're not remembered for tying him there. You're remembered as the guy who brings fresh water and rubs his ears and offers food. You're the guy who comes and frees him. You're Pup's friend, his benefactor, his saviour.

You're someone Pup doesn't ever want to lose—or displease. What if you stopped coming?

So, for the rest of Pup's life there'll be times he's snubbed to a post, or to a finger welded on your truck bumper, or to a stake pounded into the ground. Only time Pup'll be free is to go hunting, run in a trial, take a training session, have a Happy Walk, or come in and lie by the fire.

And I don't mean Pup's tied to a long chain. I mean he's snubbed up to no more than six feet of freedom. If you use a longer lead, then Pup's moving around too much and you lose the effect. The smaller Pup's world is when he's chained, the bigger it'll look when you release him.

The stakeout post convinces Pup there's no alternative to your will. Yet you've not laid a hand on him. Now when you start handling, Pup's going to more readily accept anything you want to do with him.

And when you've finished the training session, you put Pup back on his short chain. That gives him a quiet time. If you've done something out there he doesn't understand, he can think it over. There's no distractions. Plus, if you're coming back for another training session, the stakeout post gives Pup that quiet time to clear his mind.

When you come back you don't have to yell to get Pup's attention. He's attending mighty close. And he's wanting to stay out with you as long as he can. ''Go ahead Boss, throw it one more time.''

The Three-Chain Lead

There's no need spending time with Pup without training him. Say you're going to take him for a walk in the park. Well, gather up a couple more dogs and snap all three to the same lead.

Ever try to teach a pup to heel? Him setting up, rear legs tucked under, front legs braced, head reared back, all wrinkled across the back of his neck, eyes bulged out—and looking right at you?

Well no more. Put three pups on the same lead and take off. Oh they'll leap over each other and jump sideways and jerk each other down. They'll gag each other. And tangle each other. And just get into an awful mess. But never. I mean never. Is any of this discomfort or frustration directed against you. You're using other pups to train. And that's the only way to go.

When it's all finished, and I mean usually in two sessions, you've got three pups that will heel. I don't mean heel with a lead on them. I mean heel free and clear and they just sticking right by you.

Now in my book, that's training.

If you've got lots of dogs you can extend this device to a chain gang. Just put 3 or 10 or 18 dogs all on the same chain. Have each one snubbed up tight to a short drop-lead; say 18 inches. Now, when a dog moves, the chain moves, and all dogs must give to their lead. A couple days of this and you'll sensitize a dog's neck to go with the pressure.

But there's a problem. More than a couple of days and the dogs get chain-bright. They lay down, let the chain rest under their belly. Now should a dog lunge, they just get their bellies scratched.

To use this device successfully you need to keep adding new dogs.

Then, too, the chain gang really has a purpose other than the stake-out post. This is where you hold dogs to watch you train their litter mates. You think they don't want in the game? The chain gang builds a frenzy. Whereas the stake out post provides time for reflection.

One last thing. That three-pronged lead— What a way to introduce Pup to water. Walk him till he wants to drop. I mean take a long walk on a hot day. Now come along side the pond—you had this in mind all along—and let the old dog on the pond side make his move. You want to see two new pups taken to sea? I don't mean swimming water, I mean wading water—on the edge.

Those pups will cavort like seals. They'll drink. They'll splash. They'll knock each other down. And when it's all finished, the new-comer(s) will be saying, "Gee, what a fun place. I sure hope we come back." And that, folks, is making a happy experience out of Pup's first water encounter.

Now, while Pup's in water be ready to hoist him fast should he get tangled in his lead and go under. We don't want Pup sputtering out there, getting frightened out there.

Lab pup heels properly at seam of pants leg.

But on land, let 'er rip. If Pup gets knocked down, let him self-erect. Don't go babying him, reaching out to him, every time he's in trouble. He'll get to expecting it. Plus, to baby a dog makes him timid. You can only bold a dog up with discipline.

Let Pup face the world himself and work out his problems on his own. Like yesterday. Cricket and I went with one of our training duos, Bob Feffer and his Labrador, Babe, for dove in an abandoned feed lot. The dove were roosted. It was raining. So I told Bob I'd walk around the lot and spook the dove off their perch. Cricket and I took off.

In but a minute, "Boom," went Bob's Browning two-tube. Cricket nearly jumped out of her skin. She's had gunfire about her before, but the low-lying clouds, the improvements acting as amplifiers, really made the shot extra loud. I saw her predicament but I ignored her. Just walked on, paying her no mind. Gradually her tail came back out. Only to go right back under upon meeting a few remnant head of beef being fed by a tenant. Still I ignored her. Ignored her walking sideways the full length of the lot.

The chain gang, an adaptation of the horse-picket line, is one of the best things that can happen to a gun dog. Here author's string cavorts in the shade of pine trees at the farm, but seasoned pointers just lay down and take it easy, while a mixed line decides to go to sleep . . .

. . . a pup that's never had a litter box check cord or three-chain
lead will fight the chain gang. This is good. All Pup's frustration
is vented on a piece of chain, not you, the trainer. To fire a string up,
weight a pigeon to fly the line. The pigeon always stays out of harm's
way and dogs are left rattling the chain.

A half-hour later she stood beside Bob while he fired the gun and she raced with Babe for the dove. Cricket had been ignored to performance.

Now some ill-informed dogooder would have rushed to Cricket when she spooked, consoled her, and ruined her. Or seeing what I did in her predicament, the dogooder would have criticized me. It goes to show, dogooders are no good when it comes to dog training. They're not dogooders at all, they're dobadders.

7/Before The Cast

Napoleon and Mickey Rooney would have looked up to Max Evans. Yes, Max is but one finger high in a shot glass. So he suffered when he was young with the small man's disease. That's where you've got to whip everyone to prove you're mighty. Max became a sawed-off shotgun.

An infantryman in both WWII and Korea, a post-war member of our counter intelligence corps, Max, who was wounded seven times, ended his military career with a five year hitch in the French Foreign Legion (FFL) where his record shows he was in constant combat for 1,046 days.

Max ended up 10 feet tall.

But he didn't start that way. When Max joined the FFL he couldn't speak a word of French. He was taken to a barracks, directed to a steel bunk with a spring support for a mattress—but no mattress or bedding—and was ordered to undress. All his clothes, his pocket possessions, and luggage were taken from him and he was left standing naked before this naked bunk.

Max noticed a corporal sitting at the entrance to the garrison room. The corporal's desk was bare and beside his chair tilted a pick handle from a half-track truck.

There was no one else, nor anything else but rows of bunks and wall lockers, in this room. Being in the middle of the day, Max reasoned all the other legionnaires were on duty.

Eventually Max got hungry. He also had to go to the toilet. And he was getting irritated about it all, standing there without a stitch of clothes on, no food, no place to go to the john, and apparently no one coming to direct him.

So he walked to the corporal sitting at the desk and said, "Hey pardner, I want some clothes, something to eat . . . and I need to go to the toilet." Whereupon the corporal stood, saying not a word, and taking the pick handle in hand, took a Reggie Jackson swing that lifted Max from the floor and deposited him six feet away.

In one felled swoop Max's life was changed forever. His impulse was to stand and kill the man. But he knew his arm was broken. Besides he had to vomit. And terror clutched him. And he seethed with anger. And it was all so crazy.

He was in the presence of a mad man. And there was no one to turn for help.

Max staggered to his mattressless bunk.

That evening the legionnaires came in, seeing the new recruit laying on his spring bunk. It was through them Max learned the procedure, and his fate. He would be provided nothing: no food, no clothes, no toilet, no bedding, unless he could ask for each in French.

Max learned French in three days. All he needed to know, he's told me, for the next five years.

Pup in the Foreign Legion

Whenever a new pup enters a strange house I always remember Max. For Pup has just joined the FFL and you're the corporal at the desk. And Pup has nothing and knows nothing—and must ask for everything. Yet, he is without language.

What kind of corporal will you be?

Max Evans became a legend: he was one of three men out of 246 in his rifle company to survive the Algerian war. The legion—starting with the corporal—gave Max the right attitude and the right training to get the job done and live to tell about it.

But such an attitude, and such training, cannot, and will not, make a retriever out of Pup.

154

Max joined the FFL out of his own free will. Pup was adopted by you with no choice of his own.

Max was an adult and a seasoned soldier when he enlisted in the FFL. He knew it was going to be rough, he had some idea of what to expect.

Pup is a baby with no season behind him at all. He has no idea of anything.

Max could take care of himself. Pup is helpless.

Unbeknownst to many, the French government provides only weapons, ammunition, vehicles, and gas for the FFL. Being soldiers of fortune, the legionnaires must take what they can get. They fight for honor but they also fight for the prize. Their only income is their booty and profits from the many businesses bought with booty that came years before to previous legionnaires.

This is not how Pup will live. He'll not hunt for himself and set aside a duck for his dinner. He'll live to serve you, never himself.

Pup'll serve you only because he loves you. And love cannot be earned with a pick handle.

Where injustice, intolerance, and brutality can make a legionnaire. Only justice, tolerance, and love can make a retriever.

The Way It's Done

Never, never, never, bring Pup into and through the house, grab a boat bumper or a pigeon wing or a rolled-up rabbit skin or a wad of socks, and throw it on the lawn with the command, ''Back,'' and cast Pup for his first fetch.

''Back?''

Yes, that's the order given a retriever to run forward.

''Then why don't you say forward? Back is just backwards.''

I know. But here's the reason. Sometimes when dogs are sent to fetch they're stopped afield with a whistle toot and told, ''Back,'' which means go on further, and Back being an easy and distinct command to give, it just stuck for sending a dog out.

''That doesn't make sense.''

Maybe not. It's the dead hand of the past that controls so much of dog training and we'll probably always be in its grip.

''Well, Back is ridiculous.''

No more than ordering, "Come by," or "Away to me," is to a sheep dog. And that's how they're sent. But you want to discuss semantics or dog training?

"Go ahead with the dog training."

Thank you. Now as I was saying, never throw anything for Pup, right off the reel, and send him to retrieve. Pup doesn't know sick-em. He doesn't know you, the house, the yard, the dummy. Plus, he just rode to your place in a car. He ever been in a car before? Is he sick? Does he have to tinkle? Is he hungry? Thirsty? Cold? Hot? Does he want to go to sleep?

And if Pup came to you by plane can you imagine what his little mind conjectured in the black belly of that roaring thing?

And to come down a tilted ramp with the luggage?

And all the exhaust fumes?

And to be thrown on a wagon and zipped to a loading dock where the metal gates were clacked open?

Suffice to say, before we can get Pup's attention we've got to take a lot more into account than the corporal did with Max.

First we must get to know Pup and give time for Pup to know us. Plus, Pup must learn his yard. And all the smells in the yard. And all the smells in the house. And where he can lie down and where he can't. Where he eats and where he stools and where he sleeps. And on and on and on.

Max was a rifleman in the French Foreign Legion. But Max had to learn more than how to fire a rifle.

Pup is a gun dog in your household. But, he too, must learn more than serve the gun. Retrieving is but one of Pup's duties. So why emphasize throwing the dummy?

Pup will also be expected to guard the place and protect the children and keep vermin out of the yard. He'll need to learn behavior that brings you compliments—not complaints—from your neighbors. And smiles, not frowns, from those who visit you.

I Said "No" and That's Final

Pup must learn to be a good citizen.

He must learn heel, sit, stay, come, down, kennel, tinkle, stop it, no noise, lie down, and many other requirements. These are best taught when Pup is young and in the house. This is how we do it.

Always keep your commands simple, teach No first. No is a command that wipes out all other commands, that stops Pup from doing whatever he's doing. It's all purpose, all the time, and totally without excess baggage in its intent. In other words, Pup can't assume you mean *Maybe* or *Possibly* or *Later* or *When it pleases him.* No means No and that's that.

Use No when you catch Pup tinkling in the house, gnawing a chair leg, jumping on the sofa, dragging his food pan across the floor, standing on the screen and pushing it out of its frame.

No is a negative command. Matter of fact, Pup lives in a negative world. That's why you must stay cheery with him, lots of baby talk, and animation, and smiles, and swooping him up and cuddling him and cooing to him and giving him heaps of affection. For a lot of No commands is frustrating and, therefore, should be used sparingly.

Another way of saying No without speaking is just go get Pup, pick him up, and carry him away from what he's doing, shaking your head No and looking grave and disappointed.

I've never ceased to wonder at how a pup knows to look you in the eye to determine your feelings. All that can happen is the pupil dilate, or contract, and the shape of the eye lid change a bit. Yet Pup can read this.

Another substitute for the spoken word No is body language; pointing a finger and waving it up and down while your lips are pursed and your eyes showing irritation.

Try not to be a nagging trainer. It's easy to become one. Be, instead, a person who augments your restrictions to Pup's life, your denials in Pup's life, with lots of cheery encouragement and praise with anything that's done to please you.

In order to teach Sit or Come we merely wait till Pup does either then say the word. That's right, when Pup's laying in a corner and we walk into the room, we have a pretty good idea he's going to stand up and walk to us. The moment he moves, say, "Come." When Pup arrives, start scratching his ears. This is sheer contentment so you can fairly well predict Pup's going to sit and enjoy it. The moment you see his hind-side start down, say, "Sit."

Your command is always after the fact, but Pup doesn't know this. He only knows he hears a certain sound from you when he does certain things: and you look pleased in the face. About 500-or-so repetitions and you may have Pup sitting, or coming, on command. And you may not.

Margaret Dance stays at level of pup in training.

I don't care what it is you're trying to teach Pup, it'll not be taught until Pup wants to learn. Oh you may get surface performance. Pup does sit. But he's staring off, his mind is elsewhere. A butterfly will have him bounding away, unmindful he's breaking some rule of yours.

Take Cricket, the in-house Lab pup for this season, Cricket was retrieving singles somewhat mindlessly, somewhat disinterestedly. But she would retrieve. Then one day I finally saw her focus on, attend to, walk toward, stop and then stalk, and finally leap at a song bird on the lawn. I knew Cricket was ready to fetch. It was then I threw the double and she did it.

And another thing— Don't say ''Come,'' when the Come is in you and not in Pup. By that I mean, don't say, ''Come,'' when Pup's going the other direction. Why give Pup the opportunity to refuse you? Have all the odds in your favor when dog training.

One way is to reinforce what you do with tidbits.

The Treat

The British are very big on this. Ron Montgomery, my Scot friend, soaks a glove in tripe and lets Pup lick it before throwing it. Pup does run to get it back.

Knowing a tall stance intimidates pups, Margaret lets pups have mastery over her to remove fear . . .

... daughter Katherine grabs a handful of fur to press Lab down. Children make excellent dog trainers. Though Katherine is using force, the Lab looks back with total love. Ron Swoish takes pups to field when Margaret and Katherine have finished yard work.

Margaret Dance, whose middle initial is "A" so her three initials spell MAD, is not mad at all when it comes to training a pup. Margaret lives with her farm-manager husband on a government experimental sheep farm southwest of London with their seven-year old daughter, Katherine Elizabeth.

Margaret and her father, Ron Swoish, maintain a small cottage industry, turning out class Lab and English springer spaniel pups.

Margaret brings em from the nest, Ron polishes em in the field. Ron's I-gotta-do-it-to-eat life consists of owning and running an auto repair garage. With a wink of an eye he's told me, however, "One can't ever get too busy working ... to train a dog."

Before Ron's garage entrance flows the storied Thames. Many a pup has made a water retrieve between the cleaning of a carburetor and the setting of the gap in a spark plug. And, incidentally, a Thames-tuned pup can handle strong current.

160

Margaret starts pups in her house. She brings em in one at a time—for she's breeding and whelping them—and lets the little tyke do as he pleases. Then, when the pup's quite distant in the long kitchen, Margaret blows her training whistle. The pup stops what it's doing and attends. Margaret blows the whistle again. Finally the pup walks to Margaret, to learn what's making that funny noise. At that time, Margaret feeds the pup; having divided its daily intake into six portions. The pup answers the whistle and gets one/sixth its daily feed.

Back outside it goes. Another pup enters. It stands to reason each pup comes into the kitchen six times a day. And with 12 pups, Margaret is lowering that bowl 72 times between sunrise and sunset. Margaret is a very dedicated puppy trainer.

When the pup is coming to the whistle, Margaret withholds the feeding and, instead, tosses a chocolate drop to each end of the room. First she throws one right and casts the pup off with a great sweep of her hand. The pup runs, finds, and eats the candy. Now he returns to the whistle. Margaret throws another chocolate drop off to the left. Again the pup is cast with a great display, Margaret stepping off to direct the pup, waving her arm as though she were tossing a Frizbee, encouraging the pup with voice to get along.

Margaret is putting the pup on hand signals. She says, "We must do this before we send the pup to mark. For what if he should fail to find what we sent him to fetch? This way, we can help direct him to the lost dummy."

Margaret further explains, "I use the chocolate drops because they have good scent and the pups like them. Yes, they are rewards. And I don't generally give rewards, my play being reward enough. But to teach something, it seems to me, this is an easy way to do it. The pup gets his reward the moment he's done what you want him to do. He eats the chocolate drop. He's succeeded, as well. For I don't want him to bring me anything. He's catching on. Plus, this is great fun, says the pup, and he further says, 'I'm getting something out of it.'

"No, I don't like bribery and you can tell this chocolate thing sets kind of hard with me. But if that pup is hunting for something for himself then he's going to be a lot more conscientious than if he were hunting for me."

162

163

There's a right way to give a dog a tidbit. Hold it in fingertips and you may get nipped. Hold it, instead, in closed fist and let dog sniff. Then rotate fist and open palm so dog can slurp morsel from hand.

Margaret's right. She's thought it through and she's training from the pup's point of view. Not what's in it for her, but what's in it for Pup. This is the only way to train. Think pup, never human. Please the pup first, then he'll please you.

When pups are older and being fed fewer times each day, the training arena is moved to the yard; whistle, pan, and tossed chocolate drops.

Eventually Swoish takes over, training with the philosophy, "I think the basic thing is a pup has got to love you. Otherwise, it's not going to try to please you. I seek permissive, voluntary compliance. Never any punishment. And how am I going to get a pup to love me … not with food, that's for sure. Love will come by taking the pup out, being with it all the time. Letting it do as it pleases and gradually instilling a little discipline. All training is just a simple mixture of firmness and kindness.

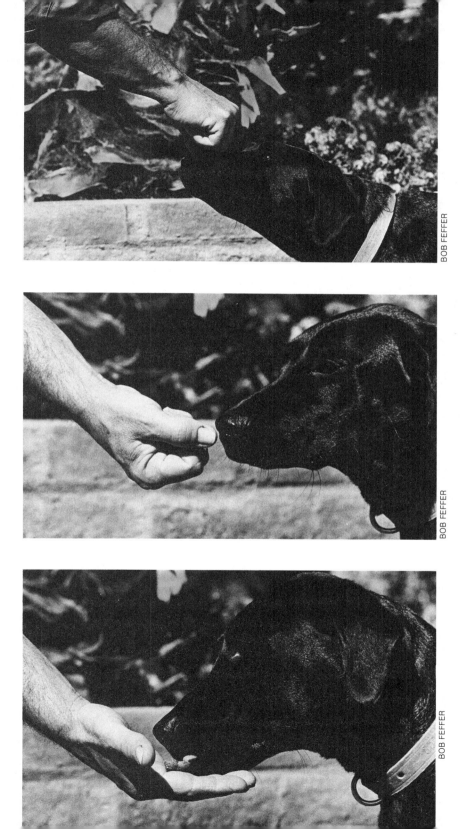

BOB FEFFER

BOB FEFFER

BOB FEFFER

"But there is this— You can't train a pup that doesn't have the breeding for it. If you want to make a first class gun stock you don't use a piece of beech, you use a piece of walnut. And there are different grades of walnut. If you're going to fit a Purdy, or a Holland and Holland, you'll want a beautiful piece of English walnut, not a piece of Spanish or French walnut. Same with a pup. You've got to have good basic raw material."

We agree with Swoish. We were very careful in selecting Pup. And in a way, we agree with Margaret, too. As she emphasizes hand signals in puppy training, so do we. When we tell Pup, "Kennel," we sweep our hand into the black recess of his crate. We point. We do the same thing every time we let Pup out a door. At first we may have to lead Pup through. Us ending up outdoors and encouraging Pup to follow. Later, we stand inside the door and say, "Outside," sweeping our arm the way we wish Pup to go.

The Hand Signal

When the American thinks of hand signals he envisions a precise, methodical, slowly evolving process. Like squeezing off a rifle round. And the dog is expected to shoot out and take a straight line. Just like the rifle bullet.

This is not the case in Great Britain. Why the handler even stands before the dog. To the side, but nevertheless, out front. And the handler makes a great sweeping move of the arm. And not the arm next to Pup. But the one that's distant. The one on the other side of the handler.

The American casts a pup with his hand beside the pup's head and the arm lifted and shot out as though the handler were throwing a bowling ball.

The Briton casts a pup with the opposite arm, with a sweeping motion as though he were sailing a paper plate.

The British method is a gross sweep, a casting of the pup in a general direction. Not so with the American. His line is precise.

But that's the essential difference in the way the two of us play this game. The American is precise. "Not a foot down wrong," he says. Yet the Briton accepts a casual approach to the whole thing. What they call, a "natural" approach.

Just look at the way the two of us go to trial. The Briton duplicates a

*British give dogs a general cast with opposite arm. American uses near-arm
and directs Pup's path with precision. D. L. Walters displays perfect
American form ...*

. . . as does professional trainer Bob Milner and amateur Mike Flannery with River Oaks Corky.

day's hunt afield. He dresses in moss green or some dull tweed. Pup may look back and not see his handler—him being camouflaged the same color as the trees behind him.

But the American? He goes wearing a white handler's jacket.

The Briton wonders if the American's selling ice cream or delivering milk—or babies. Surely, reasons the Briton, the American's not duplicating a day in the field. How could he be, wearing white?

The American wonders, too. Why do the British, he asks, make it so hard for the dog? The American wants the dog to line the blind. That is, run a straight line to the hidden bird and never require the handler to whistle him down to adjust his path with hand signals. But should it be necessary to whistle the dog down, the handler wears white to insure the dog will see him. To see his arm and body direct the way to go.

The Briton wants the dog to hunt out the blind, beating the field, quartering if you will. The Briton wants the dog to find the bird by using his nose. The American wants the dog to find the bird by following directions.

For the Briton it is a scenting test. For the American it is a handling test. The Briton's retriever must scent the bird. The American's retriever must see the handler.

Therefore, the American should never buy a fully trained British dog—he'd be wasting a lot of money—and expect him to win an American trial. The dog was trained to play another game.

But to buy a pup from Britain, the American could only be well ahead.

Introducing the Gun

Something else Margaret does when feeding her dogs is clap her hands. Clap her hands together so they make a sharp retort. That way, says Margaret, the pups are becoming accustomed to shot. Later, when the pups are fed outdoors, Margaret stands distant and fires a .410 shotgun when the pups are feeding. She prefers this, she says, over a blank .22. That, she fears, has too sharp a retort. She can visibly see the pups jump, then cringe before the noise.

Like Margaret, I have taught many a pup to sit, stay, and come with the reward of a tidbit. I, too, feel as though I'm cheating. But I really don't know who I'm cheating. Myself? The pups? Food works. Use it if you want. Americans have a tradition of training without food rewards for possibly two reasons: one, it seems to say to them they've avoided defeat by buying off the pup, and two, they don't want to go afield with a pocketful of goodies.

Yet, one of the greatest professional trainers of em all, Mr. Charles to-know-him-was-to-love-him Morgan, saw nothing wrong with coaxing a timid dog to water with shortening bread. By the way, if you haven't read his book, do so.

Now there's a way to offer tidbits to a dog so you keep all your fingers. Hold it out, as you hold a piece of chalk, and you may get nipped. Hold it instead in your fist. Lower your fist and let the dog smell it. Then slowly turn your hand over and open it. The dog will slurp the tidbit from your palm.

Once again we see the wisdom and practicality of doing things slowly with Pup. Always give Pup time to think the next move out. Never rush him. For example, don't say, "Sit," and expect Pup to drop like a trip hammer. Give him time to check with his brain, let his brain direct his body, and his body comply.

And remember what my buddy, Delmar Smith, insists we do. Always train and reward Pup on both sides. Pup's brain is split. Therefore, your training and rewards must be split. Half on this side. Half on the other side. Retriever trainers are lax on this: especially with heeling. They always want the dog on the left side if they're right handed. And vice versa.

I was fascinated to learn the decoy dog of Nacton—that's the dog that lures wild ducks up the pipe by cavorting about screens erected along the pipe's side—could only work one way. Let me explain. For a decoy dog to attract ducks he must appear and disappear. Round-and-round a series of screens he goes. Usually turning left.

But should the wind be such the decoyman must use another pipe, then it may mean the dog has to work right. That is, he must spin clockwise, rather than counter-clockwise.

Tom Baker, the man who took 200,000 ducks to market in his decoy career, tells me, "If you don't teach em as a pup to go both ways they'll never do it. You absolutely can't get an old dog to reverse his path."

Therefore, I now train all pups to heel on either side, cast from either side, sit to either side. And I always make a note to reward on both sides. Actually stroke down the left ear onto the chest. Then reach over and go down the right side.

170

Far as I'm concerned Delmar Smith and Tom Baker are right. I never argue with success. If Delmar can win 10 national gun dog championships and Tom Baker can lure 200,000 ducks to market, that's success enough for me.

Nor can I argue with Margaret Dance nor Ron Montgomery in using food, or the scent of food, to train a pup. That's the value of going back to Britain. To learn how we used to train dogs before we migrated. To learn how many things we've changed since becoming Americans. For the British gave us all our field sports and the animals to play them with.

So I say, use a treat if you want. For immediate rewards I give my pups any of the commercial dog treats. For let-em-lie-down-and-chew-and-think-it-over rewards I give those twisted rawhide sticks.

If Pup sits he gets a treat.

If he kennels for the night without a fuss he gets a rawhide stick.

The First Commands

To run through the basic commands and give specific instructions, I teach Come as follows:

One. When Pup stands and walks toward me I say, "Come."

Two. When I want Pup to come and he's doing something else, I say his name and then, "Come." Most of us are inclined to say more. We say, "Come here." Or, "Come to me." Keep your command as simple as possible. One word will do it. Come!

Three. If Pup won't come when called then I must go to him. I do this casually, picking up the pup, taking him where I was standing when I called, putting him down and loving him, saying, "Come." Then I walk distant and say again, "Come." Only I precede the command with the dog's name. For example, "Tug come." If Tug refuses to come, I go get him, bring him to the spot I gave the command, put him down, love him, and tell him, "Come." I keep doing this till Pup comes.

Four. If Pup never comes then I must attach a lead to his collar—this would be weeks later—and when I've given the pup time to fulfill my command, but he hasn't, then I give the command once more and reel Pup in. I do this gently, but nevertheless, Pup is brought to me if it means dragging him across the floor. As always, fear is washed away with love.

Ron Montgomery shows Lab pup the tripe soaked glove, gives glove a toss, and earns a fetch.

Five. Now when Pup is called and comes quickly off-lead, he's given a reward. If he doesn't come, he's scolded. Pup is now three months old. And we've had him a month. Pup is scolded and we either go get him, pull him to us with lead, or we run away. We run away, making ourselves as exciting and tempting as possible. We make of it a game. And we run away calling Pup. Telling him to, "Come." Pup can't resist. Unless— Unless you've been mean to him. Then why should he ever come?

That's why we have as a law in dog training, never create a problem with Pup. For if you do you may never get rid of it. And to correct one problem usually creates another. In actuality a dog is fully trained when a trainer has removed all the holes he can. Then it's a handler's job to cover the holes that remain.

Okay, Pup's coming. At least he's coming when you run away with your pocketful of tidbits, so let's teach Sit. And I quickly add, there's no command we should teach before another. Who says Sit can't come before Come or Down or Kennel? Teach what you want. Teach what Pup's willing to learn without a hassle.

We teach sit by saying, "Sit," every time we think Pup's going to do just that.

Later, we call him to us, let him smell the tidbit in our fist, then mold his body into the sit position, gently, and give the reward, telling him, "Sit."

I've never had a pup I couldn't teach Sit in one session.

Now to enforce the sit position, raise your hand as a traffic cop: palm flat and turned toward Pup and say, "Sit." Then love Pup to wash away the intimidation and say, "Sit," again.

Later, when Pup's standing beside you, raise your hand, make sure he sees it, say, "Sit," and lo and behold he may do it. If not, adjust him in the sit position. Always repeating the command, "Sit."

While Pup's sitting, back off, hand raised, admonishing Pup to sit. Before he breaks, get back to him and give him a tidbit.

Always with this command or any other, give Pup a chance to register. To sort out the sound you've made. To try and remember what he should do when he hears that sound—for he wants the treat that follows, be it something to eat or a pat on the side.

Still later, when all dogs are at the end of one leash and you've walked them a far distance on a hot day, just stop. Chances are good Pup will sit: he's tired. When he does, say "Sit." When you start out, say, "Heel."

After long walk, pups are content to sit.

Pups are told to sit but pan of food entices them to stand and creep forward.

BOB FEFFER

BOB FEFFER

Katherine Dance holds hand like traffic cop to get springer to stay.

But before emphasizing Heel, let's get Pup to Stay. For Stay is a natural extension of the sit position. While Pup is sitting, step back, hand raised, saying with some threat in your voice, "Stay." Pup won't do it. He'll walk toward you. Return him to the exact spot he vacated.

Remember, dogs are very place oriented. That's why they should always be fed in the same place, bedded down in the same place, trained in the same place. Think not? Just feed Pup in the same place for three days and release him from his crate in the morning. Where does he run? That's right. To his eating spot. Especially if you have a pan in your hand.

Okay, back to sit. Return Pup to the spot he vacated. Tell him, "Sit," place him in the sit position, back off with palm displayed and say, "Stay," your voice and face showing Pup how serious all this really is.

Whoops! He broke again.

Okay, we'll have to put Pup on lead.

Start all over again, only this time when Pup breaks—and now he's not breaking toward you, he wants to run away—you let Pup come to the end of the rope, gather him in, and return him to the sit spot.

Yet, too much of this and Pup sinks. He's more interested in escape than he is anything you want to teach. You're defeated. Shuck the whole thing, tell Pup, "Hie on," and go back to your TV.

Repeat all this, off lead, time and time again. Now, take your act outdoors. Maybe 500 times hence you can tell Pup, "Stay," and you walk completely around the house; Pup turned to stone, sitting and staying, awaiting your return.

If not, save it all for another day. We're just dealing with a pup. Training sessions have to be fun, you have to be pleasant, and the reward has to be love. If any of these three are missing, then don't press. You've got months ahead to get your idea across and your will heeded.

Now there are ways we can get a dog to do all these things: a dog that never had the benefit of training as a pup, but that comes later.

What we're doing now is the easiest thing on earth within the scope of dog training. Pups are clean slates on which we can write whatever we want. It's old dogs where the slates become fogged over with erasures and mismarks. That slate you'll never get clean again, but you can write on it where it will be legible.

Lab is offered mastery over walking cane. Removes any resentment he may have to being adjusted by its tip.

The Cane

So we've got Pup coming, sitting, staying, and started on heel. I always teach Heel in the company of other dogs, so any resentment Pup has to the tug on his collar is directed toward those of his own kind, not toward me.

I take all dogs walking on the three-lead leash. Or two-lead leash. Just get at least one other dog involved. It takes two to heel. And it works like magic. Or so it appears. Release all dogs from lead and they stay at heel. I've never known it to work out any other way.

I do adjust Pup's position at heel with a bamboo cane. No, I don't hit him with it, I adjust him with it. No more contact than you might press a pencil. I take the cane and touch the end against Pup, the cane saying, get over, or get back, or hurry on. I reach behind myself with the cane to move Pup back to the side where I hold the leash in hand. The cane is just an extension of my arm. And never is it brandished to cause Pup to duck. That's your index: never handle the cane so Pup cringes. And to make the cane disappear in Pup's mind, toss it out and let him fetch it. Let him have mastery over the cane. Now that neutralizes the thing.

But there is this. When you do touch Pup with the cane, don't speak. THIS IS ANOTHER LAW OF DOG TRAINING: NEVER SAY ANYTHING WHEN DOING SOMETHING WITH PUP HE MAY RESENT. Quite frankly you're trying to be invisible; not there. At least you're no part of what the cane's doing, if Pup finds the cane offensive.

My pups look upon the cane with favor: as later they will the gun. When the cane comes out that means they get let out. What matters it curbs them a wee bit. They comply and it goes away.

And carrying that cane gets Pup accustomed to objects being in your hands. Later, he'll not be so puzzled when you take along an electronic transmitter or a gun. And if you've never hurt Pup with the cane, his reasoning goes, then why should you hurt him with other things you hold? Plus, the cane means let's go have some fun. Whatever else you carry must mean the same thing.

The Nature Of Man

You can't train Pup unless you learn his nature. But you must know man's nature, as well. Reading all this you might think Pup's in training all the time. But that's not the way it is. This puppy training pops up now and then, comes and goes; it's all easy and nothing is ever made of it if things go wrong.

Suddenly, during a TV commercial, you have the urge to command Pup, "Sit." Do it. Or, you see Pup walking in your direction and you say, "Come." Then when Pup gets there you pick him up and love him.

All puppy training is free and easy. Make it any other way and you tighten up. That's right: you must remember the nature of the beast that is you, that is man. If you're out with the kids playing sandlot ball, you strike and miss and what the heck? But let that be a ball game with your company team! Now you're trying to rip the cover off the ball.

That's why we don't have formal training sessions with Pup. Oh, he might be capable of learning, but are you capable of teaching? Pup will sense you tighten up. This will puzzle him. Make him leary. And therefore, sensitive. Now should you get frustrated it will defeat Pup.

Pup isn't going to do anything that doesn't please him. Or that his instincts don't drive him to do.

Only later will he do things *to please you.*

That's why Margaret offers the chocolate drops: Pup's hunting for himself.

That's why Ron soaks his tossed glove in tripe: Pup wants to pursue that good taste and aroma.

Make puppy training anything but play and you've not only beat down a pup but you've robbed yourself of the joy of bringing a pup along, of seeing him unfold, of watching his instincts develop, of seeing him gradually do things, not to please himself, but to please you.

And as for retrieving— That, too, just comes about off-hand. And it's worked in with all we've done above. Rather than sit through the TV commercial you may want to scoop up Pup and run outside to toss the dummy.

Come to think of it, let's toss one right now.

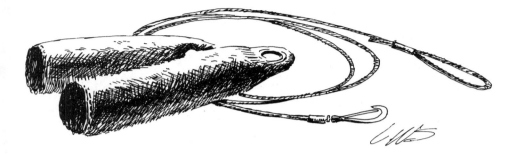

8/The First Fetch

A fly fisherman can't rush it.

Steady there. Take it easy. Work out all those holes—you'd think he was casting Pup for a dummy 'stead of a fly for a fish.

Make sure what you're offering is what the fish wants, where he wants it, when he wants it, how he wants it.

Don't jerk.

If he's come to hand, release him gently, holding him lightly, then watch him flash away.

Sit on the grass till the pool clears. Then cast again. Or store your rod and cast another day.

Read the mood of the day, the stream, the pool, the fish, yourself.

Enjoy.

And when the fish whips you don't get mad. What challenge would he be if you always won?

The First Retrieve

I don't imagine you were there when Pup made his first retrieve. What was it? A cedar chip from his bedding? A kibble out of the pan? A horse fly that died and fell into his bin?

This Brittany won't release quail so off-flank is lifted and bird plops out.

These were manless retrieves and there'll be more; some you con-
done, like the old tennis shoe you gave Pup to chew, and some you
don't, like your eyeglasses left on the floor beside your reading chair,
the hand purse your wife left on the kitchen telephone stand, the ball
your daughter left when she finished playing jacks.

Well Pup can't have these forbidden items. You must take them
from him. But how? No way can you touch Pup's mouth. Never are
you going to grab two jaws and force them apart. Not even gently, not
even silently, not any way.

So we've got a problem And now we start puppy training.

Go get a tidbit, something that is sure to work, like a piece of lunch
meat, and present it to Pup's nose in your clinched fist. There's no set
of eyeglasses or hand purse or toy ball that Pup's going to hold in
mouth and pass up a treat. When he spits out the item, pick it up
without comment, while you simultaneously give the treat, and be on
your silent way.

But let's say Pup displays a rare event. And we must consider this as well as what's common; what's expected. Pup just won't give up the purse. It's the purse he's got and he's going to keep it. Okay, reach across Pup's body, hook his flank in front of his off rear leg with your index finger, and lift. This usually dislodges whatever Pup is gripping in mouth.

If not, if Pup still persists in keeping the purse, then get directly in front of his face and blow into his nose with a great abrupt puff. This should cause Pup to drop the purse.

No matter what you do, don't use force, don't touch Pup's mouth, and don't get angry. And in the future, keep the place picked up. No need going through this again.

The First Planned Retrieve

The moment's arrived. D Day. D for dummy. And you're the launcher and Pup's the retriever. Don't you be the dummy and Pup the launcher. Or you end up being the retriever.

Here's what we're gonna do:

Go out in your back yard and look around. Pick a spot for you to stand, the dummy to land, and Pup to run between. You only need 10 feet to begin with, but these retrieves will extend to 60 or 75 feet so pick a spot you can let it all out.

If possible, pick a spot at the corner of the house. Now Pup can run down two sides. If there's a fence in the way, or a driveway, or who-knows-what, then that's that. Leave the corner. Just pick a one-path retriever spot.

Pick a spot where there's no distractions. You can't have other dogs watching Pup make these first retrieves. They'll bark and Pup'll look to them, completely forgetting you, the dummy, everything.

Matter of fact, remember, you can't train more than one pup at a time. Oh you can situate Pup among other pups to do something specific: like litter box check cording. But you can't teach Pup anything that requires his concentration with other dogs crying, and trying, to get into the act. Now there's an exception to this rule: if you have a Pup that's lost interest, you can perk him up by short-tieing him and letting him watch other dogs work. The short-tied pup will do anything to get back into the game. But this principle doesn't apply to a pup making his first retrieve.

Cricket is carouseled into casting position by swinging arm and clicking fingers ...

Back to distractions— Pick a spot where nothing breaks Pup's concentration. No kid on a bike cruising past, no milk truck, no garbage man. I don't even want Pup hearing the neighbor's radio. Ideally you'd like to rent a warehouse and throw Pup's first retrieves in its great hollow innards. Or go to a football stadium and climb the fence when everyone's gone.

But you want a spot you can go to any time and every time: just like you picked for Pup to tinkle.

So pick the best spot you can.

Okay, select a dummy. Now there's a lot to be made over what you toss for Pup to fetch. Some trainers have reasoned you don't want to use anything Pup will continually retrieve. If anything bad happens, the reasoning goes, let it happen with something Pup will never see again.

I'm not intending anything bad happens. Okay!

That's why I use a boat bumper. A small boat bumper. One I had made of canvas and kapok at a tent and awning manufacturer. Being small in diameter, Pup can get the thing in his mouth. Being extra long, Pup learns to balance his load. This is important and usually

...when positioned, she's told to stay, hand presented flat...

overlooked by the average trainer. Maybe that's why we see ducks brought to the blind by their tails, the bird sitting on Pup's nose like the hood ornament on a Rolls Royce.

The dummy has a brass grommet snapped in its top where I can tie a nylon cord. This looped cord gives me lots of versatility—I can give the dummy a good toss, carry it easily—and it also teaches Pup to hold high whatever he's carrying. If he doesn't, one of his legs ends up in the nylon loop and Pup trips.

You may toss whatever you have on hand for Pup to fetch. But it stands to reason you don't want anything so large Pup can't get it in his mouth, so textured it hangs up on a canine tooth, so heavy Pup can't lift it, so soft it encourages Pup to bite down and chew, or of such an odor it repels Pup from taking it to mouth.

So you've picked your spot and you've picked your dummy. Now gather up Pup and head outdoors, you proceeding loose and easy, not tensing, not letting Pup sense you're going to do anything but play.

Tell Pup, "Sit," or should he only be eight week's old—yes, you can start Pup any time you want, and any time he's ready—let him be wherever he wants, so long as he's near.

... to hype her up, dummy is danced before her. Then she's told to stay, once more, the dummy launched, and cast made ...

... as Cricket turns to make retrieve, author goes down on one knee to wipe out stance of intimidation, hurrahing Pup to him ...

... Cricket's pace picks up ...

Lean over from the waist, or get down on your knees, and holding the dummy by the looped nylon cord, shake it about like you were shaking sand out of your boot socks. Thump the dummy on the ground, hop it about, get Pup excited about this thing dancing before him.

Then, when Pup's got to have this thing—he covets it, you can see it in his face—give the dummy a couple of slow, false swings. That's right, false swings. Get Pup's head following the pendulum of your arm. If not, if you just toss the dummy out there, Pup's probably not going to see it leave your hand.

All the time you're making the dummy attractive, you're talking to Pup, like a shortstop talks to his pitcher, "Want'uh dummy? Huh? Want'uh fetch a bird? Gonna be a retriever? Huh? Gonna sock it to em?"

With the production you got going, the thumping of the dummy, the swinging of your arm, your voice in glee, maybe clapping your hands together now and then—this is the most exciting act Pup's ever seen. You're about to win an Oscar as the best supporting man.

Let her go. Lift off. Orbit. To land about six feet out front. And cheer Pup leaping toward it, "HEY PUP, FETCH IT UP!" Oh what a glory day! Watch him waddle. See him pounce. Now he's going to kill the thing. He's got it down and he's growling and shaking the dummy and it's surely going to die.

Or just like that, just one sweep of the mitt of his mouth, Pup's fielded the dummy and he's making his play for home plate.

What else would you expect?

You've been training Pup to FETCH IT UP since he entered your home. That's right. Pup's learned you don't lie to him when you hype him up. You did it when you served his food, "Oh boy, look at that. What a meal. Wish I had some."

Plus, Pup's been watching your arm from the start. You extended it to show him the back door, you swept it out to put him in his crate, you dropped it in disgust when pleading, "Aw pup . . . tinkle!"

All that's really new for Pup is the flying dummy. Which Pup now has in his mouth and it's time to start your second act. You're on your knees, clapping your hands, cheering, "HEY PUP, FETCH IT UP!" and you're smiling, and Pup runs toward you with dummy dangling.

BOB FEFFER

. . . she delivers to hand but author purposely drops dummy so toe-lift can be demonstrated . . .

. . . which prompts Cricket to fetch again and seat herself for a re-run.

Be ready. This is the first time your hand has gone to Pup's mouth to take a retrieve. Be ready. Don't drop the blasted thing. Don't jerk it from Pup's mouth. Don't miss it and let Pup fly by. Be ready.

And don't try to field the dummy one-handed. You're not playing center field, you're playing home plate. "Bring that bacon home, Pup!" Get both hands out and palms up. Like you were taking a drink from a pitcher pump. And keep em up. Turn em over and they're inclined to go to fists, inclined to grab. Left open, they're prone to placidly receive.

Now you're hoping you don't have to physically take the dummy from Pup's mouth. You're hoping Pup'll run to you, stop, and plop the thing into your upturned palms. If not, then go ahead and take it. Take the dummy gently and be done with it.

And I mean done with it. No more retrieves. You and Pup and the dummy go back into the house. That's it for the day. Pup's made his first retrieve: celebrate.

The Problem Retrieve

But let's say I'm painting green fields where all you've got is chat and cactus. Let's say Pup won't let go of the dummy. Well, don't pull. Have you seen those who did? They're out in the field, a pheasant leg in hand, the rest of the bird lock-jawed in Pup's mouth, and the man's pulling, and Pup's reared back, and the bird is three feet long, going on four—

No, don't pull.

Instead, push.

That's right, push.

Take a cigarette package and put it in your mouth. Pull. You can clinch it all day, right? And you can breathe around the edge. You're set to go the distance.

Alright, push. The force against the V at the back of your lips pries your mouth open. And you gag. So will Pup. Push and Pup'll be forced to release the dummy.

But if Pup's set for a siege, then as you push, twist the dummy up and back. That does two things: it stretches Pup's lips, which is uncomfortable, and it loosens the traction of the teeth. Twist, Push, Plop. The dummy's in hand.

But let's say that's not your problem. Pup's not sticky mouthed; you

192

don't think. Of course, you don't know, either. Because Pup's running in the other direction. He's off on a lark with the dummy in mouth. Well, don't do what you think you ought to do. Don't chase him. That just encourages Pup to run faster and farther. It's a game, Whee!

If any game's going to be played, make it your game. You run the other way. When Pup sees you're not following, and when he further sees you're going in the opposite direction, he'll spin about and chase you, maybe even dropping the dummy. But let's say he holds it. Be ready.

When Pup goes past—you're now running in slow motion the way you race the kids when you want them to win—you reach down and take the dummy from him. Always gently. No lunge. No jerk. To do either will make Pup head shy. Start him to dodging. And maybe the next time Pup bolts he'll not turn to chase you; no matter how attractive you make yourself.

But Pup dropped the dummy. That's okay. You and he go to the thing. When Pup's looking at the dummy, give it a lift and a short sail with the toe of your boot. That's enough to have Pup pounce on it. Now make yourself as attractive as possible if Pup's got the dummy in his mouth and he's coming toward you: hurrahing, clapping, down on one knee. Or, now get this, as distractive as possible if Pup's going the other way. That is, distract him to attend to you so you can attract him to follow in pursuit.

If it finally comes to pass that Pup just flat isn't going to bring you the dummy then go sit down and wait for him to either come by, or just drop the dummy and wander off. Either way, Pup will eventually end up beside you.

What I'd do with Pup is take him inside the house. You should do the same. And the next time you train, position your dummy toss and Pup's fetch so he can't run from you. Toss the dummy into the corner of the fence, or into the right angle of two walls. Anywhere Pup can't get by you, or run away.

But should Pup sense you're crowding him, he'll lose interest. The game is no longer any fun. So put it all away and try another day. You've got months to train Pup. Today is but one brick in the construction of his foundation.

But the next time out should Pup one, refuse to fetch the dummy from a corner, yet two, fetch it up when thrown out in the yard but persist in running away, then three, leave Pup out in the yard till you know he wants in the house, four, go out there and stand at the back door, dropping the dummy at your feet, then five, when Pup fetches up the dummy and tries to get into the house, you short stop him, take the dummy, and give with high praise.

For a while, then, always stand at the door and toss the dummy.

Or better yet, put it all away and let Pup grow up a couple of months. Should you still have trouble with fetching then, Pup'll need to be short-tied while you work other dogs.

Eventually you will win. Pup will be a retriever. You've just got to outsmart him. And that's what dog training is all about.

Besides, Pup's doing you a good service. He's teaching you what you'll need to know when it comes time to train his successor.

Whistle Versus Voice

Maybe you've noticed— I've had you shouting and waving your arms about out there, but I've not said a word regarding the training whistle. There's a reason. You'll remember Margaret Dance introduced her pups to the whistle in her kitchen. That's fine. It works for Margaret and it may work for you.

But Ray MacPherson, my sheep dog training sidekick in northern England, has mentioned while we were training border collies, "Bill, have you noticed when a dog's working up close to you, you can control him so much better with your voice than you can a whistle?"

Ray's right. Whistles are emotionless, but voice conveys your message, no matter what words you use. And you have greater range with your voice than ever with a whistle. Range from a whisper to a shout. Range from pleasure to outright anger.

All around the world I've seldom met a successful dog trainer who didn't control his charges with nearly a whisper. To have used a whistle would have been excess noise. Of course, Cotton Pershall, the retired premier retriever trainer from Nilo kennels, was the master of voice. Voice and angle water entries. But Cotton could yell. When he needed. And would his dogs attend! A yell from Cotton was something different and meant something important.

Only one man in history has won more than two international sheep dog championships. That was Jim Wilson. He won nine times. Even at a distance, Jim yelled. And as I've said before, shepherds sound like canaries with all the whistle-blowing afield. But Jim was an exception. And Jim was the greatest.

Cotton Pershall (center), father of angle water entries and soft voiced overs, heads out in John Olin's (left) quail wagon for morning plantation shoot. Olin installed aluminum wagon tongue to relieve mules' burden.

There's many reasons for getting results through voice commands: most important, when the dog's at fault you can increase your volume and put him down. When the dog's at a distance you can increase your voice and let him know, clearly, what you want. And if the dog's at fault, as well as at a distance, you've got some reserve to get his attention. You haven't used up all your voice when Pup was at your side.

But a whistle? The kind retriever handlers traditionally use—with a pea bouncing around in there—has little range in volume and less in emotion. Whenever possible use your voice to control Pup.

But teaching whistle commands is an easy undertaking. Just give Pup the verbal order, like, "Sit," then follow that with a long blast. Verbal command/long blast, over and over. This long whistle also means: Sit, Attend The Handler, and Stay.

Or every time Pup fetches a dummy give the suck-in whistle, interspersing it with the words, "Come," or "Heel." The suck-in whistle is one short blast followed by several pips.

Eventually the whistle alone will get the job done.

And I will say this about the whistle. Should any retriever trainer ever learn to whistle with his fingers and train his retrievers to cast on whistle alone—not being stopped and asked to look back for hand signals—that man is going to win it all.

Do you follow me? Let's take a minute to explain. The way the game is now played the handler casts his retriever afield, hits him with a whistle, has the dog stop and turn around, look for a hand cast, then carry on. There's no need for this. The shepherd casts his dog afield then adjusts the dog's line by different whistles—the dog never stopping and turning to look back.

MacPherson has seven dogs, each on 6 whistles, all dogs worked at the same time. Imagine, 42 different whistle signals. MacPherson is quite a dog trainer. I'd be hard put to think up 42 different whistle commands, let alone remember which one to whistle for which dog, to tell him which way to go, at what speed.

Casting Pup

There's a special reason I asked you to pick a specific spot in your backyard for Pup's dummy sessions. For the first few weeks, when training back there and not away in some field, you'll toss a dummy from nowhere else.

This will accomplish many things. One, Pup will know this is fetching country, he'll have the right mental set; two, Pup will gain confidence for here he'll never fail; three, Pup will be rammed into doubles; four, Pup will get accustomed to always delivering to hand; five, the rhythm of the cast sequence will become engrained; and six, Pup will start casting toward the area of the fall—whether or not he's seen a dummy thrown.

Here's how it all progresses.

As training sessions come and pass you'll eventually start casting Pup with the verbal command, "Pup," or "Back." The American usually says, "Back." The Briton generally uses the dog's name, for British trials emphasize staunchness—several dogs on line at the same time—and if a handler were to command, "Back," and all dogs were so programmed, the whole lot could very well take off.

At odd times, day and night, you'll call Pup to you, heel him to your designated spot in the back yard, tell him, "Sit," and hyping him up, toss the dummy.

Bob Milner works his string British style, all dogs on line honoring the working dog ...

Let's analyze your form. The dummy's in your right hand—if you're a right handed gunner—and your left hand hangs above Pup's head. So Pup's heeled to the off-gun side to avoid being in the way when the gun must be raised, or to be out of range if the gun is mis-fired.

As the right hand tosses the dummy, the left hand casts Pup to fetch it up—or holds Pup back by his plain leather collar till the dummy lands, then directs Pup to go. Or the left hand holds the end of a slip cord tied to your belt, poked through the D ring in Pup's leather collar, and doubled back to hand. The hand is then used to cast Pup, release the cord, let the cord slide through the D ring as Pup launches, and gathers it all in coil to stuff in a pocket as Pup makes his way to the fall.

Whether or not you hold Pup back is up to you. Only you can read your dog, know when he needs to be curbed or encouraged, forced to stay, or incited to bolt.

... a British national open field trial sees gallery drive tall cover while center handler signals a back. Bill Meldrum works his charges in a high wind, yelling, "Back," to distant black Lab while other dogs lounge in wait for their turn.

Ram It

We have in field trial terms the word, ramming. You ram a dog to fetch. And you ram by casting your left arm up with great vigor, booming, ''Back,'' and shooting your left leg out, knee bent, so the shoe glides over the grass. Pup will follow the cast of your arm and his launch will be channeled by the barrier, or guide, of your leg.

Okay, let's say you've been tossing a dummy for Pup about four weeks. And you've gradually started ramming your cast. To do this in the beginning would have blown Pup to side, scared him to death. But doing it now, you're accomplishing more than just launching a dog. You're putting Pup on automatic lift-off. Dummy thrown or not, Pup will launch. Which means Pup's being readied to fetch a blind.

Plus, by casting all dummies from the same spot everything is reinforcing everything else. Pup has never left that spot and not found a dummy. Pup is learning that as you send so shall he find. An absolute imperative in retrieverdom. For we never cast Pup and trick him. We never cast him for nothing.

There'll come times Pup won't want to cast. Even if he's the national champion he may not want to go. And you must be able to make him go. And this you can't do if Pup has a history of casting out there only to find the cupboard bare.

That's why some trainers seed the area of the fall. They go beforehand and lay dummies about. Then should the dummy they throw get hung up in a tree, or roll off the hill, or drop in a hole, Pup is still going to find a dummy. Any dummy will do.

Also, you've been bringing Pup out here in the dark. Hopefully there's a light overhead. Or maybe you've brought a flashlight along and shined it on the two of you. Pup sees a dummy leave your hand, and you ram. Naturally Pup takes off. And he knows where to run, and he has the confidence to run there, for he's been doing it for a month, from this same spot, with the same rhythm, with the same command—in the sunlight. Sure enough, Pup finds the dummy. Finds a dummy in the dark and that's amazing. For it takes a Pup with lots of confidence in his handler and in himself to run out there.

With two or three months of this day and night training you can eventually walk Pup out to your spot, ram him, and he'll leap forward—*without you having thrown a thing.* Pup is only six months old and he's running his first blind retrieve. What we call a repeat blind, but nevertheless a blind. Or more precisely, what we call a line to a blind, but more about this later.

Dick Cook rams his retriever to fetch, while Jim Rodgers gives a standard back.

Pup's First Double

About this time you can take Pup to your spot, hold his collar, toss your usual dummy to its usual landing, then turn about 45 degrees and throw another dummy. To state it in detail: you've got one dummy down one side of the house—where it always is—but now you're tossing another dummy down another side of the house.

Now, Pup will always take the last dummy thrown. That's the one fresh in his mind. Release him. He'll run over there and fetch it up and run back, probably trying to pass you with dummy in mouth to go get the first dummy you threw—the one we call the memory bird.

But you know Pup's going to try this so you block him and take the dummy from his mouth. So Pup stands there. He's forgotten about the first dummy thrown, he's never had two dummies down before. But you heel him to his many-times-repeated-stance, facing the way he's run hundreds of times, and ram him. Immediately all the reinforcements take over and Pup launches. When he returns with the dummy, and he will, Pup's just made his first double retrieve. Wonder of wonders!

That's why I asked you to pick a spot at the corner of your house. Remember? So Pup could run two ways and have a barrier to separate him from the two falls. Pup can't run through the wall of a house to get the memory bird. He must come to the corner and turn 45 degrees. That's where you intercept him and take the last dummy thrown. Therefore, if you don't have some wall, or fence, or similar edge, to channel Pup's path back from his first fetch, then you'll need postpone doubles till you do.

Or there is another way out. Do you have a fence where you can stand off one end and throw a dummy to either side? Pup can't run through a fence to switch dummies.

Nor through a tight hedge row; nor on opposite sides of you, one dummy left, the other right; nor on opposite sides of a tennis net—or you'll find something.

Now the classic handler moves little and says less. But we've got you throwing bowling balls on your ram so you could explode the pin setter through the back wall, and we've got you booming like an umpire. Ease off. Gradually calm your act so long as you can keep Pup's act going.

The ram is imbedded in Pup by now. It'll always be there when you need it. When Pup's confronting an ice apron about the lake or a patch of thorn bushes in the field.

A Special Place for a Special Pup

And one last word about this spot. Keep it a casting sanctuary. Don't take Pup there to tinkle or dump. Don't teach heel, sit, stay, there. For I repeat, dogs associate bad things that happen to them with places they occur. If you have something go wrong with toilet training, or yard training, let it go wrong somewhere you're not teaching fetch.

And by the same token, dogs associate pleasant things with places they happen. We've gone to great pains to make this spot the most pleasant in all of Pup's young life.

When Pup's older, say nine months or a year, you can do with him as you please in your back yard. Mix it up. Throw here. Dump there. But don't change spots, or overlap spots, while Pup's in kindergarten.

And Pardner I want to tell you something. Do you know there isn't one man out of 10,000 who ever gets a pup as far along as you and Pup are today? I mean during the dog's whole life.

Keep on the way you're going and who's to say? You may make it all the way. Make Pup one of those 90 or so dogs a year, out of 75,000 registered, to ever qualify for the national.

Or make your duck blind or those pheasant fields the way poets paint em—color it gold.

9/Some Bite With Our Bark

When mountain climbers, cowboys, and dog trainers have gone as far as they can by hand, they switch to a rope. Plus, with piton, spur, and spike, they grab ahold, take charge, enforce their position.

Until now we've trained Pup hands-off, encouraged him to be a free spirit, hyped him to performance. But you may have noticed— Sometimes, when Pup's distant, he turns us off. Other times, right at hand, he tells us, ''No.''

It's time we started using the slip lead and pinch collar.

The Slip Lead

The slip lead is a hank of nylon cord tied to your belt—we mentioned it in the last chapter. The loose end of the cord is fed through the D ring on Pup's plain leather collar. In a training situation, should you want Pup to stay, take the loose end in hand—you've now got a round-robin leash—and if Pup breaks he'll take but a couple of steps them come to a jolt when he hits the end of his rope.

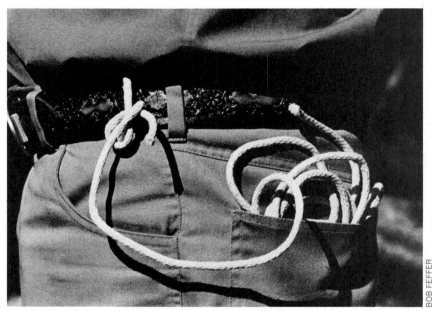

Slip lead is tied to belt loop, wadded up, stuffed in rear pocket ...

But if Pup complies and stays, he'll not feel a thing. Then, should you order, "Back," and cast Pup for the bird, you'll merely release the loose end of the cord and as Pup leaps forward the cord will slide through the open D ring.

From now on Pup won't know if he's tied to you or not. Which means, Pup will stay.

But let's say Pup's rambunctious. He doesn't care if you tumble him tail-over-nose. Okay, switch to a 20 foot slip lead. Doubled back that makes 10 feet for Pup to bolt before he runs out of rope. What a jolt? I mean his rear end shoots through, his nose points to sky, and he comes to earth like a meteor. And you? Be ready. You're going to think both arms were dislodged from their sockets.

But even with this, you say, Pup's still breaking.

The Pinch Collar

Then discard the slip lead, PUT IT AWAY, and switch Pup's plain leather collar to a pinch collar. And I repeat: PUT THE SLIP LEAD AWAY. I want you to hold the pinch collar in hand. To tie it to a rope

206

BOB FEFFER

... when Pup is told to sit, slip lead is threaded through D ring on collar. If Pup is cast, slip lead is released to zip through D ring. If Pup breaks, slip lead is held to somersault Pup before casting line ...

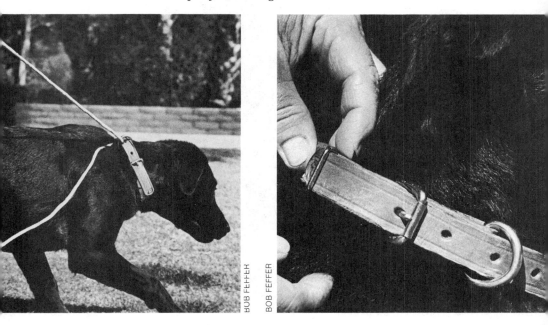

BOB FEFFER

BOB FEFFER

207

... or, a hank of rope can be permanently tied to Pup's collar —trailing him wherever he goes.

and have Pup bolt would apply so much pressure at rope's end Pup could be very seriously injured.

A pinch collar is a spike collar modified to be a self-training device. It's made of two pieces of leather sandwiched about a strip of spring steel. Inside the collar are brass studs that point toward Pup's neck. The lead-end of the collar slides through a brass roller. The pinch collar is a power training tool always worked close in hand.

As I write this book there is no pinch collar on the market. You must make your own. Later, after this book gains wide distribution and everyone demands a pinch collar, some enterprising fellow will offer one for sale. Until then you'll have to buy a spike collar, take a file, and knock all the spikes pointless. Your spikes will end up blunt brass posts.

Place the pinch collar about Pup's neck with the lead-end of the collar in hand—and I repeat, never on leash, always in hand—and tell Pup, "Heel, Sit, Stay."

If Pup obeys he'll not feel a thing. But if he resists—if he bolts, lunges, leaps to side, or rears back—he gets pinched.

Here's how it works. Any action on the collar closes it: just like the old chain-link choke collar. Only the spring steel sandwiched within the pinch collar causes this collar to spring open when pressure is released.

Specifically, you hold the lead-end of the pinch collar in hand. The lead-end slides through a brass roller attached to the other end of the collar. If Pup applies pressure the brass roller slides down toward Pup's neck, the collar contracts, the blunt studs angle toward each other gathering folds of skin, and if Pup persists in applying pressure the studs will eventually pinch the gathered folds of skin about Pup's neck.

When Pup gives in, the spring steel pops the collar open, running the brass roller back up the lead-end, standing the studs upright, releasing the folds of skin, and Pup no longer has a pain in the neck.

Used correctly—and that's imperative with any training tool—the

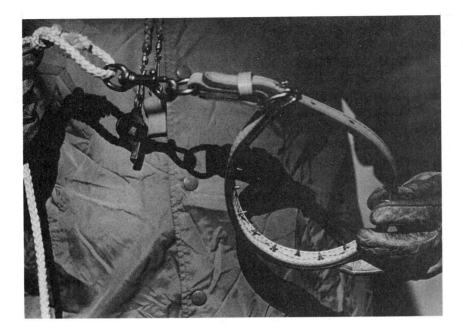

Buy a spike collar and file it pointless.

pinch collar is the most humane collar you can use. It does not gag, suffocate, cut, stick, nor gouge. It leaves no scar, no internal damage, and no imprint. Plus, it never makes a mistake.

It never applies pressure when it shouldn't. Never fails to do so when it should. The collar's timing is perfect: never ahead of Pup nor in lag. And what's most important, Pup's in charge. You have nothing to do with it. You don't pull. Pup does. You don't reckon the timing. Pup does. You don't determine the amount of force. Pup does. And you're not moving a hand, an arm, a leg—nothing. You're just standing there, detached. Pup can't perceive you as part of his plight. And Pup can hold you no grudge.

The pinch collar is a beautiful self-training device. Pup is the trainer in control. And it satisfies all our FOUR Ts: temperament—the trainer's motionless and emotionless. Timing—it's instantaneous. Transfer—your verbal command, if ignored, can be a pain in Pup's neck. And touch—you've got total contact with variable pressure.

You should know this collar is built so the pinch is not equal all about its inner circumference. Great. We can use this. The more pronounced pinch comes just off-center, toward the lead-end. That means we can place the greater pinch where it will do us the most good.

Consider the way we are: man or beast. As the head goes, so goes the body. The acrobat, the diver, the man on the flying trapeze—all attest to this. Lower the head the haunches lift. Raise the head and you tuck in your butt. Therefore, if you want Pup to lie down, place the lead-end under his chin so the pinch is pronounced behind his neck. Yet, if you want Pup to sit, place the lead-end behind Pup's neck, the greater pinch coming under the chin.

Okay?

Another thing— Do you want the brass roller on the off-side of Pup, or the near-side? To teach sit, you want the roller on the off-side. This places the greater pinch away from you. If pup resists, the pain will move him toward your knee. This will heel Pup in close: just where you want him. For that's the nature of man or beast: to move directly away from pain.

And how do you introduce this device? As with every training tool you first let Pup get the feel of it outside a training situation. Put it on Pup in the house, contract the collar, let Pup feel its bite. We did the same thing with the fly swatter. Remember?

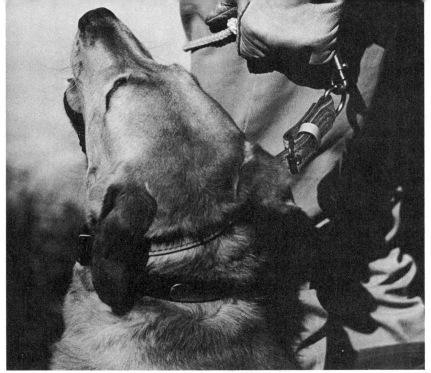

Pup's heeled properly in pinch collar — head beside pants leg seam — but Delmar Smith has rope attached to collar's lead. When you've trained several thousand dogs you can do the same. Until then, remove the lead rope . . .

The Invisible You

Dogs, and humans for that matter, expect attack to come fast. Expect anger to be accompanied with loud noises and running feet and swinging arms. The sound and the fury. Therefore, in a training situation, Pup never sees anything like this.

Sit Pup before you and slip the pinch collar over his head, position it about his neck as you want it, then gradually pull. Pup does not associate the pinch with you. Your face is neutral, you are silent, your whole being is detached. It's the collar that's got him—not you.

This detached trainer, THIS INVISIBLE YOU, is imperative throughout dog training.

Also, I repeat, you always introduce a training device apart from training. It simply does not have anything to do with what is being taught. It appears as a reality of life. It's just there. It's there and Pup must learn to live with it. You've always been Pup's friend. If you could do anything about this thing around his neck—you would. For

212

. . . Delmar shifts collar to right hand to push dog into sit position. Collar is returned to left hand when Delmar steps off and commands, "Heel."

Mindy Rodgers positions Pup perfectly, hand immediately next to pants leg seam. Ordering "Heel," she steps off, dog stands and complies. Mindy makes an abrupt turn, the dog matches her every step, her every move. Then Mindy says, "Sit," and Pup drops. This power tool guarantees perfect results and is the most humane collar ever developed. Note: hand is never moved from seam.

you've always been a helping hand, always brought comfort, always rushed to Pup's aid when he was in trouble. Now you just stand there. The pinch collar is beyond your power, like taxes is beyond a politician's. So Pup must do as it commands since there's no other way out.

Sit and Heel

Take Pup to the back yard. Put the pinch collar on him and say, "Sit." If Pup complies, fine. Stand there a moment. Now step off slowly and command, "Heel." If Pup complies, stroll about for a minute. But pretty soon Pup is not going to comply. He's going to be late. And when that happens he's going to get pinched.

And when he gets pinched he's going to fight. Hold your ground. Tighten your fist about the lead-end of the collar, flex your arm, hold your fist immediately adjacent to the seam that runs down the outside of your pants leg. Endure. And be invisible.

When Pup finally settles, say "Sit," and transfer the lead-end to your right hand. Lower your body, grasp Pup's waist just above his

215

hips with your left hand: between thumb and forefinger. Now push down and back with your left hand while your right hand lifts on the lead-end and slightly contracts the pinch collar.

Don't push straight down. If you do, Pup can stand there all day. He can lock his back knees and they'll resemble bridge pilings. By pushing back and down you break the knee-locks and Pup collapses.

When Pup's sitting, release all pressure: left hand removed from Pup's hips, right hand loosened on the lead-end. Pat Pup. Rub Pup. Coo to Pup. That's enough. Transfer the lead-end back to your left hand and step off, saying, "Heel."

Understandably Pup may be confused and he may be frightened. Do everything in slow motion. Give Pup time to comply. Later you can accelerate commands and movements. For now, step off slowly, saying, "Heel." If Pup balks, give a steady pull. He'll stand and follow.

Later, should Pup get crosswise behind you, walking sideways, his head at the side of your leg, his body angled across the back of your calves, start high stepping. Each time you lift a foot, lift it high and catch Pup in the rib cage with your heel.

Pup will work back to side. Keep going. Whenever Pup complies congratulate him. When he doesn't, let the pinch collar do your talking. Around and around you go: "Heel," "Sit," "Heel," "Sit." Short sessions will serve Pup best. Three minutes or so and put it all away.

And through it all, hold that lead-end in your fist immediately adjacent to your pants seam. That will position Pup perfectly for heel. And to repeat the obvious: never be a part of Pup's predicament. Always be detached.

How much better this method is to teach heel than so many we've used before. Especially striking Pup with a whip. Pup knows you are the culprit when he sees that arm raised and feels that whip come down. And he can smell the anger in you. See your red face. Your bulged neck. He can hear the frustration in your voice. He knows it's you that's applying the pressure and he also knows you are displeased.

Or to walk along twirling a rope before Pup's nose to keep him back. Pup sees that rope is in your hand. You're making it hit him.

Yes, we've been training retrievers wrong for a long time. We've used our hands, not our heads. And it attests to the remarkable nature of dogs that they've taken all this, forgiven us, and gone ahead to perform.

Come and Stay

My Okie trail buddy, Delmar Smith, says, "The test of gettin a dog to come is when the come's in you and not the dog."

Delmar's right.

You may want Pup to come, but Pup wants something different: like sniffing a bitch in heat, gnawing a dead toad, rolling in cow manure, going to sea after a crippled coot you spooked from the bank while walking to the duck blind.

So how do we get Pup to come?

Snap a 20 foot check cord to the D ring of Pup's plain leather collar, tell him "Hie on,"—that is, go do whatever he wants—then when Pup stops to sniff something, you walk up, pick up the trailing check cord, and say, "Come here."

Should Pup seem deaf, then reel him in. And the way to do this is not hand-over-hand. You can make twice the speed by using your off-hand as a guide and pulling the cord through it in long sweeps with your dominant hand.

Or, you can tell Pup, "Hie on," and keep the end of the check cord in hand, giving Pup 20 feet of latitude to explore. Any time you can command, "Come here," and force compliance.

And to paraphrase Delmar, when it comes to Pup staying: "The test of getting a dog to stay is when the stay's in you and not the dog." Pup may want to bolt. You're standing on the casting line and someone just threw a cackling pheasant right before him, and two shells exploded, and feathers are drifting down, and it's all so attractive Pup's saying, "I'll see you later."

Well, the best method of getting Pup to stay was discovered by my friend, Jim Culbertson, the Wichita high school coach. When Jim and I had about 20 Labs between us, and we were training most every day, Jim's football team was usually with us in the field. And these kids— I swear, they could catch an antelope, wrestle a grizzly, swim a meet with a muskrat. And they wanted to help—especially if it were physical.

So Jim or I would heel a dog on line and signal the bird thrower to toss a shackled pigeon and fire a blank .22 training pistol.

Sure nuf. Pup would break.

But what's this? Four high school football players come screaming—I mean screaming—across the casting line, throwing

Jim Rodgers attaches 20 foot check cord to Pup's plain leather collar; stepping away, Jim orders, "Come," but Pup balks. So Jim jerks rope and Pup moves to him...

themselves into a flying tackle, coming down on Pup, mock mauling him, false beating him, rolling him about.

Then during a lull in the pretended mayhem Pup's let go. He staggers out stunned, looking about to learn where he's ended up. Then seeing his handler he heads home. There he's loved and patted and cooed to and told, "What's wrong with those idiots? What did they do to you? Why poor Pup ..." While at the same time, the four idiots are walking past, positioning themselves behind the casting line—just where the judges will always stand at a field trial.

Once again Pup is told to heel, sit, stay, and the bird thrower signaled to throw the bird and pop the blank. Only this time Pup's not watching the bird. He's looking back. Wondering what those idiots are going to do.

Pup must be rammed to get the bird. And all the time he's going out he's got one eye looking back.

Jim and I never had to do this more than one time to a pup or dog. And neither of us ever had a dog break on line at a field trial.

. . . training session accomplished—Pup coming on command without rope's tug—Jim lets Pup have mastery over rope, wrapping it about Pup's nose in play, snaking it on ground so Pup can "kill" it. Pups must learn training devices are not going to hurt them.

Those idiots—the judges—were always standing back there. And Pup had learned they couldn't be trusted.

You can keep Pup tuned up to stay even when hunting—a time when things get relaxed and it's not so important if a dog breaks or not. Just run your slip lead through the D ring of Pup's plain leather collar. Pup won't know if he's tied fast or not.

Or short-tie Pup to the duck blind and release him only when you want him to fetch.

Down

There are two kinds of down. One, to lie down. The other to get down.

Lie down is taught as an extension of the sit and stay position. Remember? We told Pup to "Sit," then "Stay," and we backed off with our palm up like a taffic cop? Hopefully this drill has been engrained, but maybe not. Maybe it needs enforcement.

Okay, tell Pup, "Down," then step before him, take his two front paws and pull them toward you, breaking Pup down from the sit position. But maybe his butt is up: Pup's in a prayer position. Reach back and push his rump to earth.

Now back off as you did before, palm up, saying, "Down." Oops! Here comes Pup. It's not going to work. Okay, return Pup to the spot he vacated and place the plain leather collar about his neck. Snap a nylon cord to the D ring of the collar, run the cord through the arch of your boot that is nearest Pup as you stand in the heel position, tell Pup, "Down," and pull the cord.

Your boot sole acts as a pulley and the cord lowers Pup's head to the ground. But once again Pup may end up in the prayer position. Transfer the lead to your right hand, keep the pressure on, and reach back with your left hand to force Pup's butt to ground.

Or, drive a rod with an eyelet at the top into the ground. Run your check cord through the eyelet. Stand distant and tell Pup, "Down," as you pull the cord. The eyelet will act as your pulley and pull Pup's head to the ground. Pup will eventually drop to earth and stay there.

As for "Get down," this is taught without collar or lead. You know

Pup is told to sit and stay, the trainer takes his front legs from him, breaking dog down to stay position. Now handler steps back with hand raised, ordering, "Stay," or "Down." If Pup stands and follows he's returned to vacated spot and process is repeated.

when Pup greets you he's going to jump. Let him hit your knee. Once again you're detached from it all—no arms waving about, you're not even looking at Pup. As Pup leaps, merely bend your knee and let it meet Pup squarely on his chest.

Pup soons learns it's dangerous to jump on you. And he knows it's not your fault. It's the way you're built. You've got that bone sticking out and it catches him in the chest.

But Pup will still want to leap, so he'll cheat. He'll leap to side. Pay him no mind, but let the side of your shoe catch him in the chest. Or if Pup starts leaping up behind you, let your heel catch him in his chest.

Most dogs learn to stay distant with just one lesson, just one bump.

Now, when you arrive at a kennel gate to release Pup, you'll be saying one of two things. Either, "Stay," or "Down." For you know Pup's going to crowd the gate to bolt, or you know he's going to leap to greet if he finds you more interesting than far vistas. Bring Pup under control within the kennel run before you unlatch the gate. Tell him "Stay," or "Down," until it seems he's going to comply.

As the months go by your vocabulary with Pup will expand. Maybe he'll learn, "Get back," which means to do just that, so an in-swinging kennel gate doesn't pinch his front toes. "Get back," also drives Pup to the end of his run so you can get in there and hose it down.

"Outside," is a command taught through repeatedly going to the backdoor, opening it, pointing your arm, clicking your fingers, and encouraging Pup to exit.

By reverse token, when you want Pup to enter the house, his kennel, his crate, your car, your duck blind—snap your fingers, extend your arm, and say, "Kennel."

Day-by-week-by-month, Pup learns to watch your hands, listen to the finger snaps, follow your arm. This is good, for we're now ready to adjust Pup's platform on the casting line. When we tell Pup, "Heel, Sit, Stay," to await the bird, we want him square with the world.

On The Line

Walk Pup to the casting line, tell him, "Heel, Sit, Stay." Look at him. I mean lean back and look him all over. Is his rear end parallel to the casting line? Are his front feet equidistant from the casting line? If Pup's askew, what direction's he facing? Right, left? Pup must be adjusted.

Tell Pup, "Heel," and place your right hand out and before his nose, snapping your fingers. Slowly move your arm to the right, bringing Pup along. Now gradually turn in place, guiding Pup around you—I call this carouseling—and Pup arrives at the spot he just vacated. Tell him, "Sit." How's his platform this time? Do you need to crank it about some more?

This heel drill, or carousel, is very important. If Pup is cantered on line he'll shoot out at an angle to the bird—especially when running a blind where he's seen no bird fall. For we know, as the body is faced so shall it proceed. Also, this heeling will be done at field trials before judges and we want it all smooth and effortless. We don't want Pup flustered in competition nor you to get angry.

Incidentally, this is one reason heel, sit, stay, and down are so important. Often times at a field trial you'll be asked to stay in hold-blinds for long lengths of time. If you've got to pick, pick, pick at Pup to get him to stay, then you'll need to get tough with him, which will put him down, put him off his game—and the judges may be overhearing you.

Get all discipline down pat and make it secondary. That can't be your concern when going for a bird. Get the poultry, that's the thing, not piddle around coming to, standing at, or leaving the casting line.

Back to carouseling—

You can continually adjust Pup's casting position by carouseling him about you, or you can fine-tune Pup by merely extending your left leg, patting it near Pup's head, sliding the leg away from Pup, encouraging Pup to lean toward you. Pup can only lean so far before he must scootch his rear end about and reposition his front feet. That's exactly what you want him to do.

When Pup finally sits to please you—which is the way he must sit to address the field and get the job done—and you look out and see gunners and bird boys waiting, tell Pup, "Mark." Mark means birds are going to fly.

If the field is vacant, that means Pup must run a blind: retrieve a bird he's neither heard shot, nor seen fall. So, you'll command, "Line."

Mark and Line are terms given us by the fox hunter. A hound marks when he stops at the earth where a fox has gone to ground, tries to dig his way in, and gives tongue in a distinctive manner. A line is the trail of a running fox. Retrievers mark the location of a bird they see fall,

White terrier leaps to catch trainer's knee in chest. Cricket sits at a distance. She learned in one session the trainer can't help it, but he's built funny, and it hurts when she leaps upon him . . .

. . . yet, the British encourage their dogs to leap as Bill Meldrum fondles Sandringham Sydney at field trial and training session.

but they must be cast on a line to a bird that's fallen outside their view.

Through months of training in the field, Pup will learn the difference. Plus, you can cue him with other words. For example, you may say, "Dead bird," before you say, "Line," which lets Pup know something's laying out there you want brought to hand.

"Dead bird," is easily taught in a hunting situation. You're after quail. A covey rises. You shoot three. Pup sees one fall. He's marked the bird and you cast him for the retrieve. But Pup doesn't know two other birds are down. Tell him, "Dead bird," and cast him, or walk him about. Make sure Pup finds a bird even if you must drop the one to earth you've placed in your game bag.

Okay— Heel, sit, and stay may bring stellar performance from Pup in the back yard. But what about Pup at trial? Many a back yard champion has gone looney in competition.

That's why you must train afield with people of like interest. Pup's got to work amidst squawking bird crates, playing children, honking horns, guns going off, men yelling, dogs barking, scent all about—in other words, bedlam.

A rule of thumb in dog training is this: to put a dog right you must first put him wrong. This is vital. Pup must make a mistake in this simulated field trial set up. And Pup must be corrected here. AKC won't permit dog training on field trial grounds. If Pup goofs at a trial you can't touch him. So never let Pup learn this. Let him assume this training situation is a trial and you lower the boom. Dogs can learn the difference, you know? You bet they can. They'll do everything perfectly in training, then once on the trial grounds they tell the handler to take his whistle and—

So find a friend to train with or join a retriever club. If neither is available then seek out a pro. He trains every day and will take you on.

Fine Tuning

It's in training sessions with others, or at fun trials sponsored by your local retriever club, you can fine tune Pup on line and also drill him on everything we've covered to this point.

And it's here Pup will probably get his first birds. Now there is such a thing as a bird shy dog. That same dog is usually man shy and gun shy, as well. He's just a timid creature and we'll need to bold him up on the force retrieve table.

Professional Louisiana retriever trainer, Abele du Treil, detains derby dog in hold blind without hassle. Dog is not intimidated and has zest for test coming up.

But maybe he is bold, yet something happens in the field to turn him off birds. Maybe he gets pecked or spurred by a big cock pheasant.

Or maybe he gets confused. Maybe he finds a pheasant in the water and a duck on land.

Or maybe an accident happens. Just as Pup reaches for a pigeon he pokes a twig in his eye.

Well don't get upset with your birdless Pup. He'll retrieve. Once we run him through our force retrieving session he'll bring back a condor if that's what you send him to fetch.

10/Marks

"The function of a Non-Slip Retriever is to seek and retrieve 'fallen' game when ordered to do so. He should sit quietly on line or in the blind, walk at heel, or assume any station designated by his handler until sent to retrieve. When ordered, a dog should retrieve quickly and briskly without unduly disturbing too much ground, and should deliver tenderly to hand. He should then await further orders.

"Accurate marking is of primary importance. A dog which marks the fall of a bird, uses the wind, follows a strong cripple, and will take direction from his handler is of great value."

Field Trial Rules for Retrievers
Published by the American Kennel Club

Getting the Basics

We've got Pup marking handler-thrown singles, and maybe doubles, in the back yard. And each of us has probably gone afield and tossed a bumper, or we've joined up with others and presented Pup a pigeon, and he's heard the distant gun and felt the wind in his face and knocked down some light cover in going to fetch.

The emphasis of our yard work has been to make Pup a good canine citizen. Now, most of our effort will go to making him a good hunter and retriever. There are many mistakes to be made so let's note what they are and try to avoid them.

One. The whistle. Too many handlers are whistle happy. Just a toot will do it. Laying on the whistle is another form of nagging. Plus, judges like to hear simple, softly blown whistles—it tells them the handler's in charge. And remember, a dog can hear a whistle up to a mile.

There are two whistle signals for retrievers. *One,* the long sustained blast which tells Pup to sit—to stop whatever he's doing and sit. To sit and look at the handler.

And *two,* the come-in, or suck-in whistle: a moderately long blast followed immediately by a series of pips. The sit whistle is a dahhhhhhhhh. The come-in whistle is a dahhh-dit-dit-dit-dit.

Two. Being absent from nature the average urban dweller forgets to consider natural factors when taking Pup to field. Of primary importance is the direction and velocity of the wind. At first, cast Pup into the wind. This will give him confidence in marking: what his eyes don't see his nose will smell.

But remember this law of dogdom: Pup doesn't want to take a side-cast into the wind. Say you cast Pup from the line 90 degrees to the wind, then hit him with a sit whistle and tell him to cast directly into the wind. It's an exceptional dog that'll do it. Do it and not drift. I think it's similar to us being asked to swim upstream in a strong current. We'd rather go with the flow.

The urban dweller must also remember that different cover emits different degrees of scent. For example, a difficult cover in which to find a dummy is fresh clover. Plus, dust holds down scent. And so does heat.

From my work with fox hunters I can admit there's not a man today who knows one thing about scent. Why should dogs show good nose in dusty clover on a hot day? Yet they do.

Or why should dogs go to field on a cool, damp day when you'd think scenting conditions were perfect, and not be able to find their feed pan?

Three. The average amateur field trial trainer makes two mistakes. *One*, he overtrains his dog. Having no other dog to take out of the crate, he keeps the one he has—out too long. And *two*, he shows Pup too many handler-thrown dummies.

Consider this, the only bird Pup will generally see flushed from foot will be a pheasant or a quail. Yet, let's face it, field trials are won or lost on water. And where do ducks come from? From foot? Hardly. They come from the air, at a quarter. That's why Britons try to use another person to present dummies. And the other person is usually hidden behind a hedge row and all birds are lofted over it and Pup merely catches the arc of their flight.

It is imperative you find help. Be it your wife or husband, child or neighbor. You've got to have someone afield present the birds.

Now the average trainer who wants to hunt his retriever, not trial him, makes the mistake of not training enough. And yes, he also relies too much on handler-thrown dummies.

The hunting retriever must learn to watch for birds appearing in the sky, not originating in the hand.

Four. Another mistake made by too many trainers—especially in Great Britain—is overuse of the gas operated dummy launcher. Once again we have the bird originating in hand, plus, we've got a dummy that may turn foul. Can take on that odor of old gun powder—you've smelled as much with the catalytic converter in your station wagon—and Pup can blink this bird.

Blink the bird? Yes, that's a term which means Pup finds the bird but acts like he doesn't.

The dummy stinks, so Pup doesn't want anything to do with it.

The launcher does have limited use as a blind planter: to place a dummy afield and not leave a handler's foot trail, or to place a dummy across a stream where the handler cannot easily go.

Five. The average retriever trainer also makes mistakes we've learned to avoid. He charges Pup in the field when Pup's done wrong. He strikes Pup. Kicks Pup. He takes the dummy and slams it into Pup's mouth. When Pup returns to line the handler lunges for the bird, jerks it from Pup's mouth. This man shouldn't waste his time ruining dogs.

Six. The den of horrors for the average retriever Pup is training in water. Water warrants its own chapter—which follows.

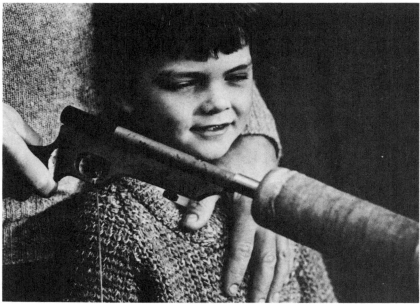

Some trainers have seen dogs spooked when graduating from hand held dummy launcher to shotgun. So on both sides of the Atlantic handlers have made their own "long gun" dummy launchers. Ron Montgomery holds his rendition in Scotland —along with his son —and American's launcher is mounted on bolt action rifle.

Presenting the Mark

Go out into your back yard, or into a mowed field, and spread dummies about 360 degrees, each 90 degrees apart. Now heel Pup to the hub of the wheel and carousel him about. He'll see the four dummies laid at the four cardinal points of the compass.

When you're satisfied Pup has all dummies marked, then tell him, "Heel, Sit, Stay," and fine tune him on one dummy. Assure yourself Pup has it marked. You can tell. For Pup will tell you.

When Pup leans forward, cocks his ears, sets his eyes, lifts his haunches, maybe even trembles—and we hope not whine—he's ready to go. Cast him.

If Pup doesn't show this concerned interest, then carousel him about, or fine tune him by patting your outer leg and adjusting Pup's platform. Finally, Pup will fine tune and focus. If not, toss a dummy to land immediately next to the one Pup's facing.

Cast Pup. He'll get a dummy and return. If not, if he starts to switch birds, that is, drop the one you threw, and pick up one previously seeded, then yell, "Heel."

Jim Culbertson carousels Pup on dummy drill, . . .

... *casts him for first dummy, takes it to hand, then casts Pup a second time. When drill is finished Jim peps up Pup by tossing dummies straight up and ...*

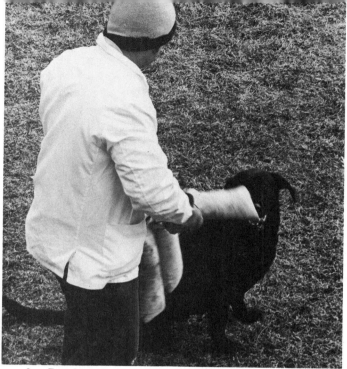

... lets Pup leap for them. See page 353.

Pup will comply. If not, go to him, pat your leg and tell him to, "Heel," direct him back to the casting line and remove the dummy from his mouth.

Also note: Pup may attempt to retrieve two dummies at the same time. Yell, "No," and if necessary, go to Pup and accompany him home.

If Pup gets confused out there and picks up neither dummy, or spits one out and hesitates to pick it up again or take another, then go to him, lift the dummy you want fetched with the toe of your boot, tell Pup, "Fetch," then accompany him back to the casting line.

But should Pup try to switch birds by running to another cardinal point on the compass, then cut him off with a booming, "No." If Pup turns you off, go get him. Slide your slip lead through the D ring of his plain leather collar and heel him back to the spot he vacated. Tell him, "Sit, Stay," and leaving him there, walk back to the casting line. Now tell Pup, "Heel."

But just a minute, you say, we're supposed to be teaching Pup to mark and you've got him running after planted birds.

That's right. For Pup to mark he's got to see.We're teaching Pup to look, to focus, to see. Pup casts from your side as his eyes tell him. He ends the cast as his nose tells him. And the general line he takes is the one you suggest. So for now, we're teaching Pup to see and to take a line off the cast of your hand.

As for his nose! We hope his mom and dad gave him a good one. We can't improve it. All we can do is give Pup ample opportunity to learn to trust it. And give him enough varied tests to learn to use it the best he can.

As always, keep your training sessions short and sweet. And never, never, never, let Pup switch birds. This can develop into a major fault: can become a way for Pup to cheat. For example, they're placing marks at licensed trials today so they end up quite close together. If Pup mismarks he can easily overlap the area of an adjacent fall.

Or in a hunting situation— There are two ducks down. One is alive and the other dead. You want the live one first and you cast Pup to fetch it. But he gets a scent of the dead one and switches birds. In the meantime, the live duck either dives or paddles away. Now you may lose this crippled bird, or spend a great deal of hunting time searching for it. All this happened because Pup switched birds.

Keep on the compass drill for as long as you hunt or campaign Pup. He must learn where you point your hand and your foot—that's where he must cast to find a bird. He must learn to hold true course.

When Pup has the four-bird-drill down pat, then start seeding the birds at 30 degrees: 12 of them. Then 15 degrees: 24 of them.

There'll come a day when you can fine tune Pup on a dummy, have him ready for launch, then saying, ''No,'' pat your outer leg, fine tune Pup's platform, and cast him for another dummy just 15 degrees away. Now you can start threading the needle.

Here a Mark, There a Mark, Everywhere a Mark, Mark

All the while you're calibrating Pup on the circle drill, you're also having him fetch dummies tossed afield: not dummies thrown by you, but by a helper.

Some tests are singles presented to fall:

In the open: builds confidence. In heavy cover: teaches Pup to use his nose. Behind clumps of thorn bush: teaches Pup to bold-up and crash through the stuff. In a ditch: teaches Pup to trust his nose and hunt close to the area of a fall. Also teaches him to rely on you and to believe his eyes. You're not lying to him. He must learn to trust you, and what he saw.

On the side of a hill: Pup doesn't know it, but it is his nature to fall off a hill. Rather than hold a straight line at an angle up a hill, he'll run a curve, drifting down. Dummies on a hill will teach Pup to compensate by staying high.

Some singles will fall close: tempts Pup to break, teaches him to be staunch. Long: conditions Pup to sustain his hunt, not give up. Downwind: Pup's running with the wind so he must learn to trust his eyes and the line of your cast. Upwind: Pup's running into the wind as a reward, or to sweeten him up after a scolding. Crosswind: hopefully teaches Pup to approach the fall on the downwind side. This is imperative and must be repeated over and over. Some pups learn. They usually make up your small lot of field champions.

Pup is worked on high ground, low ground, bare ground, covered ground, across low fences, shallow ditches, around trees and bushes. In other words, Pup must get singles in every conceivable way a bird will ever be shot to fall on land.

Now staying with singles:

Pup will have thousands of simple retrieves.

But he'll also have distractions planned and fitted in. He'll have a dummy thrown directly across his path as he's returning with his retrieve. This will teach him not to switch birds.

On a limited basis he'll have other dogs released to fetch along with him. This will fire him up, plug a competitive spirit in him, make him determined no dog is going to get his bird.

Or he'll be on line, have a gunner shoot and toss a dummy, yet, there's another gun fired and no bird thrown. He'll be told, "No," to this retort. Told he must concentrate on what he saw, not what he heard.

Plus, Pup will be returning from a simple, single retrieve and during that time the gunner will hide in the field after dropping a dummy in that spot Pup just found his bird. Now Pup will be heeled about and cast back. This will teach him to go when he's both heard nothing and seen nothing. This will teach Pup to cast only because you've told him to. This will convince Pup you're always right and prepare him for the eventual blind retrieves.

Pup will also be told to "Heel, Sit, Stay," and birds will be

launched over hedges, the gunner out of sight, presenting the bird with or without the retort of a gun. This will teach Pup that once you've positioned him something is always going to happen.

You'll think of other tests, other presentations of the single bird. The options are limitless. But what if Pup mismarks any of these birds?

Helping Pup Find the Bird

This is where the art of training comes in. There's no hard and fast science. If you help Pup too much he'll grow dependent on you. If you don't help him enough he'll lose confidence.

The best help you can give Pup on a mismarked bird is to have the bird boy walk over, pick up the bird, hurrah to Pup—that is set up a chatter, excite Pup, let him know the bird is there and everything is okay—then either yell and throw the bird, or fire the gun and toss the bird afield.

Now this hurrahing of the bird boy— Some trainers want a .22 blank pistol fired. Others want a popper. A popper? Yes, that's a blank shotgun shell made especially for retriever training. It gives Pup a thud sound instead of a crack.

Or the bird boy can hurrah! That is, yell whatever he wants to guarantee Pup attends. Jim Rodgers, former president of the Professional Retriever Trainers Association, now retired to build homes in Phoenix, imitates the squawk of a pheasant when presenting the bird. I've tried it, pheasant I'm not. Would you believe flicker?

Or, to help Pup who's mismarking, you can seed the area of the fall with dummies. Remember, any dummy will do.

Or you can go to field, pick up the dummy, call Pup to you, drop the dummy, tell Pup, "No," heel Pup to line, then turn him around and cast him to the dropped dummy.

As always your posture is firm and emotionless, never heavy handed. Then when Pup gets the bird, you're eager to praise. Now, let him have the same mark again. Signal the bird boy to throw a bird right where Pup had his trouble. Pup'll get this one and what could have been a bad memory has become a pleasant experience.

Doubles

The day arrives when Pup's ready for two birds down. And these birds are mixed and tossed to duplicate all the possible falls we accomplished with the single bird.

You'll recall the first bird down is the memory bird: the bird that will usually cause Pup problems.

The second bird down is the first bird Pup will want to fetch. In the beginning, this second bird should be the more difficult retrieve, the memory bird being fairly easy for Pup to both remember and find.

Yet, if the second bird down proves too difficult to locate, and Pup's afield any length of time, he'll forget the memory bird no matter how simply it was presented.

Now there has grown in America a group of handlers who are selecting falls for Pup. That is, they are telling Pup, "No," to the last bird down. They're picking a retrieve to avoid the hazard in the test.

For that's what judges present at trial: not simple tests, one, two, three. But tests with hazards in them so if a dog mismarks he may drop off hill into the area of another fall, or the crosswind can drift him there, or the way the cover lays—avoiding row crops, e.g.—Pup overlaps into the area of another fall. If he fetches this find, he's switched birds and out of the trial.

And the biggest hazard of all is the optical illusion: Pup can mark the degrees of a circle fairly well, but distance? That's the bugaboo. Pup will either hunt long or short. Having mismarked, he'll usually start hunting in ever-widening circles. When the circle gets wide enough, Pup's in the area of another fall.

Therefore, these handlers who line, or select, marks are simply avoiding the test.

The AKC rule book states, *"In marking tests, a dog whose handler gives him a line in the direction of the fall, provided that such lining is accomplished briskly and precisely, should not by reason of such lining be outscored by a dog not so lined. However, conspicuously intensive lining is undesirable and should be penalized."*

The question is, what's *"conspicuously intensive lining?"*

Now River Oaks Corky, Keg of Black Powder, Renegade Pepe,

Hill poses hazard in this land blind. Dogs must hold angle to blind when their inclination is to fall off to level ground.

Nodrog Penny, Deltone Colvin, and many others—were dogs and bitches who seldom needed a helping hand. They selected their own birds. As they returned from a retrieve you'd see them glance at the next bird they wanted. And seldom did any of them mismark. So you have dogs that can do it all—alone. Would then a handler's hand be construed as intensive lining?

Not so. That's the handler's prerogative. It's the dog who's told the handler to adjust his own platform. The handler is merely honoring the dog's request, giving his stamp of approval by offering his hand.

But I've judged too many AKC licensed open trials where I couldn't tell the difference between the handler casting the dog on a mark or lining him on a blind. And to select a bird? The handler's got to tell the dog, "No," to one bird, and crank his platform about to face another. Far as I'm concerned this is conspicuously intensive lining.

Plus, the handler is avoiding the test. Now if a handler avoided a water test by casting the dog upshore and gave him an over into the

Dick Cook honors Pup's request to get the bird on the left.

water the judge would say, "He avoided the test." Tell me then, what's the difference between handling the dog some distance afield or right at the handler's side?

How We Play the Game

But worst of all, this practice of selecting birds on marks perpetuates the American's apparent desire to negate a dog's resourcefulness—taking the hunt out of him—and denying the dog's confidence in his ability to mark.

The field trial handler today seeks a dog that button-hooks all marks. That's right. The dog is rifled to the bird and scores a bull's eye—he steps right on it.

No longer are dogs permitted to go to the general area of a fall then using their noses, locate the bird. i.e., no longer are dogs permitted to hunt—yet that's what they are, hunting dogs.

The British emphasize the dog's nose and encourage him to hunt. The American emphasizes the dog's handling ability. The British seek

244

to enhance a dog's natural ability, the American wants a man-made-dog. If we keep on the way we're going the retrievers will have their nose bred out of them. They'll become canine robots.

Who's fault is this? It's all a result of how we play the game. Just as some handlers feel they're justified in being brutal to a dog, to force him to do those things necessary to win a trial. They say the game demands it. I won't accept that. Don't beat the dog, change the game.

Don't be silly, my critics say. The evidence is in. The dogs can do it. Yes, as man was able to survive the Death March of Bataan, but would you recommend this over jogging in the park on Sunday afternoon?

Long ago I left the arena of man and gave my life to God and dogs. I didn't turn to God because He beat me with a BB loaded whip. He didn't force me. I turned to Him for I could see all else was false and mean and ugly. I turned to Him out of love and for love. And that's how dogs attend us. If someone's making hell on earth for a dog to win a petty game, then the game be damned.

Then you might ask, why do you emphasize the dummy drill and other training techniques where the dog grows dependent on man's cast? That's a good question. And my answer is: because the complete retriever must find and fetch birds he's not seen fall. Only man can direct him. And when you start teaching blind retrieves the average Pup falls apart, regresses to nothing, possibly never to recover.

This scuttled Pup is the one you so often hear described as a field trial dropout. The guy'll say, ''Oh he never made it on the circuit so he was given to me as a gun dog.'' A gun dog? That's what they all are. The scuttled Pup is a dog that could not give his self-will over to man. A dog bred to hunt, to mark and fetch, *on his own*.

So I teach blind retrieves from puppyhood: all those things we've been doing, the extended arm, the snapping fingers, etc., *so the transition from marks to blinds will not pose so great a hex to Pup*.

Now back to doubles—

Switching Birds

In the beginning we'll have two birds down, then three, and finally four. Jim Culbertson and I used to throw as many as six. Delmar Smith had a cocker spaniel who could mark six. But above this, both Delmar's cocker and our Labs got confused.

So we train dogs to mark. It's a long drawnout process. It takes months. And it takes lots of land. Varied land. All types of cover and background and topography. And always, we must keep Pup from switching birds.

So first, we offer birds 180 degrees apart. One in the west, one in the east. For Pup to switch he's got to run through the bird boy. Or if we have two bird throwers, should Pup try to switch, the memory bird thrower will run out, swoop up the bird, and hold it aloft before Pup can reach the area. Pup can never be successful in making a switch.

So we've got two throwers and Pup's failed to find the first bird and switched to the area of the memory bird. The memory bird thrower is holding the bird aloft. Pup's standing there, looking quizzically at the boy. We go to field and heel Pup to where he should have made his first retrieve, tell him, "Sit," then go back to the casting line and either one, have the first bird thrower show Pup the bird, or two, heel Pup to the casting line and have both bird throwers pick up both birds. We then run the test again. Or, we just throw the first bird for Pup.

Or, while in the field with Pup, we can heel him to the first bird he failed to find, lift it with our toe, and order Pup to fetch it and accompany us back to the casting line. The memory bird thrower is told to pick up his bird and we run the test again.

But what if Pup's switched with the first bird in his mouth? First, we try to whistle Pup to line. If this fails, we go to field and heel Pup back to the casting line. Then we take the bird and re-run the test.

Or, if Pup's carried a bird to the memory bird thrower, we can go out there, heel Pup to the spot he fetched the first bird, tell him, "Sit, Stay," and we walk back to the casting line. There we give Pup the suck-in whistle to join us. Then we run the whole test again.

You do as you please in all this; you know Pup. But there is this— Ideally we like to carry a dog to a spot he vacated. Pick him up and carry him. For once you've taken a dog's legs from him you've rendered him helpless. He's attending—with awe. He's yours. Same as he's the vet's when he's up high on a slick table. So carry Pup. But if he weighs too much, you'll just have to heel him.

Something else you can do when Pup's switching birds is boom, "No."

If Pup persists in switching birds then you'll need throw bird A on one side of a barrier and bird B to the other side. The barrier can be a brick wall, a hedge, a chainlink fence. Don't rely on water. Pup may try to swim across and we don't want anything bad happening to Pup when he's wet.

Over and Under

There is a test seldom seen in trialing, but it does come up in a hunting situation, where two birds land over-and-under. That is, each bird falls on the same line, yet one is several yards more distant than the other.

This can be a real problem for Pup. He'll go get the first bird, but when cast for the second he'll get hung up in the area of the old fall. Best you go to field with Pup and walk him in a straight line, all the time letting him see you drop dummies. When you reach the casting line, turn about and cast Pup for the first dummy, then the second, and so on.

But don't walk Pup down a mowed path, or a roadway, i.e., avoiding cover. Coverless routes can become Pup's nemesis. Especially near water fringed with heavy cover. At a trial, dogs begin to bore a hole, or holes, into cover and not all holes lead Pup where he should be going. Pup must learn to make his own holes, must learn to stay on line.

So never work Pup where scant cover can be attractive. He'll get hung up on roads and refuse to bust weed clogged ditches. He'll refuse to leave trails in heavy timber. He'll avoid water to run a smooth bank. He'll run down drilled crops, rather than across the furrows.

Over-and-unders will come after long practice. Just persevere.

Several years ago there was a judge who truly loved to run dogs over dirty earth to get a blind. Now, "dirty earth," is a British term meaning any place where dog's have already hunted. This judge loved to place a blind just beyond that area where the bird crates stood during the first series. The dog would be expected to run through this area and on to the blind—never stopping to honor his nose.

This test over dirty earth was wrong. The judge wanted to see if the dog would handle. And handle he'd have to, for the dog would get hung up on hot scent. But handlers can't win field trials by handling a dog on a blind. The dog that usually wins is the dog that lines the blind. That is, gets the planted bird with no help from the handler.

Pup watches dummies seeded in a row. He's heeled to casting line, turned about, and cast for the first bumper. Then the second. And so on. Such drills can force Pup through old falls when confronted with an over and under.

Therefore, for a dog to score perfectly on this test, he would have to deny his nose, run over the hotspot, and go on to sight the planted bird. He would have to place his sight above his scent. He would have to be a coursing dog, not a gun dog.

Now the British are just as prejudiced about this dirty earth business as we are: only the other way. No field trial dog in Great Britain is ever worked where another dog has hunted. The dogs and handlers and guns and judges are continually walking over fresh ground. Therefore, the British retriever has no trick tests designed to negate his nose nor have a handler impose his will over the dog's reliance on his born senses.

Consequently, as a breed, the British retriever has the superior nose. And it's to the islands we must go for new blood, since we're doing so much to breed the nose out of the stock we have over here.

Introduction of the Bird

Retrievers are trained with dummies and birds.

The first dummies were boat bumpers, usually sections of canvas firehose filled with cork and sewed up at both ends. A brass grommet was fitted to one end to hang the bumper from a pier: or to accommodate a looped cord which permitted the bird boy to lug a dozen-or-so about and give one a good toss.

Later, these dummies were molded of plastic to avoid water rot, and permeated with color to make them either quite visible, or just the opposite. It was discovered for example, fluorescent orange could not be seen by dogs.

Bumpers come in different diameters and lengths and consequently, different weights.

Always have a bird boy who's never thrown before take a couple of practice tosses with a dummy. He'll usually flip the first ones over his head—the bumper landing behind him. Later, he'll get the hang of it and be able to give you a long high glide to duplicate a bird's flight and give Pup a good look.

Birds used for retriever training are essentially pigeons, ducks, and pheasant.

Pigeons can be free—just trap them yourselves—and they're hearty. I've used the same ones for as long as two years—so they're the preferred training bird. They're also easy keepers. A pen holding a nest, a limb to perch on, a pan of feed and water, and a windbreak is all they need to not only survive, but multiply.

The British prefer rabbit to pigeon, saying the latter has loose feathers which gag a dog, and the former is common and always in season—so there's retriever training every day. Later, the dog is taken off rabbit by voice command.

You see, the British will not train, nor trial, on a pen raised, hand thrown bird. They insist on keeping things natural. Always duplicating a day's hunt, even in training.

For everyday training, the Briton takes his dog to field and hunts about until trash birds can be found—rooks, crows, sparrows, starlings—and shot on the wing. Game birds such as wood pigeon are also used for training.

For trials, pen raised pheasants released to field for at least 60 days are driven by beaters to intersect the path of walking guns, judges, handlers, and dogs. Or the field trial party walks the birds up.

The American trialer insists all dogs have equal tests; something that is absolutely not possible in Great Britain.

Also, the American insists all birds be shot dead. Yet, in Great Britain a dog may score high—and win the trial—by trailing out a cripple. What they call a runner. Yet, no runner will ever be presented an American dog for that would be an unfair test; each bird must fall and stay in that spot all other birds fall.

The American field trial bird is presented by a bird boy; a man, or lad, who actually takes the bird from a crate and lofts it by hand before the set of guns. The gunners down the birds in a precise area. Too far, one way or the other, the judges call, "No bird," and the contestant is granted a re-run.

The British cannot accept this. One, the dogs are working dirty earth. Two, no dog ever hunts a bird originating in hand. Three, every hunting dog must be strong on retrieving cripples. For four, that's what conservation is all about, plus, that's what the English kennel club and AKC both say is desirable, *"A dog which marks the fall of a bird, uses the wind, follows a strong cripple, and will take direction from his handler is of great value."*

*Pigeons are easy keepers and can be toted to field in most any container.
Here Pup makes his first feather retrieve so handler detains fetch while dog
savors his great deed.*

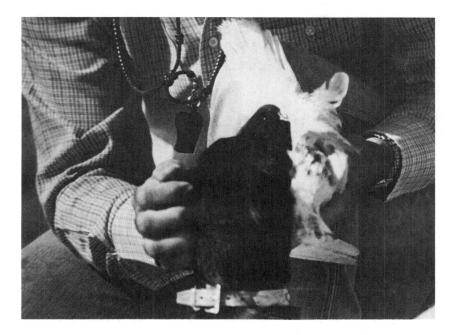

The Briton starts his retriever on rabbits then takes him off fur with such devices as this sling-shot rabbit developed by Bill Meldrum. When Pup is going for bird, Bill trips rabbit covered dummy to zip before Pup's path, tempting him to switch from feather to fur.

Yet America has now developed a game where cripples are prohibited. And dogs are never worked from blinds as mentioned in the rules, nor are they able to win a trial by using the wind on marks when another dog steps on all birds by following a cast from his handler's hand—and is given the trial.

And this is interesting— In Great Britain the guns are always immediately beside the dogs: just where the hunter will always be. But in America the guns are usually quite distant. I'll forever be amused with the memory of that time Dick Sampson, a brilliant amateur trainer who's now turned pro, co-judged a field trial with me where we asked the handlers to fire a popper over their dog.

American field trials have attracted many non-hunters. Some of those handlers viewed the gun we gave them as though it were a snake. Others didn't have the foggiest notion of how to use it.

I feel America's field trials have departed as far from the intended as God's green earth has drifted from His scriptures.

But we're supposed to be discussing birds—

Pheasants and Ducks

A pheasant has a lot of tools to hurt a dog. He can peck and he can spur. Therefore, it is imperative Pup be sent to fetch only those pheasants shot stone dead. As a matter of fact, the best way to introduce any new bird to Pup is to put the bird in an air-tight paper sack and let it go to sleep breathing it's own air. Thus Pup has a bloodless, messless, bird to sniff and mouth.

A shot-up bird can tempt Pup to literally eat it, or to clamp down and become hard mouth.

An older dog has no trouble with pheasant. As a matter of fact, a dog can handle any bird, I'm sure, even an eagle. One day Pepe and I were after quail when we came across a hawk illegally shot and left wounded by some irresponsible slob hunter.

Pepe wouldn't listen to me—I was yelling, "No." He ran to this warrior-bird and grasped it up. You know how? By a wing tip. That's right. He got the hawk by a wing tip and kept it's hardware from his face by retrieving the bird, spinning about in circles, keeping the bird distant—and sailing—through centrifugal force. Just like a matador's cape.

I took the screaming, slashing hawk from him, packed it home, and

Live mallard is tossed to cluttered pond.

nursed it back to health in a bird pen. When it was strong enough to fend for itself I opened the kennel gate and it took to wing.

Ducks are lovely, harmless creatures. I love them nearly as much as I love dogs. No matter their pain, nor terror, nor plight, they never display. They just go silently to their fate. God was really good to man when He gave him ducks and dogs. And I must add, horses.

Now geese will peck a dog. And swans—if they think a pup poses a threat to their nest—will come ashore, grab him, and take him to sea where they drown him.

Pheasants are seldom shackled and tossed afield. They're most always shot dead.

But pigeons and ducks are tethered so they may be used again and again.

There are several ways to do this, but usually the wings are pinioned and the legs taped together. Leave enough flight feathers so the bird can soar. That gives Pup a better look, plus, it gives the bird a softer landing.

Land mark is dead pheasant.

The Bird Thrower

Best way to throw a pigeon, or pheasant, is to fold the two pinioned wings upright, 90 degrees to the back of the bird, and grasp the front of the wings with your throwing hand, clutching the humerus, radius, and ulna bones: that is, the leading edge of the wing between the body and the first angle.

This gives you a strong, sure hold, plus, it minimizes injury to the bird—those wing bones are sturdy and well connected.

Be very careful in throwing ducks to fall on land. They're not built for it and can hemorrhage internally. If you must present a duck on land, either shoot it dead, or make certain it falls in foliage that forms a natural cushion.

Ducks are sometimes immobilized by taping their wings to their body: using that silver tape you see stuck on heating duct. That means the duck is shaped like a football. Toss it like one when throwing it to water, or heave it like a shot put. If a duck's legs are not taped together

255

Mallard is tethered with conduit tape about legs and rag tied about base of wings.

it'll paddle away. Also, if the wings are not immobilized it can swim away by slapping the water with its wing tips. Wings can be immobilized either by pulling the flight feathers or by tying the base of the wings together with women's nylon hose.

Remember, bird wings, even when pinioned will take the wind. Consequently, when you toss a bird aloft in a high wind, it will turn on you. To avoid this, either offer the bird at a low trajectory, or tell the gunners to fire fast if you're going to place it high. This calls for expert gunners.

Now decoys are imitation birds. And Pup must learn to ignore them. This is best done from puppyhood inside the house. Just leave a decoy laying about. Tell Pup, "No," or introduce the command, "Leave it," if he goes near it. Later, seed decoys about the back yard and walk Pup through them. Let him take a sniff of one. After that, tell him, "No," or "Leave it."

Later, when Pup's several weeks along in water, you may toss your decoys to sea. Once again, let Pup examine them, then tell him,

256

"No." You'll not have any trouble with Pup fetching decoys. But there are two things— A single decoy is the ultimate temptation. Save your single till much later. And, keep decoy cords cut short. Otherwise they'll snag across Pup's chest and he'll drag them away. This will mess up your layout and it can frighten Pup out of the pond. But we're not going to let Pup work decoys that soon in life. He'll get em when he can handle em.

To that end, let's turn to water. But one moment—

Know this about Pup. If given a choice between fetching a bird thrown dead or a live one lofted and shot before him—he'll want the live one. He'll want the flyer. Old dogs will go to a field trial casting line and look for the flyer, ignoring the dead presentations. Such dogs are like sailors on liberty. They're going for the action. They want their quarry live and hot-blooded.

You'll need to always remember this about Pup. To know he may ignore—and mismark—other birds in anticipation of the flyer. Or, he may stand for dead birds but break on the flyer. All this means Pup must have lots of live birds shot over him before he's ready for field trials. Both on land and water.

11/Water

Far as Pup's concerned, all water is the Bermuda Triangle. There have been—proportionately at least—more retrievers lost at sea than all the boats to ever leave port.

If Pup's done everything you asked till now, stand by for your first mutiny. Oh it can well start out fun and games. You'll say, "Hot dog, I've got me a natural." Then something will go wrong. Something? Best say, everything. Best say, what can go right?

But Pup can't, "Hang his pelt on a hickory limb and not go near the water." He's got to get wet. He's got to fetch ducks. And ducks aren't found on a July afternoon off Palm Beach.

They're found in ice and high wind. In stinking swamp and muck and clacking tules. They're found in flooded timber. And creeks with steep, briar-tangled banks. They're found in fast current. And turbid irrigation canals. Ducks are found any place water is found, in any condition water is found, all along the four continental flyways.

So you ask, "Why this prophecy of doom with Pup?" Simple. Pup is neither fish nor otter nor snake nor whale. He's got four legs, not

Ideally, let a pup take a pup to water.

four fins. His element is land. There he moves faster with less resistance and greater vision. In water his head is flat to surface and the element is continually holding him back, dragging him down.

Plus, there's something spooky about water. Ducks who live their lives afloat will not cross water covered by a shadow. Rabbits and cats, who can swim nearly as good as any retriever, will take to water only as a last resort. Most any animal except frogs, muskrats, mink, and turtles, will flee on land when surprised at a water hole: they'll not dive in. Water is viewed as a trap.

Now I'm not talking about cavorting in water on a hot day. That's play: Pup at Coney Island. I'm talking about working in water. The primary word is: work. And it's not hot water, it's teeth chattering cold. So cold when Pup exits he's got beads of ice hanging from his pelt. I'm talking about Pup not being asked to go get the duck. I'm talking about Pup being told.

One day Pup's going to tell you to go get it yourself. Here's the best way to keep him a willing worker.

260

Introduction to Water

Man never takes Pup to water. He always lets another pup do it. That's why we get Pup hot, along with his buddies, all of them heeling on the three-lead leash, then walk them close to pond's edge. The older pups pull Pup in. And he goes without resentment or fright. It's only natural he goes. And nothing bad happens to him and he's refreshed and water becomes something pleasant in his mind.

Or, if all conditions are ideal, let momma take Pup to water. Pup will never trust, nor love, any trainer more than this gal. Being the ultimate trainer, she can accomplish the ultimate best. But make sure momma loves water. If she's offish, Pup will sense it and may be lost forever.

But never send Pup to water with several adult retrievers. They hit water hard and play rough while they're in it. Pup can be splashed, dunked, and to his mind, drowned. Out he'll come, eyes rolled back, tail tucked under. You'll have a hard time getting him back.

Ideally, we'll first introduce Pup to sheet water. Water no higher than his knees (the carpal joint). Water found in a bend of a small rivulet. Or left by a water sprinkler. Or standing in the gutter following a rain. And let it be a hot day. Never introduce Pup to water where he comes out shivering and chattering. Wait six months if need be.

When Pup's accustomed to sheet water, let him go a little deeper. Only much later is he cast to sea where his feet no longer touch bottom.

And when this happens, Pup can panic. He may attempt to hold his head high—which tucks his butt under—and throws his front feet and legs out of the water. Then when he dog paddles the feet will strike and break the water's surface and Pup will splash himself in his face. It's all compounding. The more Pup rears back to avoid the splash, the more his legs and paws will clear water to really slap it, and splash it, when they come down.

Also, standing nearly erect in water, Pup will no longer have a rudder—his tail. Which means he will go about in circles. Whatever you imagine his plight, don't go to him. He'll not drown. Let him get ashore on his own. Make him self sufficient.

If Pup continues to swim with his head reared back—and it doesn't look like he's ever going to get the hang of it—then glide along side in a boat and gradually push Pup's neck down, which will lift his butt, and submerge his front paws. He'll probably want in the boat. Don't permit it. Just stay along side and keep him swimming—prone.

261

It's good training to have your pup work for strangers. Here, Mindy Rodgers and her 10-week-old pup, Ben, watch Cricket get her ears fondled by brothers Steve and Clay Thompkins who she's not met before. Both pups are hurrahed to mark tossed dummy, then Cricket is released for fetch. Ben watches with eagerness for he's short-tied by Mindy's hands. Then both pups are released to fetch a dummy and Cricket pulls Ben to sea (see page 264).

Incidentally, that's the way you get Pup into a boat. Let him place his forelegs over the gunwale then grasp him behind the neck and pull forward and down all at the same time.

If all goes right, Pup will start looking forward to water. When you've got him and the other dogs out Happy Timing, he'll run ahead of you and jump in. Give him a couple months of this before putting him to work. Let him have his fun. Let him learn water is not going to hurt him, that it's a good place to be when he's hot, that play can be as much fun here as on land.

I once Happy Timed a Lab pup for over a year; would never give him a water retrieve. I'd let him watch other dogs work the water for dummies or ducks but this Pup was worked only on land. I wanted to see what he'd do. I wanted to see how the retrieving impulse would surface.

And it did— Pup started diving completely under water— disappearing under water—and coming up with a fresh water clam in his mouth. That was good enough for me. I'd learned what I wanted to know. If water is always left a happy place Pup will want to retrieve. And he'll find something to get in his mouth.

The First Water Retrieve

If you're working young pups, say 10 to 16 weeks, and they've been fetching on land, just fun stuff, and you can't wait to get them wet, then toss two dummies to sea and release two pups to fetch them. One will pull the other in. It matters not if they both come back with the same dummy. A fetch is a fetch. But do this only if you've got an itch you can't scratch. Best you postpone water till you're certain Pup's ready to enter an alien, wet world.

Pups should first get sheet water.

Or you can walk the pups into sheet water—that's right, you're either barefooted or wearing tennies or waders—and you can make short tosses and encourage your charges to retrieve.

But if you're working an older Pup, say five to nine months, here's some rules to follow.

And by the way, whether or not you're requiring Pup to stay on line is up to you—and Pup. I always let my pups break until they're nine months old, or so. Once in a while I'll use the slip cord on them, but never to jerk em back. And if I did have a pup steady on land, when I went to water I'd let him break. For spirit is something you can take out of Pup, but you can't put it back in. Especially water spirit.

So the rules of the game at the stage we're in are:

One. Toss only handler-thrown dummies. Always throw dummies perpendicular to shore; 90 degrees, straight out. Never give Pup an angled water entry into water. It's too easy for him to veer from the water and run the bank. A fault that's very hard to overcome.

Two. Throw these initial dummies from the tip of a peninsula. Now there's no bank to run. Plus, the closest land for Pup to return is where you're standing.

In the beginning Pup's presented only handler thrown dummies.

Three. Make sure there's neither current moving the water, nor surface wind to blow the dummy. This must be a controlled fall.

Four. Pick water that has no submerged nor outcropped foliage. Pup must not get tangled and possibly spooked. And he must have an unobstructed view. Remember, when retrieving, Pup's eyes are not more than three to six inches above the water's surface. Only later will Pup learn to raise his head—without splashing his face—and look about.

Five. Avoid shallow water, Pup's kicking it when he runs and this makes too great a noise. Avoid deep water, it may prove too great a challenge. Ideally, choose water that's ear-tip deep.

Six. Don't put a decoy in the water for three months.

Seven. Always toss your dummy close to shore.

Eight. Make certain the shore's edge forms a gradual slope into the water. We'll save Pup's leaps for later.

Nine. Select a shore free of foliage.

Ten. Always know what's in the water you're using. Broken bottles, submerged logs, abandoned trotlines, can both injure Pup and frighten him so he'll turn against water.

Eleven. Cast Pup immediately from water's edge and also meet him there. Never lunge or grab for the dummy, but be ready and be fast. We don't want Pup developing the habit of stopping to shake off water—and dropping the dummy.

Twelve. Stay with the single, straight away retrieve for a long time. Stay with it till you're tired of it. And keep on the peninsula. Your casting line must be the first landfall Pup can reach. Then gradually work the casting line back from shore. But not the receiving line. While Pup's swimming out to the dummy, you walk forward so you'll be standing at shore's edge when Pup grabs the dummy and spins about. Be there to take the dummy before Pup stops to shake.

Thirteen. If you miss the dummy—Pup drops it—then lift it with your toe back into the water. Get it delivered to hand before you cast for another. That is, don't ever pick it up, yourself.

Fourteen. Following a water session, always end on a happy note. Take Pup to shore and toss the dummy on dry land in moderate foliage. Let Pup run and play and shake and drip and scrape and rub. Let him rid himself of that wet stuff tickling his hide.

Fifteen. Once the peninsula dummy is engrained, take Pup to a straight shore line: straight and bare and smooth. Give Pup short retrieves, long retrieves. Send him from shore's edge and from 30 yards back. When Pup's proved to you he's eager for water, attacks the edge with a straight dive, and swims directly back to you once he's made his fetch, then—and only then—can you call in a helper to toss dummies at an angle to hit the water.

When this does come to pass, tell your helper to retire while Pup's swimming to make the retrieve. The helper hides. Now, when Pup spins about, he sees only you—you're standing at shore line; once again, you've walked forward—waiting to make the retrieve. There's no temptation for Pup to swim to the bird boy.

Sixteen. Only later do you let the bird boy hold his ground. But even then, he stands motionless and silent while Pup's working. An imperative, incidentally, when any dog is working. I once lost an amateur in Colorado Springs because a gunner on line snapped his double gauge shut while the distant second bird was falling to land after being shot. My dog spun away from the fall to attend the sound. A sound he'd heard so often in our duck blind.

Seventeen. And all this time, never work in water where the opposite shore can appear close enough to Pup to be inviting. The only land available to Pup must be where you're standing.

Eighteen. And there is this— Between retrieves you can give Pup the opportunity to shake off. If he seems especially bothered by it all, even toss the dummy ashore for him to fetch. Let him run this thing out of his mind.

Nineteen. Remember sound carries on water. So heed echos. They can confuse Pup and must be avoided.

Bringing the Old Dog to Water

But let's say you've done all this and Pup's not going for the dummy. No, this isn't your Pup—not the Pup you've been training. It's a new one. One you just got in. He's six months old, was confined to an apartment, and doesn't know scat. But you've got him working singles on land, and his yard work is coming along, so you want to get him wet. What'll you do?

One. First of all, remember all cautions posted above.

Two. Now see if he'll follow other dogs in. What's that? You say he won't. Okay.

Three. What about going in with you? "No." Not even with you offering tidbits? "No."

Let dog pack Happy Time with newcomer, heat up, and leap to water. Newcomer will usually plunge in.

Four. We'll stake him out, make him watch all other dogs work. That should make him eager to get in the game. What's that? You say he'll bark and lunge but when you let him loose he runs away.

Five. Alright. Pick him up and carry him into water. I don't believe it. He still runs away?

Six. What about you standing on shore and tossing food? You say he eats the food on shore, and all he can reach by stretching out over the water. You say he looks like a rubber dog.

Seven. Well, there's nothing left to do. Work him till he's so hot he's got to go to water or think he's going to die. What's that? "It works."

Eight. Well, I'm glad it did, for there were only two more things to try. That was either stake him out in the horse tank or take him to sea and ease him overboard. For Pup must learn water is a pleasant place to be, that he's capable of handling it, that there's nothing out there to hurt him.

Nine. What's that? Was I serious about the horse tank? Sure I was. Water won't hurt a retriever. Why Jim Culbertson and I hunt our Labs in Cheyenne Bottoms, near Hoisington, Kansas, from dawn to dusk, day after day—and they sit in water above the bend of their knees. I can't say they enjoy it when there's ice on the water, but they stay and they get the job done. And when Jim and I go ashore for nature's call, or to get the paper sack lunch—the dogs stay at the blind. They came to hunt.

Ten. And dogs love to follow a boat. Do not concern yourself about easing one overboard. Why that great Pyrenees I had for so long, he'd get behind my sail boat and stay all day. Even when I'd get a half-mile ahead, he'd just keep stroking away. Of course, when I becalmed I had a 140-pound white behemoth trying to breach my transom.

In the end—we just don't know when that end will come—the Pup that hates water will work it. But here's the catch. More than likely he'll always have a little tick in his head about getting wet. He'll let you down when you least need it. You'll never be able to either trust him, nor depend on him.

That's the way with starting a dog late in training. Or trying to salvage a dog that's been started wrong, or not started at all. For these dogs have problems, and no trainer can correct one problem without creating another. That's why we must avoid problems at all cost. It's easier to avoid them than it is to correct them.

But this is not the case with Pup. The retriever we've groomed from the litter box. We have no problem. He's taken to water like a Mercury outboard, flattens it like a water ski, works it like a bass popper: hooks what you send him for and drags it ashore. This guy's ready for doubles.

Double Water Retrieves

Water doubles separate the field trial retriever from the gun dog.

The hunter who's training his retriever as he goes, will walk the bank until immediately opposite one of the birds of a downed brace, then give Pup a straight water entry. With this bird in hand, the hunter will walk the shore with Pup at heel until they're opposite the second bird down, then cast Pup for this retrieve.

But the field trial trainer? He stands at one casting line and casts Pup for both birds. Eventually, one or both casts will be angle water entries. Pup no longer hits water head on, he must veer into it. And if he refuses to veer, running the bank instead, he'll never score at a field trial.

Many a pup will run the bank. It's only natural. Land is a dog's element, not water. The retriever can get the bird ten, twenty, thirty times as fast running on land than leaping to water. So he's doing what comes naturally, he's running the bank, and you beller, "No." With this, Pup comes to a skidding halt. Where? Right by, or in front of, water.

And that's one. That's one bad experience associated with water. But it's not with water, you say. It's with Pup running the bank. And I answer, "Does Pup know this?"

And that's what it's all about. Training Pup on water without everything bad that happens being associated with water in Pup's mind.

So you let the dummy blow to shore, tell the bird boy to pick it up, heel Pup and signal for the two angle water entry birds to be tossed again. What happens? Pup runs the same line. He won't hit water at an angle but cheats, running down the bank. So you boom, "No," once again.

The birds are picked up and thrown once more and Pup is cast again. Cast? Pup refuses to leave your side.

If everything he does is wrong, he figures, he'll just not leave your side. His reasoning will naturally go: if there's nothing but trouble out there, I'll stay here and avoid it. But what trouble can be worse for you than a pup who refuses a cast?

And so it goes. And on it goes. Ever deteriorating. Until finally you've got a spiritless Pup, what's called a piggy Pup, with ears dropped and tail tucked. A Pup who ducks his head every time you cast your hand. Who walks in slow motion. Who's afraid to do anything, for in his mind, everything he does is wrong.

And this is when the average trainer beats his dog.

Beats em? Would you believe what I've mentioned before; for this is when it comes to pass. Pup's shocked with an electric cattle prod. Sizzled with an electric collar. Tied to a boat and drug across the pond. Or he's allowed to run the shoreline, only hoisted up in a tree is a log festooned with tin cans. When Pup runs under the tree the clamorous log is dropped on the back of Pup's neck. It was meant to fall in his path, but the guy in the tree misjudged.

I've seen all this and more. Man's inhumanity to life!

There has to be another way. We must either train our dogs to play the game without us being barbarians, or change the game we play.

The Plastic Fly Swatter

Now the British have a way of correcting a dog without ever lifting a hand. They walk to the dog, reach down, grasp him by the scruff of his neck—a fistful of hide below each ear—and pick the dog off the ground then hold him there. The British don't lift a hand, they lift the dog.

And we've learned how effective this is. For a dog who's lost his legs is overwhelmed by the power of the man. But the British go one step further. One step too far. They chug the dog. That is, they shake it. And there's too much chance for a blood clot on the brain.

Now this is correction through intimidation. The theory goes, Pup must learn that what's behind him is far worse than anything he'll meet out front. Simply stated, the horrors of water are less to fear than the horrors of displeasing the handler. It's hard to discount the theory. I have seen whiprun dogs win the national. But still, I think these dogs run out of some response other than fear.

If the bond between man and dog is strong enough, the dog will run to please the man. To see the man smile, to *feel* the man smile—who knows what a dog senses? That's a stronger drive for the dog than the bite of a whip.

But still, there are times when the elements are so disagreeable—
see Chapter 13—Pup just doesn't want to endure the misery of it all.
And he must go. He can't refuse. And you must know how to make
him go when he'd prefer to pass.

I recommend three things: pick Pup up, hold him before you, and
scold him. Or two, give him the big swing. Take his two front forelegs
in hand, lift Pup from the ground, and swing him in a great arc about
you—say three complete turns. Or three, buy a plastic fly swatter, and
holding Pup's collar—so he won't bolt—pop him across the butt.

I don't know what it is about a plastic fly swatter— You know it's
not hurting Pup. But dogs will literally cringe to earth when it's
produced—that's why I say the bond between man and dog is more a
motivation for Pup to do right than can ever be achieved by a beating.

Once again, the fly swatter permits man to put on a good act. And
that's how dogs intimidate each other: acting. Their bluff is always
worse than their bite.

Choose a fly swatter that's either white or yellow. That way it can
be seen from a distance. Tuck it in the back of your pants. When Pup
goes wrong afield, yell, "No," and hold up the bright colored swatter.
You'll see Pup switch to close attention and high gear.

And let's dispose of this before we go on—

I know I said never to strike Pup. I've not changed my tune. We
don't strike Pup with the swatter, we just pop him on the butt with a
snap of our wrist. Neither do we run toward Pup in anger, and never do
we raise our arm high and lower the boom.

We approach Pup slowly, almost casually. We are matter of fact, we
are determined, but we are restrained.

The man who gets our attention is not the one who shouts. But the
one who whispers. This is the guy we must strain to hear, that we must
go to, that we must lean toward.

Remember, dad could take us to the wood shed and work us over.
To what avail? We were tough. We could take it. But for mom to slap
the back of our hand at the dinner table! That destroyed our world. It
did mine.

That was because of the bond between us. A bond based on love and
trust. The same bond you have developed with Pup.

Okay, back to the doubles—

Stand on the peninsula where you've been all along. Toss the first
bird on land, the second bird to sea. Later, reverse the sequence. Still

later, toss both birds to water: one to the left, the other to the right. If Pup's going to switch birds, he must run through you.

Now go to a straight shoreline, throwing the memory bird inland and the second bird to water.

When Pup's a super performer locate a precise spot—see below—on shoreline immediately adjacent to water. Somewhere you can block Pup's path left and right.

Let's say you're right handed so Pup runs from your left. You realize your body, your extended left casting leg, and your extended left casting arm, block Pup from blowing out to the right. But the left side is open. It must be closed.

So that precise spot on the beach must either have a high cut bank to channel Pup's water entry, or foliage to channel him to sea. Something to serve as a left-hand barrier.

In the unlikely event you can find nothing suitable, then shovel out a bank, put up a wood wall, or cut a launching wall in heavy foliage. In all cases the barrier must reach to the water.

If Pup leaps upon the high bank, over the wall, or tries to break into the foliage, then you'll yell, "No." And in Pup's mind—this time—he'll know he's being corrected for jumping banks or busting cover. Not for avoiding water. Why? Because Pup's broken his casting sequence. He doesn't leap nor burrow when you send him. He shoots out free and clear. Pup knows.

Advanced Angle Water Entries

When you first move to an open shoreline, or use bird boys to toss water retrieves, make certain all dummies land far from shore. The result will be dummies lying closer to each other than either lies close to shore. Which further means the two dummies lie at slight angle from shore. Good. We don't want any drastic angle water entries for a beginning Pup. However, the dummies being close together, Pup may want to switch birds. Thus, bird switching should have been cured before reaching water.

But what if Pup switches birds? Then you must enter water and return Pup to the spot he vacated. Tell him, "Sit;" which he does in shallow water by actually sitting, and in deep water by dog paddling. Then you wade back to shore.

Let's pause—

D. L. Walters sets up test to demonstrate how Pup can quit you on a water triple. Pup's confronted with a very long memory bird. Then a poor man's double (one bird boy tossing both birds) is offered off to the left ...

The dummies are tossed far from shore to reduce their angle. And yes, you must enter water. You and Pup are in this thing together. You can't train a water dog without getting in the water.

But let's say Pup's not switching birds. Matter of fact, he bingoed both birds. It was perfect. So have the bird boys toss the birds closer to shore; increasing the angle entries. Eventually the dummies—or birds—will land fairly close to shore. But for Pup's first two years of training never permit dummies to land so close to shore that they guarantee Pup's going to want to run the bank.

It was 1969, Lincoln, Nebraska— Robert Howard, since deceased, and I co-judged the AKC licensed derby. You should remember Robert Howard. He trained King Buck as a pup, the only dog to ever appear on an American stamp, and winner of two national opens.

Now this was back in the days when big time pros carried big time derby dogs. We had 44 starters and when sundown was turning the fields gray, there was Tony Berger, Roger Reopelle, and Jim Swan, casting one derby dog after another before us. And none of these pups were putting a foot down wrong.

Bob Howard and I huddled in conference, glancing at that parting sun. Nothing else to do; these dogs had buttonhooked several triples. We'd have to resort to a quadruple. Let's face it. This is seldom done. Even at a national open. But we had a field of miracle derby dogs that had to be separated.

276

... Pup bingos both short birds but when cast for long memory bird; since there's so much water and a lot of time has passed ...

We gave them four birds. And yes, all dogs back for the final series finished the test.

Now my point in recounting this day, and those derby dogs, is twofold: one, derby dogs can mark, and two, it's better to confront them with four birds to achieve separation than to take them to water and entice them to run the bank. A bank running judge will find his winner, but he may cause irreparable harm for all dogs tested.

Never, never, never, give a derby dog a bank running test. Not at trial and not in training.

As Pup matures and gains greater skill in handling water doubles, you'll gradually pull your casting line back from shore, start showing Pup dummies that fall in high cover, start working him through decoys, and start ramming him off high banks.

If Pup's going to be your hunting dog then you must work him from a blind. He must get accustomed to looking high for his birds:

...he sucks to the point at right. D. L. runs shoreline to drive Pup back to water and gets him launched so he swims toward distant fall...

catching the apex of their fall. Most of my dogs will follow the ducks' flight: I can tell by the intensity of their gaze when it is time to stand and fire.

Triple Retrieves

Common sense tells you how to present your first triples. Return to land. Have two helpers throw a bird apiece—quite far apart. You toss one from line. Have all birds dead. Use no flyers.

Pup should have no trouble with the short bird, and you can help him with the long ones. When Pup's retrieving the hand-thrown bird, you point your casting toe toward the first of the distant field birds you want fetched. When Pup heels to deliver to hand, he'll line up with your extended leg. Should he want another distant bird, instead, then you change your stance and aim at that one.

... but Pup gets hung up on long, thin peninsula and D. L. has to drive him on to memory bird. On re-run, Pup takes a straight line to memory bird, ignoring point that drydocked him the first time around.

It's funny how we think we've got these far birds marked—yet we'll glance at Pup and when turning back to look, realize we've forgotten.

Well there's a couple of tricks— One, as each bird hits the ground, dig the toe of your boot into the soil at the casting line. Also, mark the line of the fall on the horizon. Not the spot, but the line. There'll be a tree, or a silo, or a distant fence post. Something. Some outcropping to cue you on line. And if Pup holds this line when he's cast, his nose will find the bird.

While he's hunting his second bird, move your boot toe over to fit in the other depression. Search the horizon for your clue. When Pup delivers to hand, you'll be pre-aimed at this third fetch. Take the bird and cast him.

Now dogs are very bright. They can quit marking birds and start marking guns. You'll see them run to the guns that shot the bird, then whip a sharp right, or left.

If Pup starts marking off the guns then have all gunners retire while

Pup's retrieving the hand-thrown bird. Retire? Yes, that's a field trial term which means the gunners hide.

Pup will mend his ways.

Or, another way Pup can defeat himself is to start leading the procedure. That is, while one bird is still airborne, shot and falling, Pup will swing his head to the other set of guns. In actuality, Pup's seen a bird in the air, but he's not marked a bird down. If this happens, signal the second set of guns to hold their bird and cast Pup for the bird he's turned from. This will make him honest. You'll probably have to show Pup your plastic fly swatter before the bird's found, but Pup will start waiting each set of guns through to completion.

Yet, I've had dogs that always led the guns but they proved to have all birds marked. A dog's peripheral vision is amazing.

Should Pup try to switch birds on early triple retrieves, remember, always have the bird boy beat him to it. Then you go afield and return Pup to the exact spot he vacated: the spot where he was right, but went wrong. Then you return to the casting line and direct Pup to hunt by whistle and hand signal. Or, heel Pup back to the casting line and cast him again.

Other dos and don'ts would include:

The Errant Feather Fetcher

One. If Pup must stool or hike a leg on retrieve, he must hold the bird. If he drops it, go afield, lift the bird with a toe, and order, "Fetch."

Two. If Pup stools or hikes a leg going afield then you've got trouble. Real trouble. Any dog that stops a hunt to dump has little hunting spirit—and probably should be dumped by you. I'm assuming you aired him properly before going to the casting line.

Three. If Pup freezes on the bird at hand then you must force break him to retrieve. A chapter on force retrieving follows.

Four. If Pup picks at the bird in the field; just won't pick it up; or picks it up, drops it, and jumps sideways; he must be force broke to retrieve.

Five. If Pup pops on the way to the bird; that is, stops, turns around and looks to the handler for help, then you must turn your back on him. That's right. Turn completely around. Pup must learn he's on his own. He cannot look to you for help.

When Pup exits water he must run straight to handler, not stopping to shake.

Six. Triples will eventually be taken to water. If Pup veers from water and starts to run the bank you must boom, "No," walk to the spot Pup went wrong, heel him to you and ram him to water. Then run the test again. Only this time you work from shore. Only later do you move the casting line back where it was when Pup got in trouble.

Seven. If Pup drops the duck upon leaving water in order to shake, he must be force broke to retrieve.

Eight. If Pup drags the bird instead of carrying it in his mouth, he must be force broke to retrieve.

Nine. If Pup is gun shy; that is, he cowers before the gun or runs away when a gun is fired, then you've got big trouble. We'll handle the shy dog in our chapter on force retrieving.

Ten. If Pup is impatient on line, creeps out before the handler, ends up many feet away, indicates he's just one frenzied notion from breaking, then you must command, "No," and heel him to side. You can't have Pup doing that at a trial. The judges will ask you to heel your dog and Pup may turn about when coming back to your side, taking his eyes off the marks. Or he may scoot backwards, never really coming to heel, getting you upset, never satisfying the judges.

Should this happen, work Pup in a field trial training situation wearing the pinch collar. But remember, only Pup moves; your hand is stationary.

Also, never let Pup fetch a bird so long as he's cheating on the casting line. Walk him off, have the birds picked up, start all over again.

Creepers are magnificent animals to watch but a pain to handle. The handler's always prone to a coronary; he never knows if Pup is going to break or stay. A creeping dog is a hi-flown, eager, enthusiastic, thrilling performer. He lives for birds. Can't wait for birds. But the rules of the game say he must stay at heel till the judges release him to fetch.

I keep my creepers under control by releasing the football players on them. This helps. The judges are always back there and Pup never knows when they're going to go nuts and jump him.

Eleven. Many creepers are also whiners. Once again, their desire for birds is just too much for them to control. Not only are they leaving the line before being sent, but they're begging with voice to be away. There's only one cure: a ton of birds. Especially before a trial. Matter of fact, so many birds it takes the hunter's edge off Pup. He's sick of birds and now he enters a field trial situation and you cast him for several. This may remove some style but make an honest performer on line.

Also, as each bird is shot in training, and before Pup is cast for each fetch, tell him, "No noise." You can repeat this command in a field trial situation.

There's an old adage in dog training: correct a dog on that part of his body, or at that spot in the field, where he's made his mistake. So outfit a whining Pup with a pinch collar. Now when the bird's thrown and Pup whines, rotate your fist that holds the lead-end, the collar contracts, and Pup gets pinched just as you say, "No noise." It's a flick of the wrist, done quickly and released quickly so the collar snaps open.

But this is something I'd save till Pup was 18 months or older. There is such a thing as a puppy whine. The puppy's feeling lonely or insecure. He's scared. He needs love; not a pain in the neck. Or he needs the force retrieving table.

Twelve. And then there's the dog that won't look at the bird, but instead, looks at the handler's hand, or into his face. The dog simply won't take a cast.

This is a dog with little desire. You can try to hype him up by one, force break him to retrieve, two, give him lots of birds right near the casting line; birds that will prompt him to break. Three, keep him on singles till he starts to watch the field. And four, short-tie him on line and make him watch all dogs work, day after day. Let him see you praise other dogs for their job, yet ignore him. Make a point of walking past him, not even acknowledging he is there. He'll change his ways. If not, you have a dog with no desire and you should have no desire to keep him.

The Cheater

You can't salvage all non-performers. You can hype a dog up, but you can't plug in what his momma and daddy left out. If they left out spirit, if they left out desire, if they left out birdiness—then you may fail to instill them. Even if you save this dog it's likely he'll live his life as a cheater. Know how a dog cheats? Well, they're subtle. You're teaching sit, e.g., and the dog sits on your foot. You may not even notice. But the dog is sitting on your foot for he thinks he's winning. Or he crowds you at heel. Or he freezes on the dummy. Or he piddles over the bird in the field.

Not all dogs are worth saving. Give em to the farmer down the road, to the next door kid, or the widow who wants a big dog to protect her bedroom.

Every dog has a purpose, just like every human being, but you may not want to take em all hunting.

12/Force Breaking Pup To Retrieve

Ever want a four wheeler— Every time you turned the key in the ignition it would start?

Or a rifle— Every time you squeezed the trigger it'd fire.

Or a fishing reel— Every time you cast it would unwind, smooth and easy, never a backlash.

Well we're not building RVs, rifles, or fishing reels, so we can't guarantee them to be failsafe. But we are building a retriever. And once Pup's force broke to retrieve we can guarantee he'll never fail us.

A force broke Pup just won't quit you. You get in hand what you ask to have fetched. Plus, by force breaking Pup to retrieve you convince him to hand his self-will over to you. Force breaking also bolds up timid dogs: gun shy, man shy, bird shy dogs. And makes renegade dogs biddable.

Force retrieving can also cure hard mouth, freezing on the bird, picking at feather, eating the bird, bird switching, and keep Pup from dropping the bird at water's edge when he shakes, or at field when he stops to stool.

Force retrieving gives Pup a great sense of self worth. Force broke dogs are happier, more confident, more eager, and more self reliant than dogs who've never had this training. And you may notice— Though force training forces a dog to hand his self-will over to the trainer, at the same time, it makes the dog more self reliant. This is easy to explain: becoming an honest performer the Pup is constantly pleasing the handler, which means the hassle is past. Pup only hears praise when working. This in turn makes a more confident performer and the greater Pup's confidence the greater his self reliance.

Simply stated, force breaking a dog to retrieve is absolutely the best thing that can happen to him. There's nothing bad about it. Every thing is good. No handler should ever hunt or trial a retriever that's not been force broke to retrieve.

But like the pinch collar, force breaking a dog to retrieve summons up black and forbidding pictures in some people's heads—and in many an old dog's head, too. For until now, man really hasn't known how to go about it.

The principle is this: you get a dog to say, "Ouch," which means he has to open his mouth, whereupon you immediately stick something in this open mouth, saying, "Fetch," and the instant Pup takes in mouth whatever the trainer is offering, the reason for the ouch is stopped.

Historically, dog trainers have forced an ouch in Pup by putting a reverse half-nelson on a front leg, grinding a thumbnail into an ear, outfitting a paddle-board about Pup's neck—to twist the board forces an edge into the base of Pup's skull. Or trainers have stepped on paws, squeezed them with their hands, slapped the dog in the face, taken a dummy and slammed it into the dog's mouth. And everything they did was wrong.

Wrong for several reasons. One, Pup could see who was causing his pain: the culprit was aggressive and the Four Ts declare this taboo.

Two, the trainer often drew blood and left scars. Would you believe breaking a leg?

Three, even when the trainer stopped whatever he was doing to force Pup to open his mouth—the pain stayed on. Consequently there was no immediate reward for Pup fetching. Pup had the thing in his mouth but he still hurt.

Four, trainers were teaching force retrieve with the dog on the floor, or on the earth, where he had the use of his legs—the dog didn't feel overpowered—and the handler was all off balance, being on one knee, crouched down, his legs going to sleep, his back hurting. So the trainer was miserable and his timing was off and it was all just a mess.

Well I had to find a better way. So I started searching—for 16 years, all over the world—until I found something I could modify to fit the retriever trainers' purpose.

Then I found it. Old Delmar Smith was using it in one of his lean-to barns.

Now all Delmar's life he's trained pointers, setters, versatile hunting dogs—and all others—to fetch. He's never had it easy for he wasn't working with the Big-3. He had few natural retrievers. So Delmar had to develop a force broke method for dogs that possibly had the fetch bred out of them, or for dogs that traditionally just weren't asked to retrieve. With variations, I've conceived and tested, Delmar's system is now perfect for us.

The Way It's Done

Get some lumber to build a table. Make the table top crotch high. THIS IS IMPORTANT AND I REPEAT, MAKE SURE THE TABLE TOP IS CROTCH HIGH. This will put the average dog's mouth immediately in front of your right hand when your elbow is naturally—and therefore, comfortably—bent at a 90 degree angle.

Should your arm be higher than this, or lower than this, then this means you are holding it at an angle. After a while, with this stress, the forearm will get tired and when it gets tired you'll get irritated, your timing will either precede or lag Pup's mouth, and you'll mess up the training session.

By making the table top crotch high, instead of 28 inches, or 30 inches, or 32 inches, we have designed the table specifically for you. If someone else wants to use your table—it may not fit their need.

Now build this table for stout: two-by-four legs and a plywood top. Brace it and cross brace it. This table is going to take some pressure.

There is an alternative to building a table. If you have a multi-run kennel with the dog houses within a building, you can use the tops of these houses for a long training table. But the average trainer using this book will only have one or two pups to train—not a kennel of dogs.

Okay, shove the table up against your garage wall. Where? Your garage. No need your neighbors seeing what you're doing. They wouldn't understand. Plus, you need to work Pup apart from all distractions. And finally, you need to work Pup where he'll never go again. At least he'll never go into your garage to hunt a bird. He can't associate anything bad that happens here with the field.

Imperative: table top must be crotch high.

Large kennel operations can use tops of crates for force retrieve table.

If garage wall is masonry you can substitute screws for U-shaped nails.

Now 18 inches above the table, on both the right and left hand side, drive a U-shaped nail. If your garage wall is made of gypsum board you'll need to anchor two-by-fours, then drive the U-shaped nails into these supports.

Okay, cut yourself three cords of ⅛- or ¼-inch nylon and tie snap swivels to each end. That's three cords and six swivels. One cord you want six inches long. Another 18 inches. And a third one—make it two feet, or if Pup's big, make it 30 inches.

Now rummage about the garage and find the discarded oak handle of some broken garden tool. We want three sections of oak dowel, each one about nine inches long. Saw them off the handle.

Positioning Pup

You're ready for Pup. Go get him, heel him into your garage, pick him up and place him on the table. Yes, once again, we've taken Pup's legs from him. But unlike other force retrieve training stances we've given you yours.

293

Attach Pup's leather collar to wall anchor, let him settle and reflect. Then cinch waist.

Now, snap the six inch cord to the right hand nail and snap the other end to the D ring on Pup's plain leather collar. Pup's head is facing right, his rear end to the left. Or depending on how you approach the table, Pup's head may be facing you, his rear end distant.

Step back and let Pup settle. Let him sniff and eyeball the place. Give him time to gulp.

Approach him again and wrap the 24 inch cord, or longer, around his waist; snapping both ends to the left hand (or distant) nail. Pup's roped to the wall. Once again, walk away and let him settle.

Now in the pictures accompanying this section you see a taut wire running the length of the training table. Delmar lets his charges run up and down the table to relax. Later, he heels them back and forth, getting them to launch for a retrieve. We don't need the wire since we're one, working with natural retrievers, and two, we've already got Pup casting to fetch.

Incidentally, should Pup somehow fall from this table, don't go to him. Let him find his own way back up—which he will. I've seen hundreds scramble back to stand on four flat feet. Don't worry, Pup

Retriever races down table in pursuit of dowel to illustrate use of overhead wire.

Portable retrieving tables set up in field await Delmar Smith seminar. Students teach force retrieve to all breeds of gun dogs.

will make it. And I do not exaggerate when I say hundreds. Delmar gives some 20 seminars a year with, maybe, 20 dogs attending each session. That would be 400 dogs a year on these tables—or tables like them. Plus, there's all the dogs we've trained together at Delmar's home kennels. I can tell you this, we never lost a dog. They all made it back on top the table if they fell off.

But should you think that table's shaking too much and may possibly flip out from under Pup, then remove Pup, nail the table to the wall, and put Pup back on—snapping him to the wall once again.

Now, with the three oak dowels in your right hand rear trouser pocket— "Why oak dowels?" you ask. Good question. Just as we force break Pup to retrieve someplace he'll never be asked to hunt. We also give him something to fetch he'll never be asked to pick up in the field. Plus, we want something Pup can't bite down on—we want to avoid hard mouth. We also want something small: something Pup can hold without his jaw muscles getting tired. An oak dowel is perfect.

Okay, go to Pup, put him at ease, tell him he's a fine guy, pet him, rub his ears on both sides. Now take an oak dowel in your right hand and use your left hand to force a thumb and forefinger into opposite sides of Pup's jaws. Press in at the hinges.

Touch your own jaw. Farther back. That's it, behind the teeth. Feel the pressure?

Keep pressing on these hinges of Pup's jaws and he will open his mouth. At that instant, insert the dowel. Immediately cover Pup's muzzle with your left hand, holding the dowel in position. Place your right hand as follows: hook the two center fingers under Pup's plain leather collar and place your thumb in the V under his jaw. This will slightly raise Pup's head, and since it's only his bottom jaw that can move it will hold the dowel in place. But take it easy, apply no pressure. Now we must groom Pup's mouth, must make certain no lips are being pinched. And we must move the dowel forward, just behind Pup's canine teeth.

Why forward? Place a pencil crosswise in your mouth. Toward the back of your mouth you'll feel the muscles gradually protest. Now bring the pencil forward, just behind your own canine teeth. That's right, without tiring you can hold the pencil there for hours.

Also, during all this, YOU DO NOT SAY ONE WORD. It's not time to establish transfer between the dowel and a voice command. Plus, perform all work like a dental hygenist: so careful, so gentle.

Approach training table with one dowel in hand and two in rear pocket, gentle Pup, activate jaw hinges and insert dowel, hold dowel in place with either left or right hand — whichever you're more comfortable with — groom lips, bring dowel forward to rest behind canine teeth, raise thumb and Pup will hold dowel until you ask him to leave it.

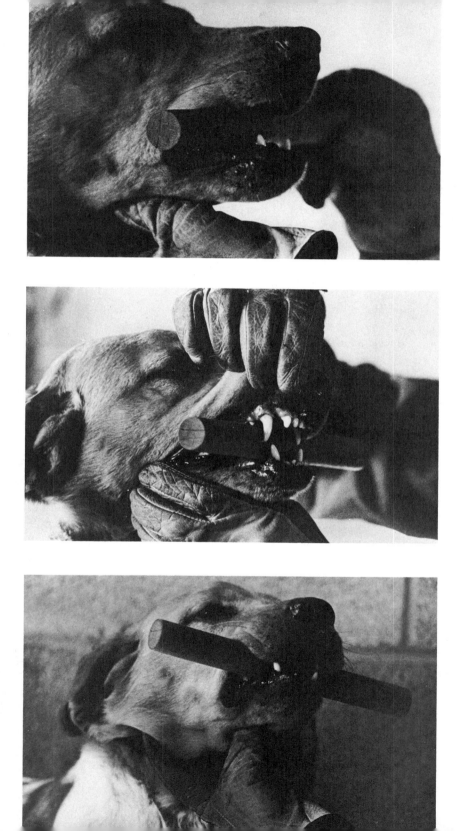

Now remove the dowel from Pup's mouth. He'll be only too glad to let you have it. Just push it toward the V of his lips and twist upwards. With the dowel removed, gentle Pup, stroke his ears, get him relaxed, then present the dowel again, and again.

A Fight On Your Hands

But what's this? Pup's flipping about up there like a fish dropped on the boat dock. He's fighting this thing and he's fighting you. Hardly likely. That's what Delmar's pointers and setters do. But we're training retrievers who've been fetching for months, or years.

Still, let's consider the nontypical retriever. As always you'll not get angry, and you'll not hurt Pup. If Pup fights you and somehow spits the dowel out, then grasp his bottom jaw with your gloved hand. Since it is the bottom jaw that's hinged, Pup can't bite. Hold it. Hold it till Pup swallows. Remember? For Pup to swallow is for Pup to sigh—to give himself over to his fate.

Present the dowel again. More than likely, Pup will fight you and you'll drop it. You have no alternative, grasp the bottom jaw and hold on. In all this, say nothing. Transmit no emotion with your face. Be detached, look the other way, but hold on.

It seems a rule of dogdom they'll fight you three times. After the third confrontation, the third fight, the third time Pup's successful in causing you to drop the dowel, the third time you hold him by his bottom jaw, and the third time he swallows—Pup's yours.

With all the fight gone, insert the dowel with the command, "Fetch," and remove it with the command, "Leave it." That's right. Now we add voice commands to both the dog that fought us, and the dog we merely had to acquaint with the process of presenting the dowel and getting the feel of it in his mouth. There'd be no need in your speaking earlier. Neither Pup would have heard you.

Pace yourself during the force retrieve session. Don't just continually confront Pup, poking that dowel in his mouth. Walk away on occasion. Let Pup think it over. Let him settle. Let him relax. Even let him get lonely—he is short-tied—and start looking for you.

And should you drop another dowel then whip your right hand back, grasp another from your pocket, and stick it in Pup's mouth. Any time Pup whips you, it merely sets the whole training session back to the beginning—or even further. Pup can't win. The dowel is always there and he must accept it.

If Pup fights you the dowel may fly, grab his bottom jaw with your gloved hand and hold till he sighs. Pup will usually try you three times then accept what you're trying to teach.

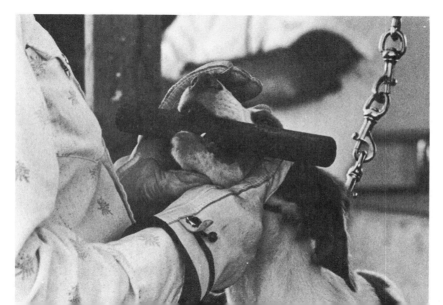

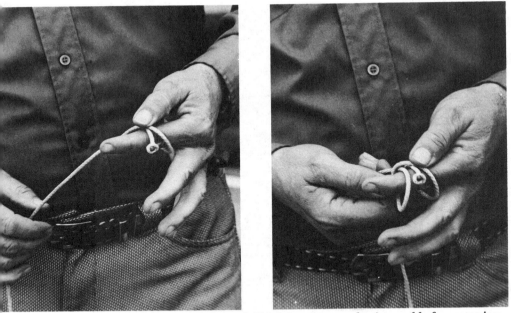

Tie clove hitch as illustrated. Trick is to loop and twist cord before running it on finger second time.

One final thing— This holding Pup's bottom jaw. No, he doesn't view this as a hostile act. Pup won't grudge your holding him. Hostile acts, as viewed by dogs, are trainers throwing their arms about, running, leaping, lunging, grabbing, getting red in the face, the neck bulging, the voice booming— None of this occurs when holding Pup's jaw.

The Nerve Hitch

Now we're ready to force break Pup to retrieve. He knows the table, he knows the oak dowel, and he knows you're not going to hurt him.

And that's the way we're going to keep it. We're not going to hurt Pup. We're never going to hurt Pup. But just like the pinch collar, if Pup doesn't do as we want him to, he can hurt himself. It's up to Pup.

Thus the nerve hitch.

Take a role of ⅛- or ¼-inch nylon cord and snip off a piece three feet long. Go to Pup, tie a clove hitch just above the carpal joint— that's what we all call his knee—on his right front leg. Or if you're

Pup's anchored to wall, tie clove hitch just above carpal joint, let cord fall straight down and loop about two center toes, push half hitch back as far as you can . . .

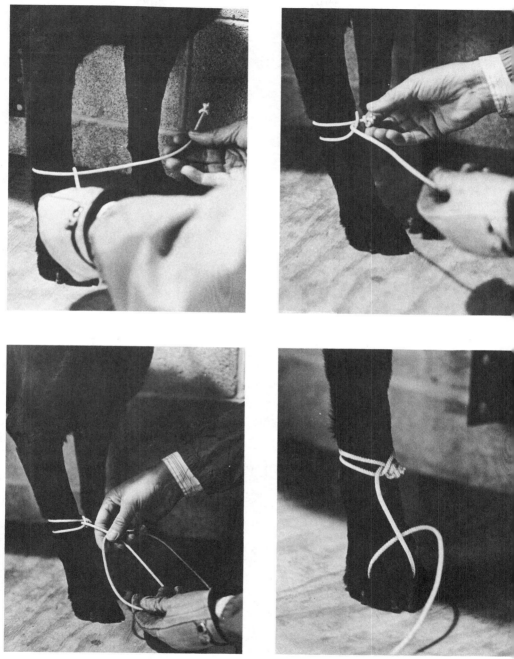

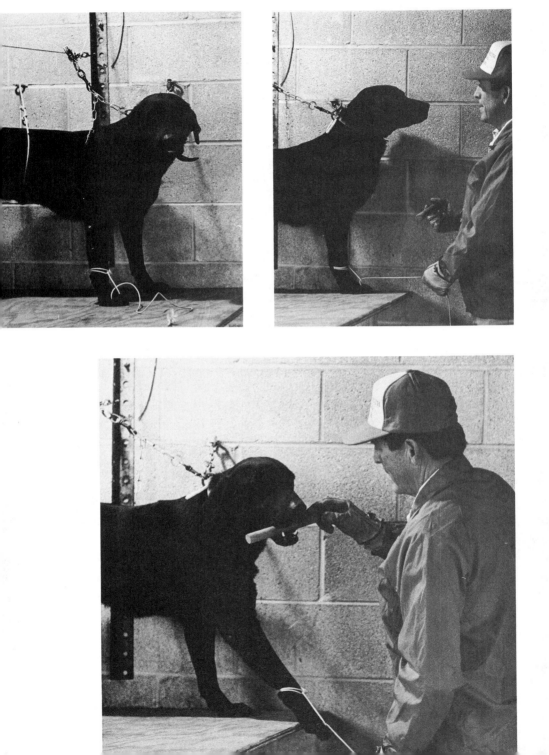

... let Pup settle. Talk him into a good nature while you prepare to pull cord that triggers nerve hitch. Present dowel. The instant Pup's mouth opens insert dowel, drop nerve hitch cord, and shoot either left or right hand under jaw and place other hand over muzzle. You may want to reach down and loosen cord when Pup's settled.

going to carry your gun in your left hand, or trial Pup from the right side, then tie the cord to Pup's left leg. Adjust the clove hitch so the cord hangs straight down and over Pup's foot. Now throw a half-hitch about Pup's two center toes. Shove the knot up tight against Pup's foot.

You're ready.

Take a dowel in your right hand—and be prepared for a fast moving dog. Place the dowel before Pup's mouth, hold it there, then gradually pull the nerve hitch cord with your left hand. The pressure will start to build. Pup will resist. Then it'll get too much and he'll leap, crying, "Ouch." When his mouth opens you insert the dowel. Pup's still tied to the wall so he can't move around too much. But still, he'll move. And he'll fight you, and he'll turn his head from the dowel. You've got to be fast and you've got to be firm.

Instant replay in slow motion—

One. The perfect fetch beats the ouch. That is, the trainer knows his dog so well the dowel is going into Pup's mouth before the ouch is ever heard. It stands to reason Pup must open his mouth a fraction of an instant before he can cry out. It's all a matter of timing—as is all dog training.

Two. But Pup's not just standing there. He's rearing back and turning his head to side and his jaws are clinched shut and he's trying to pull himself off the wall. If Pup's got too much latitude, is free enough to win this fight, then shorten all cords and press him tighter against the wall.

Three. And what if you drop the dowel? Keep your pressure and reach for another. Don't drop to the floor to find where the first one rolled: quick draw another one from your pocket.

Four. The instant a dowel goes into Pup's mouth, all pressure is released from the nerve hitch. The cord is dropped and the left hand—that's been pulling the cord—goes over Pup's muzzle to control Pup's head, then later to groom the mouth, and still later to stroke the dog.

Five. A split second after getting the left hand over the muzzle, the right hand knifes up to hold the leather collar with the thumb inserted

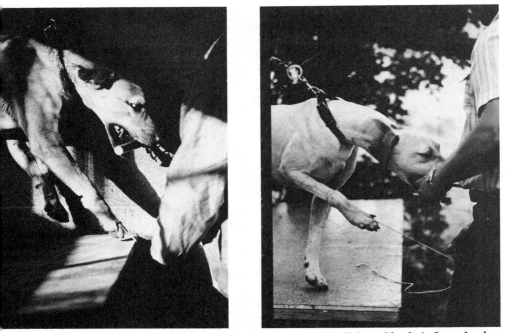

When Pup's reaching for the dowel, leaning off the table, he's force broke to retrieve.

into the V beneath Pup's chin. Pup can't be permitted to spit out the dowel. Hands are reversed for a dog that'll work on the right hand side.

Six. When the dowel is inserted the trainer commands, "Fetch," and all the time he's holding the dowel in Pup's mouth, he's saying, "Hold it."

Seven. When he removes the dowel, the trainer orders, "Leave it," then rewards Pup with a pat on both sides, lets him settle, then starts all over again.

The Fulcrum

How does the nerve hitch work? Well, weave a pencil between the fingers of your left hand. Over the index finger, under the two middle fingers, over the little finger. Now take your right hand and squeeze. It hurts? Sure it hurts. But it leaves no halo of pain, no imprint, it doesn't cut the skin, nor damage muscle, nor break bone, nor leave a scar. It's

There's not a breed of gun dog that can't be force broke to retrieve with the nerve hitch.

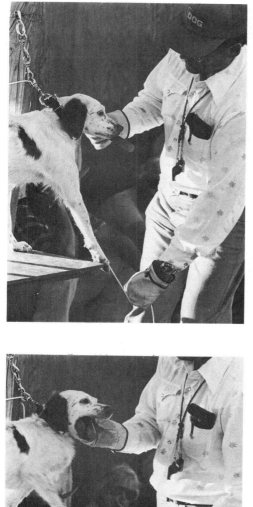

a device that works on a pressure point. Like a fulcrum. You get a lot done with a little force.

What's really important is once the pressure's released the pain stops. I mean it stops that fraction of an instant. There's no carry over. Pup's getting immediate reward for compliance.

And Pup's not viewing you as the culprit. It's that blasted thing that's wrapped around and pulling his toes. For you're not moving in an act of aggression: you're just standing there, feet flat, your left arm hanging at your side, the right hand raised, but stationary—just presenting a wood stick. Pup doesn't smell anger on your body, nor see it in your face, nor feel it in your touch. You're detached and standing there and it's all so uncontrollable and inevitable. Pup just has to take that stick and hold it in his mouth. After all, you're Pup's friend. He knows if you could stop all this, you would.

And something else that's beautiful—

Man or beast, our head always ducks toward pain. So, where's Pup's pain? At his foot! Where will Pup make all his retrieves? At his feet! Eureka! You've got Pup lowering his head to make a retrieve as well as taking the dowel in his mouth. And it's all done together.

One more thing—

After six-or-so nerve hitch retrieves you can shake the half-hitch off Pup's toes and just pull the cord as it's attached above the carpal joint. Pup will respond as though the cord were still about his toes. You can remove Pup from the table—later—and holding the cord in hand, just attached above his carpal joint, tug and get him to fetch a dowel from the ground.

Once Can Be Enough

Some trainers like to enter a force retrieve training session and get it over with. See this thing through to its bitter end. Never come back. But I'm describing trainers who are accustomed to the old dysfunctional force retrieve methods. With the nerve hitch method you can bring Pup back to the table as often as you like. String it all out. You be the judge. After all, you're standing there monitoring Pup. How's he doing?

You can tell if you're succeeding when Pup starts reaching for the dowel. That's what it's all about. Pull the cord and Pup thrusts his head forward, leaning off the table, striving to get that dowel in his mouth to stop that pain in his toes. This is when you change the six inch cord holding Pup's neck to the wall for one that's 30 inches; plus you remove the flank cord. This is when you no longer present the dowel before Pup's mouth. But instead, you hold the dowel farther and farther away. Until finally, you hold the dowel beside your hip.

You know Pup's force broke to retrieve when you hold the dowel distant and say, "Fetch," without the nerve hitch cord in your hand—and Pup throws himself forward to get that dowel in his mouth. That's a force broke dog. The dog that hears, "Fetch," and starts uprooting trees, digging holes, trampling brush to find a bird to get in his mouth.

You've got it made. You've made Pup.

You've made yourself a retriever. Did it with the nerve hitch. Take that word, "Nerve," and play Scrabble with it. One arrangement of the letters spells, "Never." You've got a dog that'll never refuse you. It's a matter of having the nerve.

What It's All About

Now take Pup afield, tell him, "Fetch," and you've got a bird in hand. But days pass, you must ignore Pup, pressing business at the office, the store, the plant. So two week's later you tell Pup, "Fetch," and he piddles. Or he drops the bird to dump. Or he drops it to shake off water at pond's edge.

Just walk to Pup's side, tap his right leg with your left boot, order, "Fetch," and all the lights will go on. To touch Pup's foot takes his mind back to the force retrieve table. Now, should Pup ever refuse you, there's something you can do about it. Just tap his foot.

Or you can tie the nerve hitch cord to the carpal joint and let Pup wear it. That's a constant reminder. Or you can carry the cord in your pocket and merely show it to Pup.

But force breaking to retrieve does more than just make Pup a guaranteed performer. Say Pup is refusing your hand cast— Remember the problem dog who just stared at the handler's face, never the birds?

Well, tie the nerve hitch above the carpal joint—you may not have to circle it about Pup's two center toes, we'll see—and placing Pup in the heel position, thread the nerve hitch cord under the arch of your left boot. Now when you say, "Fetch," and sweep your left hand up and forward, you'll also shoot out your left boot, jerking the cord forward with your heel. Watch out you don't get sucked up in Pup's jet trail. He's off to fetch.

If Pup needs a reminder while afield then make him wear the cord, tap his leg with your boot, or take the cord from your coat pocket and show it to Pup. Any of these reminders will jar him. Also, Delmar illustrates in this photo how to thread nerve hitch cord under arch of boot to ram Pup for fetch when your foot slides forward.

There's a bushel of spin-offs that come from force breaking Pup to retrieve with the nerve hitch—and they're all good.

Force training bolds Pup up. If Pup's timid it gives him confidence. Like the guy who joins the Marine Corps, or Max Evans in the French Foreign Legion. Pup and the Marine and the Legionnaire come out of their respective experiences with self respect, pride, determination, faith in one's ability, resourcefulness.

And the renegade? We had those in the Marines and I'm sure they were in the Legion. Somehow, the renegade dog, or renegade man, emerge from firm discipline with all the fire left in em but now there's an on/off switch.

Consequently, force breaking Pup to retrieve will bold him up over birds. You'll not see him jump to side again. Or pick about. Or drag

310

the thing on the trail. Or drop it while he dumps. Once Pup's got that bird in his mouth, he's delivering poultry.

By the same token, Pup's no longer man shy. He won't cower from people. As for the gun? Well a gun shy dog is really hard to cure. But force breaking him to retrieve can be part of the program.

Plus, force breaking Pup to retrieve can staunch up a bolter, or fire up a piggy performer.

I wouldn't own a retriever that wasn't force broke to retrieve. And neither will you, once you've had one.

If a force broke dog mismarks he's not going to leave the area. He's never going to abandon his hunt. He's going to stay and sniff and circle till he's found something to put in his mouth. It may be a box turtle, but he'll bring back something. I once saw a dog mismark at a Dallas trial and get confused—but he was force broke to retrieve and he wouldn't leave the area. Unable to find a bird he grabbed the bird crate that held the pheasants the gunners were shooting and began dragging the crate to the casting line.

Or what of the hard mouthed Pup? Or the one who sticks or freezes on his bird? Force breaking to retrieve is our first step in curing the clinch-jawed performer.

The Frozen Bird

But let's say Pup's gone through our nerve hitch course and he's still being rough on the bird. Well, if Pup wants to freeze on a bird, then you freeze a bird. Toss it in the deep freeze and turn it to stone: but one caution, tuck the toenails under. They're sharp as pins when frozen. Now outfit Pup with the nerve hitch cord and command, "Fetch," then, "Hold," then, "Leave it." Pup'll not want to bite that bird any more than you want to crunch an ice cube. He'll be glad to give it up when you ask for it.

Have several frozen birds on hand for this session. We want nothing but the hardest and coldest birds we can freeze for Pup to learn he no longer wants to crunch the thing.

Or, let's say Pup circles you with the bird. You're standing on the casting line and Pup returns with his fetch—only he won't give you the bird. He keeps walking around you. Slap the nerve hitch on him. He'll heel and sit. Or tap his leg with your boot. He'll remember the garage table and comply.

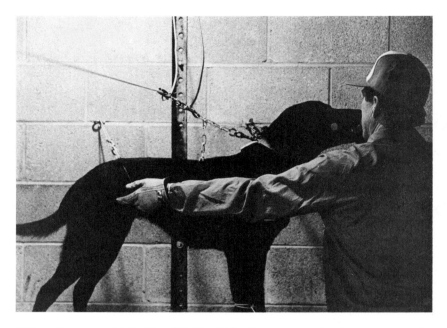

If Pup freezes on bird either lift his off flank or blow in his face as you push back and twist the bird upwards.

No matter what the problem, you can always return Pup to the force retrieve table and reinforce your will.

If Pup won't fetch, slap on the nerve hitch cord.

If Pup won't hold, grasp his muzzle with your left hand, and press your right hand thumb in the V under his jaw. Make Pup stand there till he swallows three times for three birds.

If Pup won't deliver to hand then push the bird back into his mouth and twist it upwards. Or blow in Pup's face. Or reach over and lift his flank.

You can do it all on the force retrieve table.

And by verbal command, displaying the nerve hitch cord, or tapping Pup's foot with your boot, you can gain compliance in the field.

13/The Blind Retrieve

It was one of those mornings ducks fly.

Distended gray clouds sagged like folds of skin on elephant legs: a great herd of elephants stampeding southeast.

Mad-dad wind stood somewhere on the Wyoming Rockies swinging a mace of spiked ice to beat me down each time I peered above the blind.

Frozen bark popped from nearby sandbar willows, varmints burrowed, hawks perched close to evergreen trunks, the sun gave up and headed for California.

Pepe hunkered against my leg in shudder. I ignored his complaint, his doleful gaze, and prayed hard to cancel him out. I knew what he was asking, "Please Lord, don't let a duck fall in the water."

Then they came. A wedge of mallards. The last to be blown from their northern haunts. Now they whiffle to slip wind and set. I'm on em. The Model-12 barks three times. Two drakes splash before the blind, a third one's head shot. He climbs, sets his wings and makes a death glide to the west. At 400 yards he disappears behind a hill.

I prop the gun against the hay-bale-blind and cheer to Pepe, "Come on pardner." Out we walk, leaning into the wind— Out we walk? I walk alone. "Pepe," I demand, "Heel."

Now Pepe was always a good dog, not a great dog. I bought him as a two-year-old with lots of potential. He only had one problem: he'd just as soon not enter water.

But I finally got him wet and we trialed together for many years. Never winning much, but usually finishing. For Pepe was a green ribbon dog.

Now blue is first, red is second, yellow is third, white is fourth, and all dogs who'd be called back if there were another series, but haven't placed in the top four, they get the green.

Pepe should have been an Irish retriever, not a Labrador. He papered the kennels green. The last four years I ran him I can't recall him not finishing a trial. And that was good. My need was more to learn than to win. Just like hunting birds. My need is more to see them than to shoot.

And you should know this. A good dog will teach you to handle. But a bad one will make a trainer out of you.

The Busted Camera

Okay—I'm walking out of the blind and saying, "Heel."

A mournful black head eases from behind the hay, like cards appear when sweated apart by a barrack's poker shark. No body shows, just head. Talk about a whipped dog. The jowels hang, the eyelids hang, the ears hang—

"Pepe," I grit, "Heel," the voice low and controlled. There's misery ahead, I'll need force in command at the end.

Pepe gazes at the lake's chopped surface, the jaundiced light on the horizon, the crazy tipping of the decoys. Pelting drizzle makes him blink his eyes, the wind tosses his right ear on top his head. Fretfully he relents and edges forward, though he were crossing a minefield.

A "Dead bird," I announce with enthusiasm. "Dead, Dead." I pat my left thigh. Heel the dog close to side. Now I place my left hand— fingers and thumb joined and straight, like Kung Fu delivers a karate chop—parallel with his head, moving the hand slowly up and down, mesmerizing the dog to concentrate, to take a picture.

But I can tell, no shutter snaps. Pepe's protesting he's out of film, or the camera's busted. Maybe the shutter's frozen.

I shake it all off for both of us by patting my left outer leg and pivoting, leading Pepe about me in carousel. Now we're back where

It was one of those mornings ducks fly.

we started. Once again at heel I pat my thigh in encouragement. "Dead bird," I say again, "Dead, dead."

One of the downed mallards, belly up, starts kicking its's legs in mid-air. Pepe takes a picture. He cocks his body, the ears perk, the eyes lock, the tail lifts, the shoulders angle forward.

"No, no, no," I scold. He's conning me. He knows I don't say, "Dead," for a mark.

Again we make our wipe-out circle. We needn't get those two birds out front. They'll go nowhere. It's the one over the hill we must retrieve. Each moment we delay the distant drake's trail grows more cold.

Now Pepe knows. It's not one of the short birds we're after. With grudge he gives in. He accepts the reality, "There's a bird out there and Old Ram Rod here insists we get it."

"Line," I order. "Line." My hand moves slowly beside Pepe's head with that movement of snake charmers. The dog gives himself to my will. He'll go get the bird. He takes the picture, for muscles clump on his shoulders, the ears raise so their break is parallel to the ground, the tail stops wagging and sagging, the eyes focus at the top of the far hill. I bark, "Back," and slice my hand upwards, the way duffer bowlers release the ball.

And Away We Go

Pepe launches, his paws breaking snow's crust, clawing frozen earth. But in a few feet he hits the sheet of ice rimming the lake and starts sliding. He can't stop— Splash! He otters under water. Up he comes, shaking his head to clear his ears. Now he lifts his butt, lays his jowels and ears flat to the water's surface, strokes with power.

The bicycling duck is passed 12 feet off his left shoulder. A decoy anchor line snags across his chest. The cork block heads for sea. Then slips loose, 30 yards out. The dog swims another 110 yards, crabbing all the way to hold line against the current and the wind. Eventually he reaches the far shore; another rim of ice. Back and forth he swims, looking, testing, for a place to climb out.

Each time he trys to board, the ice breaks under his front elbows. Now he curls his body like a shrimp, the hind toenails digging at the bottom of the ice cap. Up he comes. Mincefooted he measures himself across the ice. Then he reaches land and starts to shake. I hit him with the whistle. Pepe can't shake. He's using this to delay. Pepe attends the whistle, looking for instructions.

Raising my right arm as a traffic patrolman, I order, "Back," and throw my hand forward. Pepe spins and enters a tangle of cat tails, multiflora, and prairie grass. He'll be channeled by natural corridors in the cover. He'll come out off line.

Sure enough, he exits at a left oblique. Once again I whistle. When the dog stops 160 yards out and looks back, I lift my right arm 90 degrees to my body, take two steps sideways in the same direction, and yell, "Over." The dog takes a cast toward his original line. When he's near intersecting that line, I hit him with the whistle again. Pepe stops to look. This time I order, "Back," and Pepe charges up the hill, crosses a farm lane, serpentines through some red cedar, crawls under a barbwire fence, and heads for the top of the hill.

I gauge his momentum. When he tops that hill he'll be on his own. Does he have enough push to continue his line for a half-mile? I judge he does so I let him go without further command. Otherwise, I'd stop him again and ram him, "Back," with lots of voice.

Now I retire to the hay-bale-blind and wait. If anyone chanced by, seeing me sitting there with a cup of coffee out of the thermos, they'd not believe I was fetching a duck. But that's exactly what I'm doing: remote control.

And if this passerby knew nothing of dogs, or dog men, or dog work, and learned Pepe was a half-mile distant in this blizzard with ice hanging from his coat like grains of rice, I can predict one of several ways he'd react.

One type of passerby would not believe it.

Another would stand aghast at my cruelty.

A third would scoff at my laziness—why not get it yourself?

I've met em all and then some. And what few of these passersby would know is the dog and I are a team. I can't perform without him. And he can't perform without me. I'm the coach. He's the player. And we click because we've devoted our lives to training; to playing the game.

When that passerby was flying his spring kite, Pepe and I were training.

Last summer when that passerby was water skiing, Pepe and I were training.

When that passerby celebrated autumn with touch football on the lawn, Pepe and I were training.

Arrow on skyline shows where Pepe topped hill to make his blind retrieve. This photo was taken years later when Pepe was 15. The day was similar except pond is without ice.

And after New Year's, when the days seem to grow longer and winter gets stronger, that passerby will cozy with a book beside his fireplace, while Pepe and I will be training.

Bridging a Problem

But who'd pass by on a day like this? And speaking of passing by, where's Pepe? He's been gone 20 minutes. I just looked at the far hill and he's not shown. That duck must have gone a mile.

Then I hear twigs snap to the east. Probably a squirrel skittering from one cache to another. I'm looking high for a red tail when the bottom of my eye catches a black dog. It's Pepe, and the the big drake mallard's dangling from his mouth. Then it hits me. Pepe went north a half-mile and crossed the footbridge over the creek that feeds our farm pond.

My desire is to praise the dog; what a retrieve! And he showed wit in choosing the bridge. But I can't. I've got to get tough. The dog showed wit, but he didn't show grit. A retriever must backtrack his line when fetching a bird. He must come back the same route he went out. There are several reasons for this, but primarily, if he can come back from a water retrieve by land, then why not try to go out the same way?

Slowly I rise, step forward, and glare down at the dog. I intimidate him with silent, motionless wrath. He knows. He knows good and well he's blown it.

I take the bird from his mouth without a word. Then I point for him to stay—not in the blind, but out at lake's edge, out where he can see me—and I walk a half-mile north, cross the bridge, walk a half-mile south, and plant the bird on top the hill where Pepe should have reappeared. I look east to the duck blind. Pepe sits there. He watches me.

Now, a half-mile north, and a half-mile south, and I'm back at the blind. I heel the dog in soft exasperation and repeat the procedure for casting on a line. This time when I beller, "Back," the wind blast from Wyoming has met its match.

Pepe homogenizes ice, snow, and frozen dirt in departure. He leaps to water and strokes so hard he leaves a bubbling wake. There's no piddling at the far ice apron. He crashes through and bellies aboard like an Illinois river decoy overrides flowing slush. He doesn't stop to shake: no piddling. To the top of the hill he bores to scoop up the planted bird on a dead run and I must blow hard to get him stopped. Impatiently he awaits my command. I give him time to think it over. Then I trill the suck-in whistle, bend over from the waist, and wave my right arm back and forth like a railroad brakeman swings a light. All the time blowing the suck-in whistle.

Pepe bullies back the way he bullied out.

Now when he delivers to hand it's high praise. And Pepe knows. He knew all along. He was just testing me. There's not a dog running, poor or great, who won't.

His test cost me a two-mile walk. My test cost him a round-robin in the lake. But we're in this thing together. There are imperatives for each of us to make it work.

And the point to all this, what must be understood above all else, is Pepe didn't make that retrieve because he wanted to. He made it because he had to. He was forced to.

Being Pro

There's not a pro living who doesn't perform due to force. Doctors are forced from bed in the middle of the night to operate on a crash victim. They don't want to go. They're forced to go.

Attorneys are forced to defend known criminals.

Professors are forced to teach dullards.

Pro athletes are forced to play with pulled muscles, cracked bones.

That's what being pro's all about, performance in consent to force. Pepe's dead now, buried beneath a crackbar willow behind the dam that holds the pond he swam twice to make this mallard retrieve. But in his day he was a pro. Not a pet, a pro. He ran against the pros. He beat the pros. And the rules for a dog that's pro are different from those for a house dog, a kid's dog, a junk yard dog.

And the difference is this. The pro goes when he has to go, not when he wants to go.

Quite frankly, I'd never—and I've still never—seen a blind like Pepe ran that day. And I've always resented Pepe denying me the opportunity to give praise for such superb work—we'd worked hard for that one. But joy was denied me. Just another case where being pro must stand above being pals. Oh Pepe was praised for his re-run. But that's not the same thing. That's training. The other was for real and Pepe failed.

And if all this sounds like a tall story I can shorten it to fit your straightaway vision. For I wasn't alone in that hay-bale-blind that day, nor did I shoot those three drake mallards by myself. M. Wayne Willis, one of the world's greatest sporting bird artists sat next to me in that wind-blown blind.

When it was all finished, Wayne scootched about on his milk stool and with jaw jutted, brow furrowed, eyelids nearly closed to convey profound contemplation, he said, "Willy ... never in my life ... have I, nor will I ... see a retrieve like that."

Wayne's a practical man. An outdoor artist who knows a canvas can wait when a north wind starts to bend the cedars outside his studio window. Plus, Wayne's a gun dog man. And dogs were meant to spread a table, not clutter the place with silver. Wayne never agreed with my making Pepe run it all over.

And anyplace but America I'd not have had to. Only here do we make dogs perform miracles. The game demands it and Pepe was still playing the game. We were trialing as we were hunting.

How can you make your Pup equally miraculous? It all starts on the next page.

14/Never Argue With Success

To find a bird he hasn't seen fall a dog must hand his self-will over to man. He must handle.

A pilot lands his plane on a socked-in runway by ignoring what he feels, what he thinks. He lays aside intellect and instinct and flies blind by instrument.

The pilot and the retriever are identical.

Neither of them hunt for their objective. They let themselves be guided through a series of external adjustments to their destination. They both proceed out of blind faith.

Such men and dogs are unique. They have rare temperaments, intellects, and physical attributes. And they have rare training.

Both the dog and the man shudder at the consequences of failing the mission, but they do not run, nor fly, out of fear. Rather, they proceed out of faith. At no time has the system lied to them. This is proven to both the retriever and the pilot by hundreds of re-runs, pattern drills, and successful completions.

"Never argue with success," is their motto. And that's what makes them click.

Oh there are temptations to ignore this external force that guides them. For the pilot to be a barnstormer. For the dog to be a self-hunter. But they learn such impulses usually end in failure. Thus the infallibility of the system is reinforced.

Consequently, as reinforcers, and not enforcers, we instill Pup's blind faith as follows:

Semi-Blind

We've run semi-blinds before. But for the sake of the reader who flips open to this chapter first, let's run some again.

You've got Pup doing double marks. Okay. Send two bird boys afield. Have them shout, or shoot, and launch their dummies. Now cast Pup for the last bird down. While he's returning with the retrieve, signal the memory bird thrower to hide. Now when Pup turns around he'll see one man standing afield. But this man poses a hazard. His presence may suck Pup back to the old fall. Back to where he just fetched a bird.

If Pup's focused on this bird boy, tell him, "No," carousel him about you and zero him in with left leg and left arm for the memory bird. Pup should be able to see the dummy laying out there if he looks hard enough. We're training on a mowed field and we're using big, stark white dummies. Plus, the area is seeded to guarantee Pup's success: the field is strewn with dummies about the memory bird.

When you think Pup's focused on the second bird, cast him. If he angles toward the old fall, hit him with the sit whistle, or yell, "No." Ideally Pup should answer the sit whistle. But Pup's just a pup. You'll probably need to yell, "No." If Pup stops, then call him back in. If he continues on to the old fall, then you'll probably need to go to him, call him to you, and heel him back to the casting line.

When Pup's heeled back to the casting line, signal both boys to prepare for a re-run. If Pup still wants to suck back to the memory bird on his second cast then call him back to line and ask one of the two bird boys to leave the field, picking up all the seeded dummies and taking them with him. Now the boy in the field will throw the first bird and you'll throw the second bird from the casting line. While Pup's retrieving your bird, the distant bird boy will retire from sight. Heel Pup about, take the dummy from his mouth, and ram him to the memory bird in the field.

If Pup goes, and he proves successful, then he's just retrieved a semi-blind. If not, then keep repeating the drill until he does. Later we'll extend all falls. Get Pup running 100 yards for the memory bird—and farther. Get both bird boys back to the field.

Now you might have noticed— The first command we give Pup for a blind retrieve is Back. This is a command Pup knows. He doesn't know Over from Rover. By the way, I hope that's not Pup's name. Or Jack. Or Steel. Or Bit. Or Jay. Or any name that can be confused with any verbal command we commonly give. Stay Jay. Sit Bit. Heel Steel. Back Jack. That may work. But what about Stay Jack? Does Pup Stay, or go Back? What's that? You didn't say Back, you said Jack. You really expect Pup to differentiate such sounds at his age?

But back to casts. There are only four of them: Back, Come, and Over: Over to the right or Over to the left.

Over is always verbal and visual. Or it can just be visual for advanced retrievers. Come is seldom verbal, usually a whistle, accompanied by gesture.

Now I'm speaking of field trials. You say or do whatever's necessary to get Pup on the bird when he's fetching for your gun.

Now, Pup knows Back and Come. What he doesn't know is Over. Yet we've been laying the foundation for this command from the beginning. Every time we pointed with our arm or walked in the direction we wanted Pup to go, we were preparing him for the Over cast.

So that's what we teach next.

But just a minute— Remember? We prepared Pup to take a cast from our hand and hold a short line with the circle drill. We said one day Pup could handle 24 dummies, each 15 degrees apart, seeded equally about us. Well you've stayed on that drill while all the rest of this training was taking place and you've got Pup refined to 15-degree casts. That'll do for now.

And another thing— In America today all handlers wear white training jackets. No, their interest isn't sartorial. Some of these jackets were made for meat markets. The reason for the white coat is Pup can see the handler when far afield. He can see an outstretched arm. He can discriminate between his handler and the distant backdrop.

Also, after several months of seeing you in a white training jacket every time he's taken to field, Pup learns it's time to get to work. The jacket cues him. Just as the shotgun cues him when you're taking him hunting. For that reason, always remove the jacket when you've finished training. And never wear it when Happy Timing.

Loud Mouths Never Win

And one other thing— Your voice. You know how I've pleaded with you to work low-keyed, to be detached, to be nearly silent. Well there's a reason. A handler's voice must be equal to the distance of the dog, and the situation in which the dog's placed himself.

If you're loud on the casting line, you've shot your wad. There's nothing left to put Pup down when far afield.

ALSO, A LOUD VOICE COMMANDING, "OVER," WILL DRIVE A DOG BACK. NOT OVER, BUT BACK. THIS CAUSES A SCALLOPING ROUTE ON WAY TO THE BLIND, ESPECIALLY IN WATER.

Here's what I mean. The dog takes the initial side cast, the Over, but the blast of the verbal command drives him back and he ends up on his original line. And that's not where you wanted him or you wouldn't have given an Over.

Consequently, many of your better handlers say nothing when seeking a side cast from Pup. They whistle him down, get his attention, raise their right arm if they want Pup to go to his left—Pup's opposite for he's facing you—raise their left arm if they want Pup to go to his right, then they *silently* step off in the desired direction. That's right. They say nothing.

Other handlers do even more. Knowing Pup may take an oblique cast—halfway in the desired direction, but also halfway back—they say nothing, lift their arm, step off in the right direction, and simultaneously give the suck-in whistle. The hope is the side cast will point Pup in the right direction and the suck-in whistle will hold him to it, will counter a Back.

For the Back is part of Pup's makeup. That's the direction he was going when you whistled him down. The law of inertia decrees a body in motion tends to remain in motion—in the direction it was going. Plus, we all tend to move back when someone jumps us and tells us to do something. We are startled back. Repelled back.

Then there's another reason more important than all of these. Pup's

National champion Royal's Moose's Moe and Bill Connor: they shared the same bed.

a bird dog. Pup simply wants to get the bird. And that means he keeps going back, not stopping, not taking off 90 degrees in some other direction. Pup's desire for birds is so intense, so compelling, he can't take time to veer from course. So he'll give you a token Over, then get right back where he was going before you interfered.

Such a dog was 1972 national open champion, Royal's Moose's Moe. One of the greatest Labs that'll ever live.

Moose won his national championship in water averaging 38 degrees. He was nine years old.

Bill Connor will tell you—Bill is the guy Moose owned and trained—that Moose never took an Over at that national trial, nor any trial. Moose's desire for birds was too great to wait, or to probe some other direction. He converted Overs to angle backs.

So Bill would gauge Moose's position, plus the location of the bird. If Moose was off line, Bill would hit him with the whistle—early. Now when Moose took his patented oblique cast he'd come out on the

Pigeon is stuffed into remote control bird releaser. Manually activated bird releaser is available; you pull cord. The electronic collar and remote control bird releaser are triggered by this three button transmitter. One collar is a dummy.

bird. My friend Connor! He had to be a geometry wizard. But what a dog. Little wonder Moose's granddaughter, Cricket, is out there in my kennel. Like Connor, I'll always want some part of Moose around.

Electronics

Okay, Pup found the bird—the memory bird—the one the retired gunner threw, and he's heading back in. Praise him highly and put him away. He'll have more retired-gunner blinds. Right now we want to move to the back yard and get on the baseball diamond.

But what's that you say? Pup still doesn't have the bird. He refuses to leave your side. Okay, walk him out there. Stop. Let him look around. Lift one of the dummies with your boot toe and say, "Fetch." Pup must always get the bird.

What's that? Who can afford to hire all those bird boys?

Yes, you've got a point. But you don't hire them. You're a nice guy. You entice these boys to go afield with you. That's your payback for taking them camping. Or you're a prolific father. Kids all over the house. By hook or crook you get someone out there.

But you say you're a traveling salesman. Where are you going to find a kid on the road? Okay. There are ways. I want you to spring a bundle. It's really the only expensive piece of equipment you'll ever need to buy for Pup.

I want you to buy a remote control bird releaser and to save a few bucks in the long run, get an electronic collar at the same time. That way the factory can modify the transmitter to work both units: the releaser and the collar.

And yes, you're going to need the collar. But not the older model we've all read and heard so much about. Instead you'll get the new sound-blast electric collar. I'll tell you why, later.

And if this is too much money for you to spend then split the cost and go partners with a buddy. Besides, we said training Pup would be fun, not free.

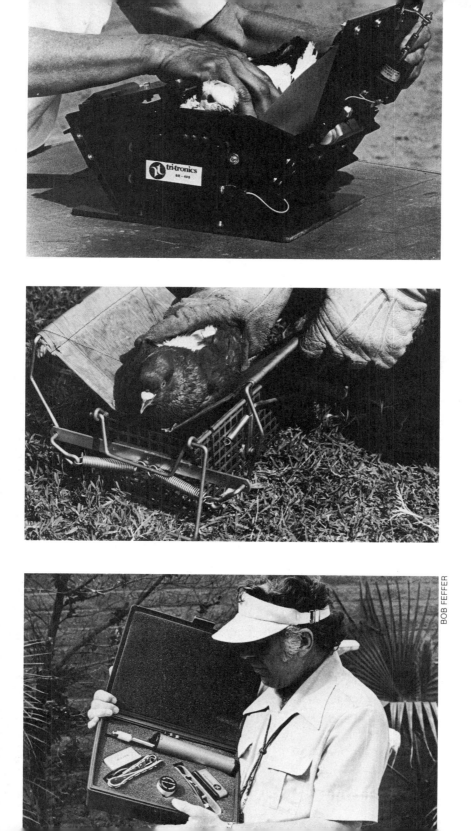

So why the remote controlled bird releaser? Because it's the bird boy you can't find.

Place the releaser in the field. Say 20 feet out. Drop a bean bag in its sling; or a pigeon will fit in there, nicely. By the way, you have to make your own bean bag. At the time I write this, the factory's not in the bean bag business. Okay, drop the bean bag—or pigeon—in the sling and snap the two flanged top flaps shut. Walk back to the casting line. Tell Pup to mark. Press the transmitter button. Up pops the bean bag.

It's beautiful. No gunners for Pup to mark; instead of the bird. Pup has to mark the flight of the bean bag. Plus, Pup has to pay attention at all times. The releaser doesn't fire a cap when it catapults the bird. The only sound is similar to the clack of a pump gun being shucked. And when Pup gets in the area of the fall, once again there's no guns to mark-off from. No one standing out there to give Pup field orientation. Pup's got to mark the fall. So he's got to know where he's going when he leaves the line. And since the releaser is somewhat silent, Pup's got to pay attention when he's at heel on line.

Two other benefits, among many, offered by the releaser are, one, should Pup be preceding the guns, that is, looking to the next set of guns before the first set of guns has dropped the bird to the ground, then you can place the releaser to the left of the first set of guns—the second set of guns is to the right—and release a bird, signalling the right hand set of guns to hold their bird.

This'll make Pup honest and get him to watching the whole field rather than the men who stand out there. Why, birds can pop up anywhere.

Also, two, the bird releaser is perfect for practicing walkups. That is, you have Pup at heel and you walk him through a bird field. This is the way all British trials are conducted and such tests used to appear in American field trials prior to large entries and the drift away from hunting tests. While you and Pup walk through the fields you press the transmitter and a bird launches—right in front of Pup's nose. What a staunching test. Then you fire and down the bird. Pup must wait until he's cast to fetch. This is the ultimate training drill to staunch up a dog. And it's the best of all training drills to bring along a hunting retriever.

Introduce the releaser by placing it in plain sight, up close, and pop Pup a few singles. Later, pop-up a bean bag but keep Pup at heel.

Throw a dummy off line. Send Pup for the dummy, then cast him for the bean bag.

Gradually move the releaser farther and farther away from the casting line. It'll respond to electronic impulse 170 yards out.

There are other uses for the releaser. Say Pup's fetched a bird and he's heading in. Oops! You hid the releaser out there in the tall grass and now you've triggered it and a bean bag pops up right in front of Pup's nose. Does Pup switch birds?

Or say you've got Pup working a tough blind. You predicted this one would give Pup trouble. So you placed the releaser next to the planted bird. When Pup quits you, you give him the sit whistle, then a cast. Say Pup must take an Over. Give that command and at the same time release the bean bag. This should convince Pup that as you point, so shall he find. The evidence is flying in the air.

Poor People Have Poor Ways

In the old days we didn't have a remote controlled bird releaser. What we did—since we had no help, either—was cast Pup for a blind, then toss a dummy we held hidden behind our back, out and over Pup's head.

Now why did we do this? Why not plant the blind in the first place? Well these were water blinds. And we never give Pup a water blind on land, nor in cover. Therefore, there's no place to plant the blind. The dummy must be out in open water. And if it's out there, Pup can see it, and that's no blind retrieve.

So we'd cast Pup to open water then throw the dummy out and over his head to plop before him. Know what that caused? A popping Pup. That's right. Pup'd wonder if the dummy was coming from behind so he'd turn around to look.

Well, poor people have poor ways. And popping Pups.

You might well ask, why didn't you plant the water blind in cover, or up on land, say the opposite shoreline? Pup couldn't have seen the bird there. Well there's a law for successfully running a water blind. And in the words of my old buddy, one of the finest professional retriever trainers who ever lived, "You don't get a water blind by sending the dog directly toward the bird. Oh no! You get a water blind

Culbertson sits Pup at pitcher's mound, returns to casting line and gives an over. Pup looks that way, but won't move. Jim goes to third base, lifts and drops a dummy, . . .

by sending the dog directly away from all hazards.'' That's D. L. Walters talking. And like E. F. Hutton—everybody's listening.

Cover and shorelines are Pup's hazards. Therefore, we can never have Pup find a bird there. We have trouble enough keeping him out of such places, off such places, we don't want him compounding our difficulty by fetching feather two places he should never be.

Oh, he can be there later in training. He'll have to be. But not now.

The Baseball Diamond

A baseball diamond is composed of home plate; first, second, and third base; and a pitcher's mound. It's here we put Pup on pattern drills to run blinds.

There are many variations.

One. Heel Pup at home plate. Walk him to the pitcher's mound. Drop a dummy. Heel Pup back to home plate. Turn him around and cast him for the dropped dummy.

Two. Do this at first base, second base, third base.

Three. Leave Pup someplace he can't see. Put dummy, or dummies, at pitcher's mound. Go get Pup. Heel him to home plate. Tell him, ''Line,'' and cast him for the pitcher's mound. Repeat the same sequence for first, second, and third base.

Four. Your series of commands go, ''Heel, Sit, Stay, Line, Back.'' Or, one long whistle blast will tell Pup to sit, then a verbal Line and a Back casts him for the bird. Always use the suck-in whistle when Pup's returning with a bird. Other commands can also be useful, such as ''Dead bird.'' Or ''Find the bird.'' And finally on fetch, if Pup is sticky mouthed or keeps leaping after the bird once you've taken it to hand, command, ''Leave it.''

Five. However, when we start stopping Pup afield and giving him Overs, don't say, ''Get over.'' Or if you want a dog to go Back, don't say, ''Get back.'' Too many handlers do this and too many dogs leave

. . . returns to the casting line and gives the over one more time. So what does Pup do? Run to third base? No! He heads for handler. Sessions later, Pup will get it right.

336

Pup's stopped at pitcher's mound and told to take a back. He won't move ...

on the word, "Get." These dogs don't wait for the hand signal, nor the second word. And the direction they usually go is Back. But you may have wanted an Over. So forget the, "Get." Just say Over and Back.

Six. Now if Pup won't go get the dummy at the pitcher's mound, then toss one out there. He'll fetch a mark. Then turn him around and send him for the dummy pile.

Seven. When Pup will run to first, second, third, or he'll stop on the pitcher's mound and take a Back cast to second base for a dummy, we're ready to start Overs. What's that? Pup won't stop at the pitcher's mound. Then we'll have to go to the option posts.

The Option Posts

Trainers who stop by my diggings to work their dogs have named this system the TOP method: Tarramoor Option Posts. Tarramoor is the name of the farm.

. . . so Jim drives him from the mound with voice and hand signal and bearing-down-presence. Pup fetches the dummy.

TOP's a mishmash of the old stubbing post used to control wild horses, or whoaing post used to break bird dogs. It's my remembering a city dog run up and down a clothesline. It's watching a trainer stand distant as he teaches a horse to neck rein. Even a depression child's amusement of sending messages up a kite string. I just put it all together, got some fence posts and pipe and whatnot and welded it all up.

When I first described this system in *Field & Stream,* a couple of professional trainers poked fun at me, saying, "A man don't need all that junk ... and all those ropes." I nodded in agreement. You sure don't if Pup's going to get everything right at the ball diamond. But later— I was both pleased and amused to find at least one of my critics running his dogs through the TOP program.

To get all this stuff rigged up here's what you do: cut the bottom section off a steel fence T-post. The section that's got the arrow head welded on it so you can stick this post easily into the ground. Then weld this section inside a two-inch metal pipe. At right angle to the post, weld a section of angle iron so you can stomp on it and drive the point into the ground.

Atop the post is a pivoting metal arm made free with neoprene washers. Attached to the metal arm is the best ball bearing pulleys you can find. Cheap pulleys make distracting noise and offer resistance to the pull of the rope by both handler and dog.

When your two posts are all welded up and outfitted with pulleys, then paint everything fluorescent orange. You can't lose em in the field and Pup has a hard time seeing this color.

Now get yourself some ⅜- or ¼-inch nylon rope—good quality that won't kink or fray—and make sure it has sufficient strength for all work to be done and all dogs to be trained. We need, say, 150 feet of rope to start. When Pup's coming along, we may go to 300 feet, or more.

Now place the option posts side by side, 10 feet apart. Thread one end of the cord through both pulleys. You'll have a bundle of cord on one side and a short end on the other. Attach this short end to Pup's plain leather collar. An aerial view of all this will show Pup sitting there with a cord leading off his collar to a post, then the cord going on to another post, and finally, back to the handler. You're standing out front and you've got the long end of the cord in your hand.

Now tell Pup, "Stay," and start backing away, feeding the cord

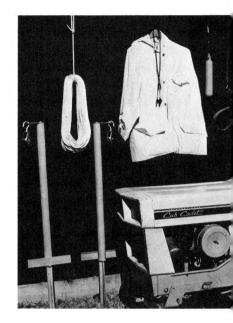

Tools required for TOP posts and baseball diamonds include: Lawn mower to mow a great, flat expanse; never a lane. Two option posts, a bundle of cord, white training jacket and whistles, dummies and pinch collar. Pup wears his plain leather collar for all work except when he just flat proves obstinate and won't do what he's been taught to do.

through your hand as you go. Should Pup try to follow, hit him with the Sit whistle, raise your command hand like a traffic patrolman, and grasp the cord with your non-command hand. That'll stop Pup in his tracks, for the cord attached to Pup's collar and run through the two pulleys will grow taut and hold him.

Our aerial now shows a figure 7. Pup's at the tip of the left hand downstroke of the 7, the option posts are at the top angles of the 7, and you're at the end of the long right hand downstroke of the 7.

So Pup's sitting by the left hand pole and you're backing toward the casting line. Finally you stop and blow the suck-in whistle. If Pup balks then toss a dummy behind you. Catch Pup as he tries to go past. Incidentally, as Pup runs forward you release your grip on the cord and let it run freely through your open hand.

As Pup runs he may be confused by the trailing cord. It sizzles through the pulleys and whips along in pursuit. And Pup may get

The advantage of two posts is evident: Pup's not confronted with two cords to tangle.

spooky and freeze. But that's not likely, not a pup that's been litter box check corded and walked on a three-lead leash and short-tied. Pup's an old hand with the ropes. You can see why all training is pyramiding and sequential.

When Pup comes all the way to you, heel him back near the option post and repeat the drill. Incidentally, you can see why we're using two posts instead of one. The rope you hold is offset from Pup's path. He can't get tangled.

Alright, with the long section of the rope in your non-command hand and Pup eagerly coming to you when you blow the suck-in whistle, start him toward you—THEN BLOW THE STOP WHIS-TLE. Raise your right hand as a traffic patrolman. But, Pup's not going to stop. So you'll need to help him. Grab the cord that's running through your hand—this requires gloves. The slack will snap out of the cord, it'll tug Pup's collar, and Pup will stop. Repeat this drill until Pup stops on the whistle with no tug on the line.

So now we've got Pup sitting, coming, and stopping on command. Let's cast him. First a Back.

Take Pup to the option post at the left hand top of the figure 7. Stand next to him, holding a handful of dummies. Command, "Heel," and start walking, Pup at side. Drop dummies as you go. Pup has to see them hit and bounce, you're working on mowed grass. When you're as far as you want to go—or you've used up half your rope—then heel Pup about so he's facing the line of dummies you just seeded. The cord's in a configuration of an inverted U.

Cast Pup for the first dummy in line. If he balks, pull the cord you have in your non-command hand. Better yet, have a helper standing to rear do the pulling. Coax Pup out. All it usually takes is a suggestion with the TOP method. Tug Pup, he gets the idea and takes off. Soon Pup'll be racing back and forth after the seeded dummies, going more distant for each one with each cast.

Pup's placed at option post and told to stay. He's whistled in and leaps forward, ...

... then told to stop and sit. Trainer backs away, enticing Pup to break.
Pup holds his ground, so trainer walks back and whistles him to side.
Should Pup break he'll be stopped by check cord in handler's
non-command hand ...

... handler throws a dummy toward post and casts Pup to fetch. Later he seeds the trail with one dummy following another, teaching Pup to retrieve over and unders.

Between Pillar and Post

Now, place your option posts 40 feet apart. Pile dummies at the base of the right hand post. Sit Pup at the base of the left hand post. Make a round-robin of your check cord, snapping both ends to Pup's leather collar. Pup is cross-tied between posts. You take a position several yards away from the two posts, equi-distant between them. The cord is now stretched to form a triangle with you standing at the apex.

For this you can use a helper. He's behind you and he's standing outside the triangle. Whistle Pup to sit. Doesn't matter if he's already sitting. That's not the point. The sit whistle is given before every cast command. So, whistle Pup to sit. Then when he's looking at you, step off to the right, your right arm raised perpendicular to your body, and tell Pup, "Over."

Pup probably won't move. So you return to that spot you vacated, give the command once more, only this time, your helper pulls the cord in his right hand, nudging Pup to move to his left (remember, Pup's facing you, all directions are reversed).

Tell your helper to milk the rope with his back hand, the front hand serving as a guide. That's the fastest way to retrieve rope—as we've already discussed.

Yet, some dogs offer resistance, they're not moving, so the helper must pull hand-over-hand though he were lifting heavy sail.

Pup will eventually move. He'll get the dummy. And you'll whistle him in to your side. And it stands to reason, when Pup runs toward you he jerks the rope from the handler's hands. So you stand far enough in front of the handler the rope doesn't hit you in the back of your legs and stop Pup. Or keep an eye on the rope's progress and jump as it goes under.

Of course there's another way: two helpers. Lay the rope out in the configuration of an upside down U. Now, no rope is going to contract and come racing toward the back of your heels. Yet, help is hard to find. You'll probably stick with the triangle and keep jumping, though I admit, it's not ideal.

When Pup's taking these right hand overs on his own initiative, the helper merely lets the cord slip through his hands.

In a later session you'll place Pup by the right hand post and pile dummies to the left.

Still later, you'll place Pup equi-distant between posts and pile dummies to both sides. Now you can cast him either way.

Pup's heeled to right hand post, dummy tossed to left hand post, handler retires to casting line and gives cast for a left hand over. Pup refuses cast and heads toward handler. Assistant tightens rope and stops Pup short. Handler positions Pup again and throws dummy toward left hand post. Assistant tugs left hand rope as handler gives over. . . .

Getting tougher, we place the posts 50 yards apart, or however far you want to work, leave Pup in the center, and perfect your overs to either side.

Finally we take the rope from Pup's collar but still work him between posts. That's right, we have no contact with Pup but he'll be inclined to follow our directions because he's working in conditioned territory.

And last of all, we work Pup without ropes or posts. Out on mowed ground. Then off to grass covered fields.

Most of the Big-3 retrievers won't need the nudge of the TOP method. But when training dogs you've got to account for the rare event and be prepared to handle it.

346

. . . Pup takes over and fetches dummy. Assistant drops rope and handler jumps so rope clears heels. Dummy is delivered to hand and Pup's eager to make a repeat retrieve.

When Pup's taking left hand overs he's positioned at left hand post and given right hand casts. This proves no problem: Pup's got the picture . . .

World Series Ball Diamond

It stands to reason since we've got Pup taking overs, stopping to the whistle, coming to heel when told, and casting without hesitation —we can now return to the baseball diamond.

All we have left to teach Pup is to stop anywhere in the field and take a Back.

With you and Pup at home plate, cast Pup to the pitcher's mound where there's a pile of dummies. Do it over and over again. Now put Pup away.

Take your dummy pile and place it at second base. Drop one dummy at the pitcher's mound. Get Pup. Cast him. Hit him with the stop whistle when he gets to the pitcher's mound. He'll fetch the dummy and return to heel. Cast him again. Once again, hit him with the sit whistle at the pitcher's mound. He should stop. Stop so you can give him a Back to second base where all the dummies are piled.

350

. . . when training session is finished handler sweetens Pup up, letting him attack dummies, and tossing them high for a cavorting fetch.

DELMAR SMITH

354

Delmar places swivel on telephone pole to cast Pup on round-robin check cord. Here a reluctant Pup is taken to water.

If Pup won't stop then outfit him with a trailing check cord. Let it zip through your open hand as Pup runs to the pitcher's mound. Hit the sit whistle. If Pup won't stop, then grab the cord. Once he's stopped, drop the cord, give Pup a Back and he should head for second base. He can see the dummies waiting there.

You may have to do this once. You may have to do it 30 times. Finally, Pup will start stopping at the pitcher's mound when you hit the sit whistle.

Now place your dummy pile at first base. Send Pup toward second base and hit him with the sit whistle at the pitcher's mound. Make him sit. He'll want to run on to second base. Say, "No," if you have to. When Pup's settled, give him a cast to first base. If he refuses to take the cast, loft a dummy over there. He'll run for that.

When Pup finally takes a cast to first base, and it's all down pat, then repeat the procedure using third base.

Now, place a dummy pile at first, second, and third. This is what we've been working for. Line Pup where you want. Hit him with the sit whistle where you want. Start him for second base, stop him at the pitcher's mound then cast him any one of three ways.

Or let him pass the pitcher's mound, near second base, and hit him with the sit whistle. Now give him the suck-in whistle. When he's near the pitcher's mound, cast him to first base.

Pup's playing world series ball, now. He's handling. But there's something we haven't emphasized and this you should know. Whenever Pup's taken off marks and started on blinds, his marking goes to pot. So you've got to mix dummy drill with marks. And you've got to give Pup leeway on marks: he's confused. He never knows when you're going to blow that whistle.

And when he really gets confused is when he mismarks and you whistle him down, take away his hunt, while you try to direct him to the bird. That's what it's all about: getting Pup to hand his self-will over to you. For Pup to handle.

So be kind, be tolerant, and be knowledgeable of Pup's predicament.

Handler sandwiches Pup against brick wall to get a straight cast. Then runs him down chainlink fence, barbwire fence, and lane of shrub intermixed with fencing. In it all, Pup's never run down lane which conditions him to avoid cover.

Holding a Line

When Pup no longer needs the impetus of the TOP system, nor the regimen of the ball diamond, take him to field for his blinds. The test now is one, for Pup to take an exact cast off your hand, and two, to run, or swim, a straight line for as far as you want.

Sometimes Pup will start to kick out on you at the upswing of your casting arm. Pinch this in the bud. Heel him so he's sandwiched between you and a barrier. When you cast, he can't kick left.

Take him to field and run him down fencing. An excellent place to practice this is your local high school. All that fencing built around the athletic fields.

But don't do what many have done before you. Don't mow channels in heavy cover and run Pup down these corridors—not on the simple baseball diamond, the world series diamond, nor afield. You'll curse

A pecan grove makes excellent place to start land blinds. Pup's channeled by tree trunks and when given an over, he'll hold a straight 90 degree line.

the day you did. There'll come a field trial where Pup will refuse cover and run a trail, or head down a road, or run down a bank, and that'll be all she wrote.

To extend Pup's run, take him out on an abandoned runway, or to some great, flat stretch of land, and seed your dummies from your car window as you drive along. Start your casting line a half mile away. Jim Culbertson and I regularly run our dogs a half mile to a mile. The dogs like it. It's good exercise. And it's good practice.

Well, Pup's off and running, but you've not tricked him—as yet. He's had no diversions, no suctions, no hazards. These, the field trial judges will hand out. And we must train for them. But first, back to water.

15/A Wet Pup

Men and retrievers! Their great victories come on water.

Washington crossing the Delaware,

Mike Flannery's dad stripping down in dark of night, strapping a .45 to his head and swimming the Marne to free a French prisoner,

Dog Hero of the Year, a Chesie named Chester, pulling his five-year old master from a raging Livingston, Montana, creek,

And Lab bitch, Ripco's V. C. Morgan, winning the 1964 national open at Weldon Springs, Missouri, with a high ambient temperature after the first day of 13 degrees and the water's frozen so a motor boat is kept twirling about to keep it chopped open.

Men and retrievers! Their great defeats come on water.

Captain Ahab and Moby Dick,

The Spanish Armada,

And Pup running his first 1,000 water blinds.

Moon Shots and Water Blinds

Let's be practical, testy water blinds are for field trial contenders, not shooting dogs. If you and Pup are after feather, not silver, and you drop a bird that Pup's not seen fall, then more than likely you're going to heel him along shore till you're near the bird then ram Pup to fetch it.

If Pup's a typical shooting dog he'll probably run up and down the bank, refuse the water, see you getting angry, then go fetch a dead carp to try and appease you.

Being a typical wildfowler you'll be more interested in getting the downed bird than training Pup so you'll take the carp from him and toss it toward the duck. Or you'll throw rocks, or clumps of mud, or shotgun shells—or even Pup—out there and hurrah him to go fetch.

Finally, you and Pup will sit and wait for the wind to blow the bird to some shore.

There isn't one wildfowler out of 10,000 who enters a blind, or a boat, with a trained retriever. More sad to report, many wildfowlers hunt without a dog. And let's admit it, most field trial retrievers are seldom taken on a hunt. So great gun dogs are not usually seen with men out hunting.

Now in all this I make no complaint. I'd rather see dogs trained for silver than trained for nothing. There's too many anti-dog, anti-gun, anti-hunt groups gaining strength today. Dogs, and men who love em, need all the help they can get.

If you own a shooting dog and you want him to run water blinds, then read on. But the fact is, and you must know this, water blinds are harder to achieve than moon shots. And like a missile that goes cockeyed and the space scientist presses a button to destroy it, so too do dog handlers destroy cockeyed retrievers. Only they do it out of ignorance. From now on you've got to be much smarter than Pup to get the job done.

Water Blind Philosophy

In a field trial open stake you're never going to be asked to fetch a water blind that Pup isn't snookered. You get no straight-in shots at this game of water billiards. This is an absolute fact you must remember. An absolute fact you must plug into all your training. Always there will be something between Pup and the bird. And whatever this something is, should Pup touch it, he's probably out of the trial.

Consequently you must train Pup to avoid hazards, not to fetch the bird. Let me explain. In water blind training you don't drill Pup to fetch anything. You drill Pup to avoid everything.

This duck pond offers minimal challenge for tough blinds but specially designed training pond (below) has points, peninsulas, islands, pincers, and channels to tempt a dog.

DELMAR SMITH

363

Which means all water blind training is negative. Pup's like a poor dogface told to cross a minefield and enter a village. The soldier must forget about the village. It's the minefield he's got to maneuver. The soldier's real mission is not to reach the village. It's to avoid and survive the minefield.

Understand? If so, you're a member of a minority. All the average handler has on his mind is get the poultry. To get the poultry and receive a high score. The score's foremost in the handler's mind. He knows how judges look at these things. They want a water entry straight toward the bird. They want a retrieve with no whistle or hand signals. They want the dog to stay wet. And they want the dog to return the same way he went out—by water.

And if Pup doesn't run this water blind just this way then the judges are back there scribbling. You can hear em; sounds like someone opening a thick cardboard crate with a dull knife. And you know they're deducting points.

But to run your dog exactly as the judges want will probably cause the dog to fail the test. He'll suck to a decoy, get on a bank, bend toward an old mark he's retrieved, refuse an angle water entry and run the bank. He'll do that for the test is designed to tempt him to do that. So the handler can't run the test as the judges want. He must run the test within his dog's capability. And to do that he must avoid all hazards. Avoid all hazards the judges want to see the dog handle.

Too often the real blind in a water blind is the handler's view of the test. The handler is blind. All he can see is a direct route from casting line to bird. And pardner, that may be the way the first place dog wins it. But first place dogs are— What are the figures up front? Seventy thousand retrievers registered each year. And maybe 170 field trials. So that means 170 first place winners: and great dogs repeat. Therefore, first place dogs are miracle workers.

So don't be blind. Don't cast Pup for the bird. Cast him away from all hazards. Don't bank on miracles. And just hope the judges assume you're running their test and marking you accordingly.

What the Judges Will Give You

To snooker Pup judges will offer:

One. Some test where you just picked up a water triple. Pup ran three routes, brought back three birds. He remembers all three routes, he remembers all three birds. Plus, and please remember this, duck scent stays and floats on water. Just like smoke from a stack bending out over the land in a slight wind—that duck scent is out there.

Now the judges place a bird between two of the old falls, only back another 50 yards—back through the old scent. So what's the test? To ram Pup between the two old falls—where he was successful before—and get him to carry a line another 50 yards. That's the test. That's the minefield. The test isn't getting the bird. The test is threading the needle through two old falls: and remember, Pup is mighty place oriented. He knows exactly where those old falls were. And remember the hovering scent.

A good way to train for such tests is run Pup down irrigation ditches where you've seeded dead birds on each bank. Yep, once again Pup must *not* honor his nose. He must swim until you whistle him down and give him an Over to land.

To keep Pup in a channel you'll probably need to walk a man on each side, keeping pace with Pup's progress. The helpers are needed to drive Pup back to water if he wants to emerge.

Two. It's the second day of the open. Pup's still in the trial. You drive to the field trial grounds and discover the judges are going to give you a cold water blind. No, that doesn't mean the water's cold—which it probably is—but that Pup must start cold. You know? He walks to the casting line; hears nothing, sees nothing, and you cast him for a bird. Pup's starting out cold.

What's the test in this situation?

Well there are many. *One,* Pup's got to believe you. Far as Pup's concerned he's heard nothing, seen nothing—so how can there be a bird out there? Pup must run out of faith.

Two, there may be a strong cross-wind from the right. But the bird is planted on the right hand shore. That means Pup must approach the bird from the left if he's to stay wet. Consequently, at the end of the cast, Pup must take an over into the wind. Pup doesn't want to take an over into the wind. That's the test.

Or *three,* to hold a straight line to the bird, Pup must enter the water at a drastic angle on the shore. Let's say the bird is to the left, yet on the casting line there's heavy foliage to the right—which repels Pup—and a smooth bank to the left, which invites him to cheat. What's to keep Pup from running the smooth bank. That's the test.

Train Pup to run cold water blinds by releasing him from crate and ramming him to run. Over and over. Sweeten him up by having him run 300 yards and suddenly a gunner appears who throws and shoots a squawking cock pheasant. Or a pigeon is lofted from the bird releaser. Now that's some reward to keep pulling Pup on.

Or, walk Pup through a public shooting area during duck season. Go early in the morning. Slob hunters without dogs will have left many dead ducks from the day before that will float to shore during the night. Pup will have the reward of maxi-harvest.

An incident I'll always remember— I was returning from a trial at Cheyenne, Wyoming, where I'd run Jim Culbertson's Keg of Black Powder, and my own string. Off to the side of the highway near St. Francis, Kansas, I saw three pheasants fly into a stand of cottonwoods and shrub a half mile from the highway. What a beautiful cold blind retrieve.

I pulled off the road, let Powder leap from her crate, heeled her and gave her a cast over the plowed ground to the scrub island holding the three pheasants. Powder flew. And when she hit that cover it exploded like a hand grenade. Must have been 30 pheasants blast out of there. Powder took off. Two miles later I ran her down. The lesson: some dogs are just too birdy to practice cold blinds on live and non-gunned game. Especially Powder who would run a flying pheasant until it pooped out and she caught it.

Three. All around the pond there's heavy cover. Pup's entered and left this cover three times finding three marks. Now the judges place a bird—make it a pheasant since Pup's been fetching ducks from this water—on a shingle, attach it with a clothes pin, and anchor the rig directly in the middle of the lake where there is no cover. The pheasant rides so low in the water Pup can't see it till he's on it. The blind floats 100 yards away from the casting line.

You cast Pup for the floating pheasant. But remember, to be successful till now, Pup's hunted cover. So Pup doesn't want to swim a blank sea. You can't get him out of the cover. That's the test. Finally, Pup breaks into the open. Now he's looking, coursing instead of scenting. But he sees nothing. And you keep driving him farther into a coverless sea. Pup must really believe in you to keep going. You have to know something he doesn't. And he has to grant you this super knowledge. In other words, for Pup to be bright he must admit he's dumb. That's the test.

Finally Pup winds the bird. But it's not a duck. It's a pheasant. Pup refuses to honor his nose. He's fetched three ducks from this water and duck is what he's after. That's the test.

Four. It's cold and there's ice on the water. That's the test.

Five. To line this water blind Pup must swim through the pinch of an hour glass 150 yards out. That is, the shore of the pond forms a figure 8 but does not touch at the center. There's a channel like this:)(. The bird floats on a shingle near the center of the top o in the 8. Ram Pup through the two pincers of land and not have him dry dock. That's the test.

Six. To line this water blind Pup must swim along side an irregular shore that has several fingers of protruding land. Like this: VVVV. The handler must drive Pup past each finger and not have him beach, nor suck into the void within one of the Vs. That's the test.

Seven. To line this water blind Pup must enter water, climb on an island, abandon the island and hit water, climb on another island, drive across it, and enter water again where the bird is floating on a shingle. The test? To get Pup to touch land after you've trained him never to do so when running a water blind. Plus, to drive across each island and not hunt them out—or to turn to you for help; to pop. That's the test.

Eight. There are two water blinds. One's in cover, the other's at sea. Or there are two blinds in a straight line. Or one bird's on land—a duck. And another's in the water—a pheasant. The tests are self evident.

Nine. Or the water blind is across a rapidly flowing river and the current will drift Pup off line. Pup must crab to hold a straight line to the bird. That's the test.

Ten. Pup is heeled to the casting line and told to Sit and Stay. Off to the left of the pond a gunner stands and fires a gun. The handler tells Pup, "No," to this retort, then carousels him about, lining him to the right hand side of the pond where the bird is actually planted. The test? For Pup to ignore the gun. To once again have blind faith in his handler. To grant the handler is right when the world would seem to indicate he is wrong.

By the same token, most of these water tests can be presented on land: except for one occasional water test which is called sluicing the duck. It's a breaking test. A duck is shot near the casting line, then there is silence. But both gunners then fire down at the duck. That's four shots fired for one bird. Some dogs will break to all this commotion, plus, remember—dogs are rhythm oriented. Break their rhythm and you throw them off their game.

Anyway, most water tests can be run on land. And that's where they should first be confronted. In each instance there is a hazard. And in each instance Pup must place the handler's knowledge above his own.

He must cast and hold a line out of blind faith. He must give up his instinctual urge and skill to hunt and say, "No, I won't do that. I'll do what this guy who can't run, can't see, can't smell, can't swim ... I'll do what he wants me to." We ask an awful lot of Pup, don't we?

And how do we train for tests three through ten? You analyze the hazard, duplicate it afield, and work around it. That's why Rex Carr of California, D. L. Walters of Kansas, John Olin and Cotton Pershall of Illinois, and David Crow of Louisiana—to name a few—have designed and built field trial ponds in their back yards. Designed and built land and water configurations until every conceivable field trial test can be worked out in training, accomplished in advance.

The Winner Is Always Wet

For remember this— Field trials are won or lost on water. And the clincher is the water blind. Don't care what anyone else sputters about this statement: it is true. And field trials could, in practicality, just use a water blind to find the winner. Run it first. Get it over with. But that's not possible. Water blinds take too long to finish: that's why they're saved till last. Saved till 80 of the 90 dogs entered have been eliminated. And the AKC book does say, dogs must be tested on land and water, on marks and blinds.

Nevertheless, all field trial tests are merely prelude to the final water blind. Like each test in the trial was the football season and the water blind stands as the superbowl for the finalists.

Why is it this way? We've already analyzed the reason: water is Pup's Waterloo. It's a foreign, drag-back, suck-down element. It's spooky in there. It's all slow motion. Plus, blinds require the dog to hand his self-will over to a handler. Combine all this and you've got the ultimate test in dogdom: no other breed trial can come close. Nor should it. We ask too much of retrievers. We've gone too far.

If God had actually wanted us to play the retriever game as we play it today He'd given us an animal with a remote controlled brain triggered by the handler's ESP, plus a solid state computer to program angles, and a switch on the side of its rib cage when turned to "WET" would transform the animal into an 80 pound otter and when turned to "DRY" would produce a soft mouth cheeta.

But we're on our way— Dogs have stomachs designed for meat, yet we've converted them to eat grain. We'll make em what we want before it's all finished.

Now let me hark back to the beginning of this chapter. Do you see why the average hunter ends up throwing a dead carp at the duck? To train Pup for water blinds calls for great thought, great time, and great outlay. By the same token, do you see why the typical field trial champion is seldom taken hunting? For the same reason you don't usually see Indy 500 cars parked at shopping centers.

And if you're curious why Britons are not big on water blinds, the answer is simple. One, they're grouse and pheasant shooters, not wildfowlers. And two, no field trial bird can originate in hand. All birds must be flushed wild and shot dead. This makes for some lucky flushing and a long death glide for the bird to land as a blind in water.

The First Water Blinds

It stands to reason— If an old, thoroughly trained, highly experienced retriever can run a water blind only by avoiding hazards, then a young, partially trained, inexperienced Pup should be trained to run water blinds without any hazards. We must build Pup's confidence before we confront him with his torment. We must start positive even though we will end negative. Therefore, remember and plug into your water blind training all the cautions you exercised in first bringing Pup to water for marks.

For example: One, all blinds will be presented straight away from the bank. No angle water entries.

Two. All blinds will be presented out in the middle of the pond. Not in cover, nor up on land where Pup wants to go, anyway.

Three. Never close to the area of an old fall where Pup's just retrieved a mark.

Four. Never between, nor between and beyond, the area of two old falls Pup has just worked.

Five. Nor is Pup given a double water blind.

Six. Nor is Pup worked in moving water, nor placed where he must take a cast into the wind, nor run in shallow water where the splash he makes drowns out the handler's whistle.

Seven. Nor is Pup asked to fetch a land-fall close to shore then asked to run a water blind. Why not go back to land? That will be his thinking.

Eight. And never is Pup run on a blind where he must leave water and touch land: be it point on shore, or an island.

So what's left to work with? Plenty. And here's the way we start.

Use big, stark white dummies that float high in the water.

Pup can see them out there. If he refuses to launch, then toss another dummy to land in the floating pile. Okay?

Heel Pup. Have two bird boys throw two water marks. When Pup's returning with the first retrieve, have the memory bird thrower retire. Cast Pup for this semi-blind memory bird.

Take Pup to shore. Turn him about. Send him for a short, simple land blind. Turn him again. Cast him straight from shore for a short, simple water blind. Pup's got blind retrieve on his mind because of land: exploit this momentum.

Place large, stark white dummies directly in front of the casting line. Say they're floating 30 feet out. Now, have someone on shore dry-fire. This gunner who fires at nothing, who dry-fires, who shoots nothing, is called a popper. Remember? And the shell he shoots that contains no shot is also called a popper. Tell Pup, "No," to the sound of this retort. Cast him for one of the floating dummies.

If Pup refuses to go, if he's hung up on the gun shot, looking at the gunner, then tell the gunner to fire again. Convince Pup there's no bird over there to either be seen or fetched. Once again tell Pup, "No," to the retort and cast him for the dummy.

If Pup still refuses to enter water then throw a dummy to land out there with the others. When Pup eventually retrieves, Happy Time him to the gunner. Happy Time? Yes, let Pup bound along doing as he pleases, toss the dummy for him in play, have everything relaxed and easy.

When you get to the gunner take the dummy from Pup and ignoring him, start talking to the guy. Let Pup think you're paying him no mind. Let him wander off. He will. He'll want to hunt about for that bird, or those birds, this gunner has shot. But Pup'll find nothing. And this is important; you didn't tell Pup to hunt. Nor did you cast him into this area. It just so happens you took a break and Pup followed you, then sniffed about. The result: Pup learns on his own that a gun shot does not mean poultry. There is no bird to be found.

Now take Pup back to the casting line and run your popper sequence again. This time Pup knows it's all a game. The guy over there firing the popper is just making noise. Pup has learned a gun shot doesn't mean a bird down. And Pup knows you didn't lie to him. He found that out for himself while you were talking.

There's a reason I take the time to emphasize all this: Pup must be told, "No," on the line to a dry-popper (the shooting of a shell that

370

holds no shot). And to tell Pup, "No," is negative. And this, "No," can put Pup down on the casting line when there's a blind water retrieve before him. This can't be. Pup needs everything going for him and everyone behind him when he launches. He can't crumble to a "No," and become dispirited, doubtful, and dejected.

By the same token, Pup also hears, "No," when the handler see's Pup's sitting wrong for a blind and many other times on line. Get all the, "No," commands handled in basic training. Never have them be a factor at a trial. Nothing negative can come up before Pup launches to water.

As with marks, we gradually extend the distance of the blind retrieve away from shore, and we gradually pull our casting line away from the water. Later, the planted dummies are placed behind, or in, heavy cover. Still later, they are planted on the opposite shore. And then that distance is extended until Pup's going 100 yards inland to make his water retrieve; making it on land as Pepe did the mallard drake.

As the days and weeks and months pass, the hazards are brought nearer and nearer to the path Pup must swim to retrieve the planted blind. Plus, the blind is placed farther and farther away from the casting line. And the dummies get less visible, the angle water entries more acute, the water colder—until one day Pup flat quits you.

What? Pup flat quits me? Yep, just like that. I know of no retriever that didn't eventually turn off his handler when learning blind retrieves on water. The reason is simple: the game demands too much of the dog. It is all too negative, and too difficult, and too dedoginizing. Dedoginizing? Yes, same as dehumanizing. We subtract so much from the will, from the instinct, from the common sense of Pup. We go so against the grain of his soul. We ask him to proceed out of blind faith, never thinking for himself, and to ignore a real world that's purposely built to tantalize and trick him into doing wrong.

So, Pup quits you. And how do you then enforce your will?

Well, there are ways. But before that, let's look at the process which results in Pup saying, "No."

If It's All the Same to You I'll Just Sit This One Out

See our training pond in Lou Schifferl's diagram? The pond's shoreline is shaped like a 1979 Chevy Suburban. But no wheels. Well, we're training Pup on water blinds so let's walk him to spot V. That's

The Suburban training pond:

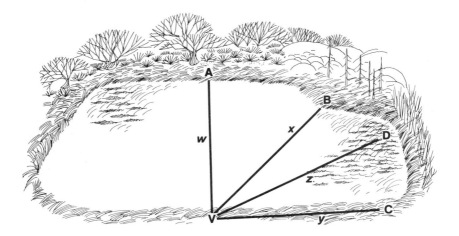

For pictorial sequence of Pup trying to fetch bird at spot D, see pages 375–380.

our casting line. Our test is to get the bird floating at spot D.

Now, let's tell Pup, "Heel, Sit, Stay," and by carouseling him about us and fine-tuning him we get him zeroed in on spot D. When we think Pup has the picture, we command, "Back," and ram him to water.

What does Pup do? Well, to take a line to spot D Pup must make an angle water entry. But Pup doesn't want to do this. It's his nature—all dogs' natures—to leap to water with both front paws parallel to shore. Exception: every animal has a dominant lead. Dog, man, horse: all lead out with one foot preceding the other. Check to see what lead Pup favors. It'll usually be the lead foot that strikes most distant in water upon a leap.

What you should know about the lead foot is this. Upon making a leap, Pup'll usually pull off line toward his lead foot; on water or on land. That is, this is the direction he'll veer.

Apart from lead-foot considerations, Pup—and all pups—will leap in our test pond to face spot A. Now, this happens to be the closest shore and this fact naturally draws Pup to swim for it: once again, it's

372

Every animal has a dominate lead:

Scot Lab leads with left foot (Britons demand dogs leap walls at most trials), . . .

the nature of the beast to exit water as fast as possible. If Pup were playing in water he could stay all day. But this isn't play, it's work, and Pup wants his work done quick. Sort of like some humans.

But, we don't want Pup to beach at spot A. So we're whistling to get his attention and giving hand signals to cast him across the pond to his right. What's the use? Pup ignores us. And we can't stop him.

If we leap to water, or run around the Suburban's rear end, by the time we get to Pup he'll have hunted the far shore and done Lord-only-knows-what-all-else and should we discipline him when we get to him he'll not have the foggiest what he's being disciplined for. For hunting? No. But that's what he may think. He's been out of water too long to associate a cast refusal with your anger.

So we heel Pup back to spot V, tell him, "No," to spot A—once again a negative—and cast him for spot D. Note: this is our second cast for spot D.

So what does Pup do? Pup knows he must avoid spot A. So he's in the water looking around. And what does he see? Well that piece of land jutting out at point B—where the Suburban's windshield meets

... single Lab hits water with left foot lead, and duo jump to sea with the one on the left favoring his right foot and the one on the right favoring his left foot. As expected, these two dogs hit shoulders as they surfaced and started stroking for dummy.

the hood—is the nearest shore; dogs always want to hit the nearest shore. So, once again we're whistling and waving our arms— To no avail.

We get Pup back and tell him, "No," to spot A, and, "No," to point B—now there are two negatives—and cast Pup again for spot D. Cast him for spot D a third time. But this time Pup's got it figured out. He's convinced we're upset because he keeps entering the water. So when we order, "Back," Pup runs down the bank to spot C, taking line Y. Great, now we've got a bank-runner.

We get Pup back and tell him, "No," to spot A, point B, and shoreline C—three negatives—and cast him for the only place left to go: spot D. We command, "Back," and what does Pup do? That's right. He sits there. Pup's turned to stone. He refuses to leave your side. Why shouldn't he? Everywhere he's gone—as his natural inclinations would lead him—has resulted in our saying, "No."

So now we've got a bank-runner that won't enter water. And why? Because we've got to train on tests where the dog would naturally never go, for that's where judges are going to place the bird.

Jim Rodgers runs Sauron through pond shaped like our diagram. Blind is planted behind and to the left of white stake in distance . . .

. . . Sauron refuses cast and heads for near shore.

He's heeled and cast again . . .

. . . this time sucking to the left hand point . . .

. . . heeled a third time and cast, Sauron runs bank . . .

. . . now there's no place left to go but down the middle . . .

. . . yet, Sauron sucks to right bank, . . .

. . . and stops when Jim hits him with a whistle . . .

. . . and gives him a left angle back, which Sauron converts to a 90 degree over . . .

. . . Jim hits him again to keep him off the point. Now a back puts dog on line and retrieve is accomplished . . .

. . . poor Sauron, he could have lined this blind, but author's need to illustrate diagram had him going every which way.

The Whiprun Dog

And that, according to some trainers, is what they've been waiting for. For what they planned for. For Pup to refuse a cast into water. Now is when the water dog learns the last place on earth he wants to be is beside the handler. This is when the handler gets so rough with Pup the dog decides that nothing out there could ever be so bad as what's standing beside him.

Pup now runs out of fear. He doesn't run to something, he runs from something. And what does he fear? He fears being kicked, cursed, shocked with an electric cattle prod, hooked to a cable and drug by Jeep across the pond. He fears all this and sometimes, more.

But what about our Pup? The one we've been training since page one? All we have available to those of us who train by the humane principles requested by this book are one, mock rage, two, lifting Pup from his feet and chugging him, or three, swatting him with our fly swatter. And will any of this be sufficient to drive Pup into a negative, and what he considers to be an optionless, world? If all your training till now has been in accordance with this book IT WILL BE. But what of the new dog you just bought. He's three-years old. He's not had the benefits of thoughtful training. The type of training you've given Pup.

Such a dog will eat fly swatters. And mock rage? He returns it 10-fold.

So now it's time to go to the electricity: the electronic collar that can reach out over water and bite Pup in the neck. There's no doubt about it. The most important discipline tool ever devised by man to correct a dog is the electronic collar. Yet, it is also the most incorrectly used tool man has ever devised to force a dog.

Yet it's all really so simple to understand. YOU ABSOLUTELY CANNOT TEACH PUP ONE THING WITH AN ELECTRIC COLLAR. BUT YOU CAN ENFORCE YOUR WILL ON PUP SO HE DOES WHAT HE HAS ALREADY BEEN TAUGHT TO DO. Get it? You only use an electric collar on a dog who already knows what he should be doing—BUT REFUSES TO DO IT. That's when he gets the juice. He gets shocked for being DEFIANT, not for being CONFUSED.

To state it all again: when Pup knows he's doing wrong, and he knows you know he's doing wrong, and he knows you know he knows he's doing wrong—that's when he gets bit by the electric collar.

Sauron wears electric collar for land blind. Jim adjusts dog with riding crop on casting line. Training session over, Sauron's given command of the crop.

The Electric Collar

First off, just what is this contraption, this electric collar? Well, it's a black box that receives radio signals and it's rigged onto a plain leather, or miracle fiber, collar. When the black box is triggered by radio impulses coming from a transmitter held in the trainer's hand, the dog gets shocked in the neck through two domed studs with a jolt of high voltage, low amperage current. The amount of shock can be predetermined by the length of time you leave the black box on charge. Yes, these units must be continually recharged at home.

Today, electric collars are nearly failsafe. Seldom do such collars pick up extraneous radio signals and shock the dog in error. Seldom do they get water soaked and fail. Matter of fact, so far as my own experiences go, I've not had a collar do either. But I can't speak for all collars nor all trainers.

I repeat, the collar is triggered by an electronic transmitter held in the handler's hand. The transmitter has a telescoping antenna to increase or decrease its range. You'll recall the transmitter I asked you to buy has three buttons: one, to trigger the remote controlled bird releaser, two, to shock Pup while at the same time emit a sound-blast, and three, to emit only the sound, the dog being conditioned to react to the sound-burst as though he'd been shocked.

How to use the electric collar:

One. When Pup first feels the bite of this contraption he's going to panic: he'll want to dig a hole or leave the country. That can't be in a training situation. Nor can it be when Pup's out running loose. So put the collar on Pup and shock him in his kennel run, you being distant and detached.

Two. This collar is expensive and Pup can tear it up; or his kennel mates can chew off the collar, or damage the case. So you outfit Pup with a dummy collar—same size, shape, weight—and Pup wears this dummy for a week. He forgets he has it on.

Three. When Pup's conditioned to wearing the contraption, substitute the real thing for the dummy and shock Pup in his kennel run. Just a bump. And you be distant, detached, no part of Pup's plight. Bump him again. Let Pup think about it. Bump him again. Walk off and let Pup relax. Later, come back and bump him again. When Pup settles to the shock, doesn't panic, doesn't climb the chainlink panel, you're ready to take him to field.

Four. Release Pup from his kennel, take him to your land blind area, and run him for some planted dummies. Pup's going to learn on land you can reach him—no matter where he is, you can reach him.

We stay on land until Pup is perfect: he answers all signals, takes all casts, holds all lines. Pup knows how to run a blind. We know he knows how to run a blind. He knows we know he knows how to run a blind. Okay? Now if Pup refuses us on water we know it's not confusion: it's obstinancy and we can tell him we don't approve by touching our button.

Five. So we're off to water. And sure enough, Pup's giving us cast refusals. Cast refusals we don't get on land. But now, here they are. So what can we do about it? Well, you're tempted to bite Pup the instant he pulls your leg. Right? Well, don't. NEVER SHOCK PUP IN WATER. If you give Pup a hand cast to get over, for example, chances are you are trying to drive him away from land. So, if Pup's refused your cast, chances are he's standing on that land you wanted him to avoid. Now's the time. Hit him. Hit him either with the juice and sound-blast, or the sound-blast, alone. You know your Pup. It's up to you. And hit Pup the moment he steps on land: let him know exactly why he's being corrected.

And so it will always be. If Pup refuses an Over, or a Back, or tries to return from a blind retrieve by land instead of water—hit him with the juice. BUT ALWAYS HIT PUP ON LAND, NEVER WATER.

This may mean you must switch water blind training to long narrow ponds. To irrigation ditches; canals. For if Pup refuses an Over and then swins 50 yards, that's too long to wait to hit him.

Also, if Pup's a totally knowledgeable dog who just insists in defying you, then you can hit him with the sound-blast while he's in water. Not the juice, but the noise. Then use both juice and noise when Pup touches land.

Sure you're going to see top trainers hit Pup with juice in the water. I know of more than one national champion who was sizzled while wet. But I don't recommend it. Not when the sound-blast becomes a conditioned substitute for electricity, and not when you can save the juice for the worst of all water blind faults—touching land.

Far as I'm concerned the electric collar is worthless in trying to stop Pup from popping on a water blind: you know, turning around, treading water, looking at you for help, and you've not whistled him to do so. In that case, as pointed out up front, all you can do is turn your back on Pup, wait till he casts somewhere on his own, then whistle him down and give your command. For a popping Pup is a confused Pup and such a dog is never shocked; only a defiant one.

In all water blind training we make land Pup's nemesis. We also make water Pup's haven. The only place Pup doesn't get shocked is in water. We make water the one place Pup wants to be, the one place Pup wants to stay. That way you're going to win some water trials. For they're designed to trick Pup out of water and onto land.

Six. At no time do you ever associate yourself with Pup's predicament. You never yell while shocking Pup. And electricity is always your last resort. Let's say Pup won't take a left hand over. But Pup knows what a left hand over is. And you've walked around the pond several times to tell him about it.

Okay, here's your sequence of correction: whistle Pup down to turn him around to attend, give him a left hand over which he refuses. Whistle him down again. Give another Over. Still Pup refuses. You yell, "No," and while Pup's attending you give him another Over. Pup knows what he should do but he just won't do it. Okay, let him go. Say no more. The minute Pup puts one paw on land, hit him with the juice and sound-blast, or the sound-blast alone if Pup's totally familiar with the collar.

Incidentally, this sound-blast noise is an irritating sound. Kind of like a French taxi horn with a sore throat. Even when I know it's coming the thing startles me: it has to get Pup's attention.

The collar's bite, or bite and blast, will do one of several things. One, it will stop Pup in his tracks, two, it will drive him back to water, or three, Pup will bolt across land. So be ready to hit your stop whistle if Pup bolts, get him stopped, let him think it over a few seconds, then give the left hand over he's continually refusing to accept. If Pup won't take the cast then shock him with the collar.

Should you think Pup is going to bolt you may station a helper to cut him off. Pup must realize there is no way out. He must take the left hand over.

Eventually he will. But probably not today. Pup must be put away and rested. Short-tied and given an opportunity to think it over. Or chain-ganged and forced to watch all other dogs work. Eventually he will answer the whistle and take the cast. And when Pup does get it right, sweeten him up and put him away. That'll be all for that day. Then, keep running the same test till Pup is perfect. Now move your test grounds somewhere with right hand suction and give the left hand over. If Pup accepts the Over you've got it made. If not, either start rebuilding on this pond, or go back to the success pond and sweeten Pup up.

Seven. If you've ever doubted Pup's brilliance he'll teach you something now. Pup can't live the rest of his life wearing that electric collar. Nor can he have it on during a field trial. And Pup's going to figure out when he has it on he can get bit, but when he's not wearing it you can't touch him. So in the end you've got to get wet. You've got to whistle Pup to sit—he just refused your cast and dry docked himself on shore—and you walk around the shore line, get Pup by his plain leather collar, or nylon collar if you prefer that in water, and drag him back into the water and out to the spot he went wrong.

This Chesie displays lackluster return. Black Lab shows confusion. Both dogs could be Happy Timed to pep them up, or chain ganged, or short-tied, or even placed in solitary confinement. Each dog's different. You've got to use your wits.

Tell Pup, "Heel, Sit, Stay," and swim, or walk, out of the water, around the shore line, and back to your original casting line. "What?" you ask. "Tell Pup to sit in water?" Yes. We don't have a command for float. So tell Pup to sit. He knows that means to remain stationary and he'll tread water till you're ready to release him. If not, if Pup wants to bolt, then have a helper position Pup in water and hold him while you give your command. Or, place Pup on TOP posts with check cord strung out and over the water.

The point is, Pup must learn that no matter where is is, and whether or not he's wearing an electric collar, you will reach him. Unlike the game of kick-the-can there's no place on earth, or water, where Pup can stand free.

387

This is what it's all about.

Jim Culbertson lays out decoys at dawn, guns down a pair of gadwall, casts Pup, ...

Mopping Up

We've been through so much, you and Pup and I. It's a blazed trail behind us. So there's no need repeating everything applicable to water blinds that we learned on land, or while throwing marks. Like, never yell at Pup on an Over, it merely drives him back. Or, Pup must always return from water by water. We all know that. Even Pup knows that. If Pup's permitted to return by land from a water blind then his thinking may go, why not make both trips the same way?

But what if Pup insists on coming back by land? Then stop him short. If you know he's going to make for shore, or follow the shore line if the blind retrieve were found on land, then hit Pup with the sit whistle, get his attention, then while giving the suck-in whistle extend your arm to cast Pup to water. It doesn't always work but it's worth a try.

If Pup ignores you, yell, "No," and when he's looking at you give him the suck-in command and hand signal, once again.

If all this fails, then run Pup on water blinds attached to the round-robin check cord fitted in the TOP posts.

. . . stops him in decoys and gives a left hand over, . . .

. . . accepts retrieve, and casts Pup for second bird. A gun dog that'll take whistle and hand signals makes the day and the hunt a rich and rewarding experience.

You'll hear it said at field trials, "He's an honest dog." The term implies the dog doesn't try to cheat. It's honest dogs that line water blinds, they don't cheat and head for shore. But should they go off line—these honest dogs—they'll usually heed the whistle and take a cast back where they belong. Such dogs seldom refuse a command, they seldom cheat.

How did they get this way? They were trained that way. They were never allowed to cheat. They were always forced to take an Over, always forced to heed a whistle, always forced to come back by water, always forced to never step on land. Pup must be similarly trained. And he must be built of similar stuff. It takes a tough, bright dog to graduate from a handling course.

And something else, you'll be seeing a hand cast at field trials I've not mentioned. It's an angle-back. Pup's in a predicament so you should give him an Over to avoid the hazard, then another Back to drive him on to the bird. But you know the judges are counting whistles. Therefore, you want to keep the number of whistles down and you decide to do two things at once. That is, on one whistle, give two casts at the same time—an Over and a Back. An angle-back.

Well, I advise against it. We've learned it's Pup's tendency to continually want to go back in the first place—and yes, in the last place. Plus, your voice drives him back. And Pup's desire for birds drives him back. And his momentum drives him back. The result is, angle-backs seldom work. I know there are exceptions to the rule. There always are. For example, angle-backs may work on land, when never on water. Or, great dogs can take angle-backs, when dry or wet. But how many great dogs are there?

You've probably only got a good dog and for you to win you've got to do everything right, while the great dog's got to beat himself by doing a couple of things wrong. I advise you to always give an Over and then a Back. Go ahead, let the judges add up whistles. But none of the whistles they've marked as demerits could be nearly so serious as their looking up and seeing Pup standing on land when he ought to be in water.

Angle-backs are usually used by Mississippi riverboaters. By gamblers. I can see him now, Joe Schomer, the Conroe, Texas, pro who won the national open twice with Spirit Lake Duke. I can see him sitting in the cab of his dog truck, reading the newspaper baseball reports, glancing over the hood of the pickup now and then, shaking his head, smiling at an amateur running on Sunday morning, saying, "Mississippi riverboater."

Joe, like every professional retriever trainer I ever met, would do anything to help an amateur run his dog and win a trial: even if the amateur were competing in the open against the pros.

In the old days the pros would stay at the Leaky Faucet Motel while Mr. Moneyfeller—the well heeled amateur and all who would emulate or cultivate him—stayed and played at Sterling Manor. It was a matter of economics only in part. It was more a desire on the part of the pros to be off alone with others of their own kind, for they were country boys and kept things simple.

I always stayed with the pros, picking their brains, inspecting their gear, listening to their tales. Never once was I ignored nor resented. That's the way with the pros.

And always they'll invite you to come train with them. Like Cotton Pershall helping Bill Connor train before the 1972 national open that Connor won and Pershall lost.

Yep, there's not a pro who won't help you beat him.

I can't count the times I've approached D. L. Walters and asked him about the suction in a test. D. L. always told me right and in great part helped keep me in the trial, competing against him. So did Schomer. And many others.

But there's one thing— Pros know you can't win an open on luck. You can't wish the dog to the bird, you've got to handle him there. And you can't do that gambling. No Mississippi riverboating.

Drying Out What We Mopped Up

Some final pointers for training Pup on water blinds should include:

One. If you cast Pup to water and he's swimming an incorrect line you've got to figure your odds on when's the best time to stop him and correct his line. If you stop him too soon you intimidate him. You bring back all those bad sessions when you were asking him to get the bird at spot D.

Yet, if you let Pup continue on this incorrect line too long he'll become convinced this is the way to go. Then when you whistle him down you'll have a hard time changing his mind.

So, if you hit Pup short, give him a silent Over. Less intimidation.

But if you hit Pup long, you've got to really jar his mind, so a voice-over is in order.

392

Two. At all times a handler must think for, and think ahead of his dog. For example, Pup's in running water, the splash of his movement will drown out your whistle. So you must wait till he enters swimming water before trying to get his attention.

Or, to think ahead of Pup, you will whistle him down short—hit him with a whistle before he enters tall cattails—so Pup can see your hand cast. If he's in heavy cover he may not be able to see a thing. Also, heavy cover usually means shallow water. Not only can't Pup see, he can't hear.

Three. Remember, voices make echos on water. If you see Pup twist his head around upon your verbal command—now he's looking away from you—he's getting a boomerang feedback. Switch to silent overs.

Four. Always end every training session on a happy note. If Pup's done miserably in water take him to land and throw him some kindergarten singles.

Five. However, if Pup turns sour, nothing goes right, then rest him Isolate him. Don't work him. Or, short-tie him on a stake and make him watch all the other dogs work. You know your Pup. You know what's best. But my point is, Pup can literally give up, deep down inside he can quit you and quit himself. He has to be psyched back up.

Six. All dogs like to piddle about when emerging from water on a water blind. It's a form of cheating. Nip it in the bud. Be ready with the whistle. Drive Pup on to his business.

By the same token, Pup can start cheating on you when emerging from water with the bird in his mouth, standing there shaking. Once again, whistle him to your side.

Seven. Be careful where you work Pup. Water can cover a junk yard. And one great leap to water, just to smack his chest into a submerged log or discarded hot water heater, may take the leap out of Pup forever.

Eight. If you're finicky about getting wet, if you chill easily, if your wife resents mud-stained pants, then wear a pair of plastic leggings, or rubber rain pants, when running Pup on water blinds. I've seen handlers stand like matadors trying to avoid the pass of the bull as they try to take the bird from Pup and not get wet. As a result, they sometimes drop the bird. Or they get the bird by a wing tip and while lofting it Pup's enticed to leap after it. It's all for a bad show. And a bad score. With plastic leggings these handlers could hold their ground and get the job done.

Nine. It's one thing to tell Pup to line and cast him on a blind—then whistle him down and give him a hand cast. Pup's prepared for this; that's part of handling. But it's something else, entirely, to cast Pup for a mark then whistle him down and handle him to the bird. This is when you're going to get whistle and cast refusals: especially when Pup is young.

Here's what you've got to know. You're usually granted two mistakes before you're dropped from a trial. Okay, Pup's just made one mistake. He's failed to mark. That's why you're handling him. Now don't let Pup make two mistakes, both on the same bird. When you start to handle, then handle. So often the handler will be wishy washy about handling on a mark. Maybe he figures he's already out of the trial, what does it matter? But it does matter. It matters a great deal for two reasons. One, always be definite and mean business when handling Pup, and two, many a Pup that's handled goes on to win the trial: even the national open.

Ten. And should you ever care to be bold, don't put Pup on a pea whistle like all retriever handlers presently use. Use your fingers to make a whistle, instead. Make up whistle commands: one blast for stop, two blasts for cast right, three blasts for cast left, a descending blast (changing tone) for Pup to get back, whatever. This way Pup will never have to stop, turn around, look for you, wait for your command, then turn back around and go on.

As Pup takes his outrun he can listen for commands to adjust his line—as the whistle tells him to do. Such a Pup will never pop.

This is the way shepherds handle their dogs. And as sheep dog training becomes more popular in America and more retriever handlers view the end results—which seem miraculous—I predict this will be the handling technique of the future. After all, handling Pup by remote control was the shepherd's gift: they did it first to control their stock then gave it to the sportsman to fetch his bird.

And two final thoughts—

Experienced handlers know an acceptable line to a blind is not a rifle bullet—as I've said up front. But instead, each line lays within an acceptable corridor. Liken it to a bowling alley: stay between the gutters you're going to score. Decide in your own mind where you think the judges have drawn the corridor for acceptable work. Work the edge of this corridor to avoid the hazard as much as possible.

Finally, a field trial test that's rare today because of the cost of pheasants is the flyaway. A bird is actually lofted, all cackling and wings beating, and the guns either fire and miss, fire poppers, or don't fire at all. Then the handler is asked to fetch a blind. You'll need to work on this: no matter the expense.

You'll need to work on this not only to cast Pup for the eventual blind, but you'll also present such a bird to train Pup for a no-bird at a trial. That is, a bird the gunners wanted to hit, but missed. The judges will give you a re-run, if Pup doesn't break. A cackling, wing beating flyaway is the ultimate temptation for Pup to take one look and say in departure, "I'll see ya." And where he'll see you is back at your truck, because he'll be dropped from the trial for breaking.

16/The Problem With Problems

You and the boys are building a duck shack, tight and sound for winter's blast, tucked away from vandal's sight, no propane tank nor electric hookup for you wish to escape the human condition.

To warm the place and cook your meals you build a fireplace.

Cement, sand, and brick are hauled to the site and you pour a foundation, build a hearth, run up a stack. It's time to celebrate. You clean four ducks, run em through with a spit, stick em in the fireplace, and sit in smoke. In smoke? Yep. The thing won't draw. You designed it wrong.

Now you can either endure a smoke-filled room or tear the thing down and start again. Or worse yet, you can eat cold food.

Men bring dogs along like this: design em wrong and the dogs won't work. So they're left at home or traded off or the hunter ends up gunning without a retriever.

But let's say the fireplace draws. That's not your problem. The problem is the mortar's cracking, some bricks are splitting, and other bricks are popping their veneer. Well, you can chip out and grout in new mortar, even replace a faulty brick—but what about the mortar and brick in the guts of the fireplace? Back where you can't reach.

So it goes with gun dogs. Sometimes the foundation is weak. The stuff of which the dog is made is defective. The breeding produces a crumbler. Or the material in the dog was great but the dog trainer was a poor do-it-yourselfer. He should have contracted the construction of the dog with a professional trainer.

So it goes. The problem with dogs are the same as problems with anything man builds: good or bad raw materials, expert or poor craftsmanship.

So what to do? Fireplace or dog? If the fireplace won't draw and the dog won't fetch you may have to abandon both. Or start all over with the raw material at hand.

But let's say both work, they just have holes in em. Well, to replace a brick you've got to chip and brush, maybe hammer and pulverize. And while this is occurring, the whole fireplace may separate. For certain you're going to make a mess of the duck shack.

Maybe you get the faulty materials replaced. But the thing never looks right. You can see where you patched.

Plus, you always know the fault is there. The pride is gone. And, when will it all crack again?

So, in training a dog or building a fireplace it's easier to avoid a problem than to correct one.

But there is this difference: you may be able to build a perfect fireplace but never a perfect shooting dog. There's always going to be some holes, some cracks, in your final product. And some of these holes and cracks are major, some minor. Some can be corrected, some can't. Let's run through those specified by AKC as major faults, plus those any hunter can't abide, and see what we can do to correct them.

The Gun Shy Dog

The gun shy dog is a pitiful thing. A timid thing. A spooky thing. Afraid of man, bird, wind, car—everything. You see such dogs walk through fields as though they were strewn with tacks.

What to do? Well, traditionally a trainer offers such a dog food, stands distant while the Pup approaches the bowl to eat, then the trainer pops a cap. In other words the pup must endure the retort or go hungry. He cannot shy from the gun and eat. Upon hearing the shot the average gun shy dog will bolt to his dog house or jump sideways and turn to stone. The trainer enters the kennel and removes the food.

Later, the food is offered again and when the dog approaches the bowl a distant shell is fired. This can go on for days, even weeks. Dogs can go hungry much longer than you can imagine—it's their nature to do so in the wild. God gave them that kind of fasting and feasting ability.

But no living creature can go for long without water. That's why I substitute water for food in trying to cure a gun shy dog. Without water the average dog is in bad shape within 48 hours. He's got to drink, no matter how frightened he is of the gun.

So offer Pup water, stand distant and fire a gun: a cap pistol at first, then a .22 blank, and finally a .410 shell. If Pup ducks back into his dog house, i.e. stops drinking, then remove the bucket of water. To do this right you need a helper. That gun must be distant, plus, you must get the water out of the kennel in a hurry. Pup must know he's going to be denied until he bolds up.

Pup will finally drink. But that's not to say he'll stand to the gun in a field situation.

Now with pointers and setters in a field situation you can direct the blast away from the gun shy dog by always walking around point, kicking the birds out yourself, and firing away from Pup. But a retriever, by the very nature of his work, is usually standing at the gunner's side when the gun goes off.

It may be, for a while, Pup should be worked by a handler who has no gun, and Pup be asked to retrieve only those birds shot at a distance by other gunners.

But that's an awful lot of trouble for a doubtful Pup. Just as some other remedial techniques are a lot of trouble. You realize some trainers tranquilize a pup and fire a gun over him? Yep, a doped dog, all senses dulled, the gun retort muffled by the muddled state of the dog's mind. Pup'll endure. And if enough care is taken, and enough time, Pup will gradually accept the gun.

But who wants to go through all this? If Pup won't respond to water denial and firm up to the gun, then I'd give him away. My point is, why go through all this to salvage a doubtful performer? It takes a bold Pup to finish training. With a timid Pup you've got too much against you at the start. The dog's breeding is defeating you before you ever get started.

That's why knowledgeable gun dog men advise a newcomer to stay arm's length from Pup till it's proven he's going to make a gun dog. Many a worthless dog has been kept for life because the man, his wife, and kids became attached to him as a pet. The dog was kept as a matter of heart. And that space he occupied in house and heart may well have kept some hunter from having a gun dog he could take hunting; there was just no more room for another dog.

Hip Dysplasia

Many assume dysplasia to be a genetic fault. Others say, ''No, it is brought about by dogs growing too heavy as a breed for their underpinning.'' Whatever, or whichever, hip dysplasia simply stated is a result of the ball of the femur (femoral head) becoming too loose in the hip joint (acetabulum socket). The dog is crippled: mildly or critically.

As I write this book there is no cure, no corrective surgery, for hip dysplasia that is 100 per cent effective. The only way we can control this affliction is through selective breeding. Only those parents who x-ray free of dysplasia should be used to whelp litters. Yet, we've seen up front, even certified parents can throw pups with bad hips.

To be as safe as you can in buying your pup select him only from a breeder who's had both the sire and dam certified dysplastic free by the Orthopedic Foundation for Animals, Inc. (OFA).

Such certification is obtained by having a vet x-ray each parent and forward the film to OFA where three independent radiologists interpret the bone formation. If the hip joints appear normal the dog is given a certification number. If not, the owner and attendant vet are notified.

I just bought a pup that came with papers saying, ''If at the end of two years this pup shows bad hips, send me the pup's death certificate and I shall refund your purchase price.'' That's mighty grisly business. What a shame. Can't you see the kids standing in the driveway when you pull out—taking Pup to his execution? Should this pup I just bought prove dysplastic I lose two years of care and love and training, the breeder loses his purchase price, and Pup either loses his life or I end up caring for a cripple till he dies. I like nothing about it. But what are the alternatives?

And one other thing— If Pup hurts in the hips the way arthritics hurt in their joints, then he is indeed to be pitied.

Please be careful when you select your pup. And take your chances: not willy nilly chances, but calculated chances. We now live in a society, so much of which seems to ask to be able to live risk-free. No matter what happens to some people anymore, they want to sue some one else. Sue some one else even though the plaintiff may have been stupid, careless, or vindictive.

Be responsible for your life, for the chances you take in it, for the decisions you make. God envisioned no risk-free life when He made this world and let us step upon it. What risk-free life did He grant His own son?

And one final thing. Do you know dogs have won the national championship with hip dysplasia? The dogs may have run in some pain but no other dog could duplicate their day, their way, their grit, or their excellence. There's more to a dog than hips, there's also heart.

Heartworms

I've told you before, your Pup can be born carrying heartworm. Keep him on a monitoring schedule with your vet. Plus, should you live in an area where heartworm is prevalent, put your pup on heartworm preventative. Heartworm can kill. And it's a horrible death. Don't let this happen to Pup.

Hard Mouth

When we were force breaking Pup to retrieve you could see how this could avoid hard mouth, or stop it in the bud before it ever became a factor, or ease it out of a dog that was confirmed in crunching. Same as training with frozen birds and oak dowels. But you're going to pick up some book that tells you to wrap a bird with tacks and force Pup to fetch it. The theory goes, Pup won't bear down on this porcupine bird. If you want to try it, it's your pup.

Me? I've seen dogs ram the tacks right into the roof of their mouths.

So I keep returning the hard mouth Pup to the force retrieve table. Plus, I hand him birds in my gloved hand. Pup's not going to bite my hand. Then later, I wrap the glove about a bird in the field and send Pup to fetch it.

And with a birdy dog—I repeat, a birdy dog—not a timid dog, nor a bird shy dog, I've started hitting them with the sound-blast in their electric collar. Just when they pick up the bird, but before they can clamp down on it, I buzz em. The buzzer is a reminder to take it easy and it works.

You may have heard you should never put electricity, nor sound-blast, on a dog when he's working a bird. The dissuader goes: it'll make Pup bird shy. For some dogs that is the case. But I'm talking about a birdy dog. Nothing is going to make this dog blink his bird; or pick it up, drop it, and leave it in the field. The sound-burst can remind Pup 100 yards out to carry that bird gently. And I repeat, the buzzer is a sound. Not a shock. A sound conditioned to take the place of the shock.

Herb Holmes, field trial hall of famer and owner of Gunsmoke kennels, was the first man to prove to me you can use electricity—this was before the sound-blast was invented—on dogs around birds. Herb uses it to force an honoring dog to back, to keep the pointer or backer from creeping, and to hold both dogs steady to shot and wing.

I don't known how many nationals Herb's won, but I do know it's a potful and I don't argue with success. You can shock a dog on birds.

But there's one thing you should note about hard mouth. Pup may be crushing the bird with his drive, not his mouth. He may be smashing it when he hits it, not munching it on his retrieve. Such a dog was Beau of Zenith, one of seven dogs to finish the 12-series national open won by Spirit Lake Duke in 1957, at Smyrna, Delaware.

Beau died before his prime, he was only two years old at Smyrna, but was he a gallery pleaser. He'd hit that bird like Earl Campbell smashes through an opposing line or Ty Cobb used to slide into home plate.

If only my dogs could be this way: I'd put up with broken bird bones.

And before closing this section you should know how most dogs become hard mouth. Their handler grabs for the bird and pulls. The dog pulls back. The next time the dog is sent for the bird, out in the field he makes up his mind, "I'll just hold on harder this time . . . that way he won't get it." And so it goes, ever deteriorating. That's why we never pull a bird from Pup's mouth. Always push. Nor do we lunge. Always we wait with hands upturned. We seek a delivery, not a tug of war.

The Dog Fighter

If Pup's a confirmed dog fighter you're going to live the rest of his life with a pen-pulled hand grenade. Never can you go to a trial, nor to a duck blind with a friend and his dog, but what it's duck hunting in Pearl Harbor. When the attack?

And if you don't know this I want to warn you now: when Pup's in a dog fight he don't know you, he don't hear you, he don't feel you. Not even if you're beating him with a steel pipe. What else on earth can be so intent as a dog in a fight?

Some trainers will tell you, "Spray the dogs with a water hose." If it's a preliminary card that might help. But not if it's the main event.

Scoop, my great old Lab who wants to keep his jewels dry, and Moby—that leviathan great Pyrenees—never meet that they don't honor some life oath to kill each other. It's simple to understand. Moby runs loose at the farm; he loves to kill skunks and I have a wealth of them burrowed about. The farm is Moby's territory. But when Scoop is released from his kennel run, the farm is his. The result is a range war worse than the one that spawned Billy the Kid.

In one fight Moby broke Scoop's lower jaw and extracted a canine tooth. The vet told me such an extraction took him, maybe, 20 minutes. Moby did it in a fraction of a second. Another time Moby ripped Scoop's right front paw from toenail to heel. Still later, Scoop bit Moby's tongue nearly in two. And so it goes. I keep em separated when I'm home but I must leave now and then and always the kennel boy will not believe what I tell him will happen.

Just as he won't believe my warning about the coyotes. They don't bite me, so the boy figures they won't bite him. Yet, every time I arrive home the health department is waiting for me. The coyotes have bitten the kennel boy—they must be quarantined. Which is always amusing to hear: they think I let em run loose? But the kennel boy— You know where he's always bitten? Right on the butt. I think that tells us something but I'm not sure just what.

Anyway, if you've got a real dog fight on your hands you can get bit. Or you can jump in there kicking and break those little bones on top your feet.

There's only one way to stop a dog fight; and a dog fighter. And it takes two men. Each man grab a dog by its two hind legs and give it the big swing. That'll stop the fight, for that day.

But there's such a thing as territoriality, Pup wants to defend his home. Or possessiveness of a bitch in heat. Pup wants to perpetuate his own kind. And you can swing till doom's day and Pup's still going to fight.

So, forever you've got to keep an eye on Pup and short circuit his hostility. You can tell when he's about to attack, give a sharp command, "No," and do whatever else is necessary. And this is the only time in this whole book I've written, " ... whatever else ... " For it will take all that. Maybe even the legionnaire's pick handle.

The Trash Chaser

Pup can have a fondness for poultry. Oh, he'll mark and fetch game birds, no problem there. Why he'll never muss a feather. But leave him alone in a barnyard and he starts acting like he had a contract to supply Colonel Sanders.

Same with chasing cars, or sheep, or deer. Pup can run for hours in pursuit of anything that takes his fancy. And yes, rabbits can take Pup's fancy.

So how do we stop this marauding, this eating between meals? With the electric collar. Not the sound-blast but the real juice. Every time Pup nears a chicken, rabbit, car, deer, whathaveyou, hit him with the charge. *Never say a thing. This is important. Pup must be convinced this thing he's after—is after him. One session should do it.*

The Big Faults

In a pocket-sized pamphlet entitled, "Standing Recommendations of the Retriever Advisory Committee," published by AKC, it is written, *"SERIOUS FAULTS. In and of themselves, these are, as set forth in the "STANDARD", usually sufficient to justify elimination from the stake."*

In other words, if Pup does any of the following, he's out of the trial. What are these faults and how do we correct them?

One. POOR NOSE: Well, momma and daddy put that nose on Pup. He's got what they gave him and you can't add to it. All you can do is give it lots of opportunity to be used.

Two. RELUCTANCE TO ENTER EITHER ROUGH COVER, WATER, ICE, ETC: You can bold up a timid Pup by Happy Timing him his first year, letting him learn the territory and discovering nothing out there is going to hurt him, plus, you can increase this boldness by putting Pup on the force retrieve training table. And you can put zip in him by running him with his litter mates, or short-tieing him and making him watch his colleagues work. But once again, desire is basically determined by the seed and the womb.

Three. RETURNING TO HIS HANDLER, ETC: If Pup returns to you without a bird, gives up his hunt, finds the bird and leaves it; all this shows lack of desire. Maybe confusion for a young pup but we're past that stage, now. It may be Pup's breeding was inferior, or maybe, he had improper training. If you can't keep Pup from blinking the bird then send him to a professional trainer. If the pro says it's worthless then give Pup away and get yourself a contender.

One Happy Time diversion is to cast all dogs for the same dummy, or, place one dummy for each dog on distant shore then cast all dogs to fetch: yes, they do race each other.

Four. STOPPING HIS HUNT: see number three above. Force break.

Five. SWITCHING BIRDS: see number three above. Force break.

Six. BLINKING THE BIRD: see number three above. Force break.

Seven. RESTRAINT BY TOUCHING OR HOLDING A DOG, ETC: Back to basic training. Get your football team behind the line.

Eight. OUT OF CONTROL: Both basic and advance training have been insufficient. Pup must answer all voice and whistle commands, take all casts. This isn't one brick that needs replacing, the whole fireplace is faulty. Start all over with Pup or send him to a professional trainer.

However, there is one way a dog can be out of control that has little to do with basic training. I'll never forget competing against 1967 national field champion Butte Blue Moon owned by Bing Grunwald, trained by D. L. Walters, and handled by Brownie Grunwald, Bing's wife. No dog could ever beat Moon at a trial: only he could help you by beating himself. There were times on a blind when he would tell Brownie to take that whistle and whistle her own tune—something incidentally Brownie can do quite well. But did Moon know this? Did he know Brownie was an excellent entertainer, an artist, a skilled musician with her whistle? Or did Moon just decide once in a while to bug out? Bug out? Would you believe finding him four miles distant?

Yes, Moon ran out of control when he wanted to run out of control. Take him back to basic training? Why? He knew more than most trainers. Take him back through advanced training? That is the definition of advanced training: to be the national champion.

No, Moon, like some men I know, just decided once in a while to take off. What a great guy he was, though. I hope he enjoyed those outings. And I thank him for leaving, so my dog and I could vie for part of the winnings he left the also-rans to dibby up.

But even then it was a rough row to hoe: I had to hope Marge Johnson's great dog, Jetstone Muscles of Claymar, would also jet out of control. Honest folks, I grew so tired following that dog's blue-ribbon tail year after year—

But I will say this, I never won much against the likes of such immortals, but I learned what good work was and how to achieve it. And I learned something even more important: second best just ain't ever going to make it. You don't luck into a championship.

Nine. EXTREME FREEZE: Force break to retrieve.

Ten. RETRIEVING A DECOY: Back to basics.

Eleven. BREAKING: Get your football team behind the casting line.

Twelve. HARD MOUTH: Force break Pup to retrieve.

Thirteen. LOUD AND PROLONGED WHINING OR BARKING: Now this is a tough one. There have been some great dogs that never would shut up. Their owners had their voice box removed. Harsh! Yes.

First we must determine why Pup's whining. Is he timid? That's one set of problems to be cured as we did for two above. But it may be Pup's bold; he's whining because he wants to go, he's birdy and he wants to fetch, he's whining because he can't stand to wait on line. Should your pup's whine be so caused then outfit him with a sound-blast collar. Everytime he whines on line, give him a buzz. He'll stop. But it'll take a lot of birds. A helper afield with a crate full of birds day after day after day.

Seldom do we speak when disciplining Pup: we are detached. But this is one time when Pup must transfer your verbal command to the sound-blast. After all, Pup can't wear the electric collar in a trial. So you say, "No noise," each time the sound-blast goes off until Pup associates your command with the blast.

You'll be permitted to say, "No noise," on line at a trial. Remember to do so or you could well have a whining Pup and be thrown out of the trial.

But what of the barking dog? He's not whining, he's barking. And he's not on line, he's in the kennel, or in your station wagon, or standing on leash in a public park. The same company that makes the bird releaser and electric collar also makes a no-bark sound-blast collar. I've never put one on a pup that didn't shut up.

That's not to say the pup won't bark when the collar's removed. But by then he's learned the command, "No noise," in conjunction with the sound-blast, so my voice, plus my pointed finger, and my scowl, will shut him up—and lay his ears down and tuck his tail between his legs.

Continuing with serious faults that can cause ejection of Pup or handler from a trial—

Fourteen. WATCHING BLIND RETRIEVES BEING PLANTED, ETC: Poor sportsmanship on the part of the handler. And there are some of these guys, and gals, around. They can't train a

Mindy Rodgers honors her dog on the same side as the working dog: the ultimate test for staunchness.

dog to win so they cheat to try and get the job done. The theory has always been such a person would be reported to the field trial committee and there would be a hearing. But too many people figure you can't kick a pile of manure without getting a little on your boot. They don't want to stop for a shine. So they go their own way and let the cheater cheat. But I can tell you this: I've never known one of these guys to win. They don't have the stuff to win, no matter how they go about it.

And you should know this: there are times when the field trial committee will eliminate a handler from contention but his dog can go on and compete with another handler. An example would be a handler who gets angry and verbally abuses a judge. The handler's out but his dog's done no wrong. The dog can go on running.

Fifteen. WATCHING BIRDS BEING SHOT OR RETRIEVED BY ANOTHER DOG IN A WATER TEST, ETC: Same as above.

Sixteen. DELIBERATE BLOCKING BY A HANDLER SO THAT A DOG WILL NOT SEE ALL BIRDS AND ALL FALLS; THIS APPLIES BOTH TO THE WORKING DOG AND THE HONORING DOG: Once again, poor sportsmanship on the part of the handler. Why? Well, the handler's afraid his dog is going to break. Maybe there's a squawking pheasant to be shot right off line. That's too much temptation for this guy's hair-trigger dog to stand steady. Best the trainer get him a football team to the rear of the casting line.

As for honoring— I've not mentioned this. Offered no training technique. Heck, I haven't even defined it. Saw no need. If Pup's steady to shot and wing, he's honoring at your side on the casting line. He's honoring you. Whether or not another dog is working is irrelevant.

But I have done this with a jealous dog. You see, the dog that's totally staunch when he's the working dog may bolt on honor—if you're the apple of his eye. Such a dog can't stand to see another dog get the bird.

The best way to cure the jealous dog is to place your football team to rear, then you take your buddy's dog to run, and let your buddy take your dog to honor. That is, you switch dogs. Now that's really going to give Pup something to be jealous about.

Sure he'll break. But the football team will put an anchor in him. Then when it comes time for you to honor with Pup there'll be nothing to it. Try it and see.

Seventeen. THROWING ANYTHING INTO THE WATER TO PERSUADE A DOG TO ENTER OR TO DIRECT HIM TO A FALL: This pup's never been trained. Run him through boot camp.

Eighteen. FAILURE TO FIND A DEAD BIRD WHICH THE DOG SHOULD HAVE FOUND: This rule was made up for two types of dogs: the one who had no desire and the other who didn't know scat. We'll bold the lackluster dog up on the force retrieve table and give him lots of birds afield. As for the one who doesn't know scat: we'll run him through our whole program. You see this rule was essentially made up for days gone by when an occasional hunting dog showed up to run in a licensed trial. The handler didn't know the difference: "Ol Rover there can do it all!" he thought. Poor Ol Rover. All he could mark was fleas.

Nineteen. NOISILY OR FREQUENTLY RESTRAINING A DOG FROM BREAKING EXCEPT IN EXTRAORDINARY CIRCUMSTANCES, ETC: Once again, call out the football team to keep Pup from breaking. And what are those extraordinary circumstances referred to? Well, if the judge calls, "No bird," then you're permitted to bark, "No," at Pup and get him off that casting line. You're still under judgment so if Pup breaks you're on the way home. Also, if the honor dog breaks the test is over, the judge will boom, ''No,'' which clues you to do the same, and you get a re-run. But until you get off that line you're still in contention and under judgment. If Pup breaks you're out of the trial.

So those are the nineteen major faults that can cause ejection from a trial. One of them represents deficient breeding, three are caused by inadequate basic training, three by a combination of deficient breeding and/or basic training, five by failure to force break the dog to retrieve, four because the handler had no football team, one because he didn't use the sound-blast collar, and two because the handler was a poor sport.

The standing recommendations also list eleven moderate faults and fourteen slight faults. These twenty five minor faults have been dealt with as we proceeded to train Pup. They, too, represent faults stemming either from poor basic training or poor breeding.

As Taken From the Nest

So in the end, it's just this simple. The way you finish depends on the way you start. The pup you pick. The way you bring him along.

And during the process of training, if Pup develops a problem, like the fireplace popping its glaze, it may destroy the dog, or wreck the house, to fix the thing.

So all problems are not corrected. It all depends on what you can live with, win with, hunt with. There may have been a perfect fireplace but there'll never be a perfect dog. The high point dog of them all, River Oaks Corky, took a whining problem with him to his grave. Royal's Moose's Moe would fudge on an over. Renegade Pepe would prefer to go by land. Not by sea.

But tell me, who was ever the perfect trainer?

And tell me more. Who ever wrote the perfect dog training book? As Frederich Buechner stated in his inspirational text, *The Faces of Jesus*, ''If we are determined to speak the plain sense of our experience, we must be willing to risk the charge of speaking what often sounds like nonsense.''

And tell me last. Who would have it any other way? What you can't train out of Pup, or into Pup, you can handle around. Field trials then become a game like, ''I've got a secret,'' and you try to win the game with no one learning what your secret really is. But they always do. The weaknesses of dogs are the grist of trial mills as the weaknesses of men are the stuff of which politics and religion are made.

So each time you go to the line it's always a new event, and the game is always exciting, and yes there'll be times you know you're doomed. The test is designed to trip Pup. But lo and behold, Pup steps right over the test and goes on. And you're standing there with tears in your eyes and a lump in your throat—or heart, they seem to be the same—and you know Pup did this one for you, for the gipper. And you love that Pup. You'll love that Pup the rest of your life.

And for that love, for mine and yours, I wrote this book.

17/Health, Education, and Welfare

In 1689, Tom Fairfax, late of England, some 300 years late, wrote:

"You can't begin too early to teach the water spaniel obedience, when he can but lap, for that is the principal thing to be learned; for being made to obey, he is then ready to do your commands; therefore so soon as he can lap, teach him to couch and lie close, not daring to stir from that posture without your commands, and the better to effect this, always cherish him when he does your will, and correct him when he disobeys; and be sure to observe, that in the first teaching him, you never let him eat any thing, but when he does something to deserve it, that he may thereby know, that food is a thing· that cometh not by chance, or by a liberal hand, but only for a reward for well-doing; and this will make him not only willing to learn, but apt to remember what he is taught without blows; and to that end, have no more teachers than one, for variety breed confusion, as teaching diverse ways, so that he can learn no way well."

Tom, I wish I'd known you. I like your ways with dogs, though not necessarily your way with a sentence: 182 words! But you meant well for you trained well and you cared well. You say much to be heeded today. And you did much you did not say. For we read between the lines and thank you.

Housing

Housing should teach as well as shelter: just as Tom got double mileage out of food. He nourished but he also trained.

Make your dog house a combination school and gymnasium. How's that? Well, the house should teach Pup all those attributes he can learn when short-tied. Plus, it should exercise him instead of just prompting him to lie around and grow soft.

Now many a seasoned old retriever man is going to gasp on this— THE IDEAL DOG HOUSE IS MADE FROM A BARREL. That's right. Not a wood house, nor one of concrete blocks, but a barrel.

The barrel can be made of either wood or steel. The last wood barrels I bought originally held whiskey and I found them in Grand Junction, Tennessee, and had them shipped prepaid to Wichita, Kansas, for 15 dollars each. Now I bought 30 of the things so I may have gotten a quantity discount. And interesting to note, the last wood dog houses I built had 24 dollars worth of raw lumber in them: that much money before I ever pounded a nail.

The way to prepare a wood barrel for Pup's house is to saw into and knock out half the wood lid. This half you remove is then reinforced and hinged to the half that remains in the barrel to make a flap you can close when the sky forewarns blizzard. The house is mounted—on its side, balanced halfway back—on a section of four inch oil field pipe, about 18 inches off the ground, and around the pipe is fitted a revolving steel collar to which you can attach Pup's four foot chain. Or you can just snap the chain about the pole. Atop the pole is a rectangular and slightly curved plate to bolt to the barrel.

Now Pup's short-tied to teach him self reliance, and his house is elevated so he must leap every time he wishes to enter or exit. This helps build up those hind quarters important for leaping to water, driving in muck, or breaking heavy cover.

The wood barrel is the perfect house since the material is a natural insulator. But wood barrels are becoming scarce and you may have to settle for a barrel rolled from steel. No matter. Steel barrels work nearly as well.

You prepare a steel barrel house—these presently cost about 10 dollars—by removing half the top with a welder's torch or a cold chisel. The ragged edge on the half that remains must be crimped over and pounded flat. The half that's removed is probably destroyed so

The ultimate in dog houses, the hi-rise barrel.

House is stationed inside block niche to ward off sun. Flooring is placed in steel barrel with platform roof.

toss it away. Then if you wish to build a flap to attach to the bottom half as a door you can build it of wood and hinge it on.

But we can't have Pup lying on cold steel when the chill factor's 45 below. So we build a wood pad and angle it through the opening then place it to form a floor in the steel barrel.

Whether wood or steel, both barrels are elevated on a four inch pipe, and both collared so Pup can run around-and-around and leap in and out of his house. We leave the bottom half of the lid intact to keep bedding from being scattered about.

At the outer circumference of Pup's circular world drive a post into the ground on which you've welded a platform to hold a water bucket. Position this post just outside Pup's length of chain so Pup can't, one, knock the bucket over, two, lift a leg and tinkle in it, and three, try to get his front legs in it and thrash about when he's hot.

During the summer Pup can move about the post, always staying in the shade of his barrel. When it rains or snows he can jump inside his

416

These pointers live their lives rebounding — the same thing's accomplished with an elevated barrel.

Pups enter and leave elevated barrel by ramp: starts building strong drive muscles.
If you want conventional housing then here's the best you can do. Offset door with hallway, slanted roof, and elevated floor. Pup enters, turns corner, escapes wind's blast.

barrel. When it's cool he can sun on the roof—if you elevate the barrel in scaffolding with a flat plywood platform top.

This scaffolding is probably attractive to you who would like to experiment with a barrel house, but still keep it in your kennel run. You can erect a rectangular platform to encase the barrel and provide a flat roof where Pup can sun in spring and fall, momma-dog can leap up there to escape her pesky brood, or either Pup or momma can lay up there to take the breezes.

The platform top is also good for grooming Pup, examining him after a hunt or training session for foreign matter wedged between toes, stuck in eyes, or lodged in coat.

And how do pups get into our barrel house? By placing a board from barrel opening to earth, we let them scamper up and down a tilted ramp. This is good for em, bolds em up, gets those legs exercised under stress.

Most people who own highfalutin retrievers think of a barrel as that abode of a junk yard dog. Far from it. If Pup were a contractor this is the home he'd build. Ask my buddy Delmar. He explains, ''I've been training and boarding dogs all my life. Probably had my hands on 20,000 of em. And one time I had a great pen and I got to thinking ...

''I put every kind of dog house I could imagine in that pen. Then each day I'd let a different dog go in there. Next morning I'd go check. Where did that dog spend the night?

''Know what I found? Well, more than 95 per cent of all those dogs were sleepin in the barrel.''

In conclusion, there can be no substitute for a short-tied Pup. A kennel run provides too much room to goof off, to get in trouble, to let the mind wander, to fence fight, to do many things I no longer want done. From now on all my dogs are going in barrels. You do as you please.

Far as I can figure, everything's good about a barrel house. Why else would Bob Wehle, owner of Elhew kennels, probably the finest kennels in the world, use them? Field Trial hall of famer Wehle has the funds to build whatever he wants for his dogs. Bob wants barrels.

419

Kennel Run

I'll never again ask a dog to stand on concrete. I won't do it. Why should Pup? Concrete's not natural. And it's hard on Pup's feet. Either too hot or too cold. And it puts callouses on elbows, causes feet to splat out. Concrete is just no good.

If you're going to house your dog in a kennel run, which I strongly recommend you don't, then use pea gravel for your runway. It doesn't creep out of the run and call for constant grooming and replacement, it hoses down well, and it keeps Pup from digging.

Dirt's good, too, but it gets urine soaked. Of course you can always sanitize a dirt run with salt—but too much and you will burn Pup's feet.

Sand helps build good tight feet, Pup's always standing there flexing his toes. But sand can get mighty hot in a summer sun. Yet if you live in a cool clime sand may be your choice. It toughens and tightens Pup's feet. It invites Pup to dig. And when he's but a few inches down it provides a cool place to lie. Water drains from it fast. And nothing much grows in it. Plus, it's easy to groom with a rake.

But there is a problem. Pup can dig out if he's not short-tied to a pole. Yet if you're going to keep Pup in a run then no bother, just build a concrete foundation about the run, or bury the chainlink and bend it under Pup's path.

If it is a run you prefer then please make it at least six-feet wide. Few people do this; they go four feet. And with this narrow a run Pup's always having to walk around, or through, his leavings. Plus, he beats his tail against the wire fencing and can abrade the tip. If you've never tried to cauterize a bleeding tail, then you've no idea of the chore before you.

Be sure your kennel run is covered. Pup can climb like a fox if there's a bitch in heat. Plus, rabid foxes can, and will, climb over.

Now if you have all your dogs on poles and sleeping in barrels, you will still need a security fence about the area. A dog can conceivably break loose from his chain; there must be perimeter fencing to hold him. And every kennel run needs compound fencing to stop the bolter when he's released from his run and escapes your grasp, or for the dog who exits a gate that wasn't latched shut.

420

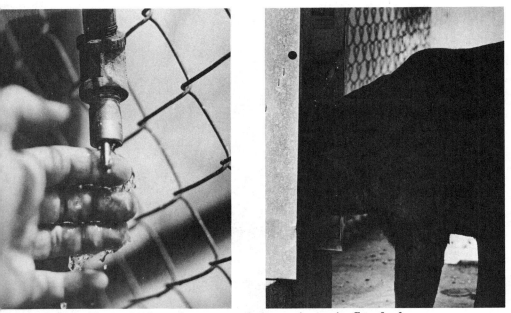

Tongue activated waterer and automatic gravity flow feeder.

If at all possible all dogs should be fed dry food with gravity flow feeders. And except where it freezes, all water should be automatically dispensed. Oh there's electric probes to keep water buckets open when the temperature hits zero, but can Pup reach the insulation on the electric wire and chew it off? And if you live in a hot climate and don't bury the water lines leading to each dog's bucket the water may be so hot the dog can't drink it.

Sanitation

If you're a city dweller who's decided to use a concrete run you better connect the drain trough to the sanitary sewer. Otherwise, Pup may generate too much stuff to spread around. And yes, though I prefer gravel, the city dweller will find cement easier to clean and keep free of feces, ice, snow, and dumped food. Plus, the concrete will satisfy snoopy city inspectors.

Make sure the shovel trough at the drained side of your run is both

422

This kennel has excellent drain: can accommodate shovel.

wide enough and deep enough to accommodate a standard shovel. Most people make these troughs too small. Design yours at least 12 inches wide and 12 inches deep. That way most shovels will enter the space and grass cuttings or blown leaves won't clog the drain and overflow the trough.

If you live in suburbia, or on a farm, disposal holes may be dug with the auger on your tractor's power take-off, or they can be stabbed in by hand with a post hole digger.

Drop Pup's feces in the hole, top it with a little dirt, and keep building.

Shipping Crate

To save the interior of your station wagon—from all that water and mud Pup will shake—buy an aluminum crate. Not one of those wire things, but a four-sided aluminum crate with an aluminum bottom and top. To give Pup a comfortable ride throw a couple of boat cushions in there, or some cedar chips, or straw.

If you can't road your dogs, then walk em.

Remember! These crates can get mighty hot. Keep plenty of ventilation circulating about, especially when your car is parked.

And should you buy a crate that has no holes at the top, get a punch and open it up. That's where heat goes. Up. Let it escape.

Roading

By the time Pup's placing in the open or amateur he's fairly well trained. Your function now is to keep him conditioned: both physically and mentally. So road him. I've never known a great champion who didn't hoof it out in harness. Corky did. And Don Beauchamp's Buddwing, the hi-point red setter of all time, and all of Delmar's national champion Brittanys and all of Bob Wehle's national champion English pointers—they were all roaded.

Here's how it's done:

Buy Pup a sled dog harness. Proper design calls for all load be borne by the chest and front curve of Pup's shoulders. Snap on your check

424

Cricket poses in sled dog harness. Check cord's snapped. Cricket pulls trainer about back yard. Heavier the pull, greater the value.

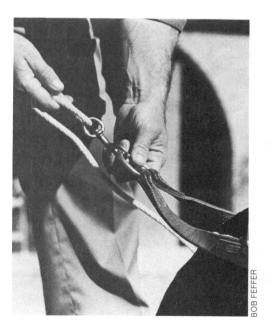

425

Pointers pull pickup with motor turned off.

Yellow Lab falls behind on treadmill as operator raises speed: note pull on dog's collar.

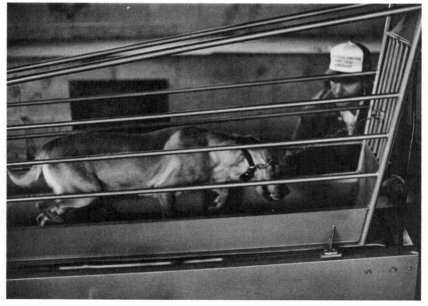

cord and tell Pup, "Hie on." Let him pull you about. You walk along and lean back. Matter of fact, to pull is imperative. That's why you can't road Pup with a bicycle, for example. You set up no resistance. Pup must pull against something.

When Pup's pulling against your hand, or arms, then transfer him to car, tractor, pickup. Put the vehicle in low gear, edge along about eight-miles per hour, and watch Pup pull. Quite frankly, this becomes an obsession with most dogs. And generally speaking, one-hour's pulling in harness equals three-hours running free, and I mean running hard.

If it's a hot day, don't put Pup in harness. Instead, make him swim along behind the boat as you paddle about the pond.

Most trainers road one day and train the next. It's a good routine. And how can you tell when Pup's had enough? When he drops his tail. It's that simple to monitor.

I'm pleased to report that after several years testing there's a new product on the market to help you keep Pup conditioned. It's an inclined variable drive treadmill which permits you to road Pup inside a building come rain, ice, wind, or heat. It works. And it works not only for Pup but for the trainer as well. Matter of fact I want you to get on the treadmill before you stick Pup on it. Learn what's happening to him. You'll not leave the timer on so long when Pup's first started after you've come out of there—exhausted.

Birds

You can't train a bird dog without birds. The easy-keepers are pigeons. Trap your own in barn lofts, atop flour mills, in church belfries, railroad roundhouses, under bridges, wherehaveyou. If that's too much trouble, contact your local pigeon racing fanciers. They always have culls they wish to sell.

As I said up front, all a pigeon requires is a pen, a limb to perch, a nest, a pan of food, another of water, and some place to get in out of the wind. Pour a concrete floor for easy cleaning.

You can transport pigeons about in a gunnysack or make yourself a pigeon tote: wood or metal, with inner-tube sections overlapped to form an entry through which you can stick your hand and clutch a bird.

If you're not in a building mood then buy a pigeon trap from any gun dog supply house and make it your portable crate.

Gamebirds can go to field in most any container. A pigeon trap: note swinging bobs. A wood box. Or a homemade contraption with innertube strips for reclosable door.

Bill Connor carries typical poultry box on top his dog trailer. Note holes at top of trailer compartments to vent air.

Margaret Dance's Lab chews bone midst promenade of poultry: old fashioned European barnyard staunches a dog . . .

. . . Maury Smith maintains such a barnyard in downdown Phoenix: ducks in pond, birds in hutches.

Shipping

The fast way to get Pup from point A to point B is airfreight. There's hardly a spot in America, anymore, Pup can't be at a nearby airport in four hours.

Always send Pup, just Pup, and nothing else. No food. No water. And never any tranquilizers. Food he can go without for days. Water for hours. And dope forever.

Buy Pup one of those molded plastic shipping crates sold by all airlines. They may be the biggest dog house bargain in America today. That's why some of the airlines will no longer sell you a crate unless you've got your dog in hand and ready to ship—they've had a run on economical dog houses. I can only criticize this crate on two points: one, pups will eat out the pressed paper flooring, and two, there's no need for the water dish. It sticks in the door like you were keeping a parakeet.

The reason these crates are good for airfreight is their sides are not straight up and down. They angle out to keep adjacent boxes from cutting off Pup's circulation. Besides, the front's wide open; just a cross wire gate, and Pup can get air there, too.

We've all heard horror stories about pups on airlines. Some stories claim Pup was lost. Or crushed. Or asphyxiated. Even that he froze to death.

Now I've had dogs miss planes because ground crews wouldn't move out. And I've had dogs miss planes because airlines refuse to ship several hi-priced dogs on the same flight. But all in all, I've never lost a dog. I've had em end up in strange places. But heck, I've had airlines do worse than that with me.

Breeding

If you own a stud worth having there's going to be bitches sent for seed. Now some of these gals can come in mighty bulled up. And a dog is helpless before an aromatic bitch. So help your dog. If necessary, hold the bitch's head. Don't let her turn and snap. And when the two are finally coupled, don't let the bitch run into a dog house and leave Pup spread-eagled against the front wall.

Also, put the bitch in a secure kennel. Dogs can climb the highest mountain, swim the deepest sea, when there's sex involved.

And give the dam's owner his money's worth. Stand the bitch twice in case the first mating doesn't take.

431

Dr. Jake Mosier with mongrel pup in Kansas State University research center.

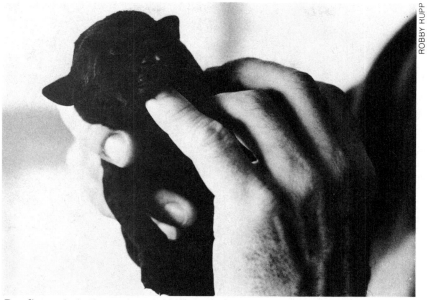

Put fingertip in Pup's mouth. If he's an effective nurser you will feel the suction.

If you have a mistake; a bitch gets bred by the wrong stud, you've got 48 hours to get her to a vet for a shot that'll knock most pregnancies.

Whelping

And should you own the bitch she may need help·in whelping.

Dr. Jacob Mosier, head of the veterinary school, Kansas State University, possibly the world's foremost expert on keeping puppies alive from inception through weaning—and a class act as a human being—tells us:

One. It's imperative a dam have animal protein in her diet to help assure a healthy litter. An ounce of liver per meal may reduce litter mortalities from 60 to 20 per cent. And Doc says, if you think 60 per cent mortality is high then you're not keeping records on your litters.

Two. The first puppy born is usually large or normal in size. It's later pups in line that can, and will, be the runts. Maybe it all relates to how pups are stacked in the uterus, but it's later pups that will need your attention.

To give Pup artificial respiration open his mouth with finger tips. Hold him before you at arms length then throw him toward floor with arms swinging between legs. Centrifugal force will throw foreign matter from respiratory tract.

Three. Runts indicate insufficient animal protein in the dam's diet. Small placentas carry small pups and it's not known for certain but chances are the size of the placenta is also determined by the dam's diet.

Four. Runt pups are usually weak pups which means they are ineffectual nursers. They just don't have any suction. They quit nursing not because they're full but because they're fatigued.

Five. The first 48 hours are critical for puppy survival: one portion of the litter will gain weight at the 12th hour, but at 24 hours another portion will have lost less than 10 per cent of their body weight. And still another portion will have lost more than 10 per cent. It's this last group that's in trouble: 30 per cent of them usually die.

Six. Ineffectual nursers have no suction due to poor muscle tone, deficient energy. But also, ineffectual nursers are pups that never get a good first-gasp in life.

Seven. Runts don't breathe well. Therefore they become hypoxic.

434

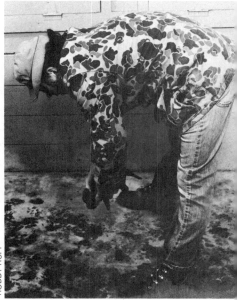

435

That is, they don't get enough oxygen to supply the muscles of their body which in turn means they'll not achieve proper muscle tone.

Eight. It takes a burst of air sufficient to raise water in a tube 23 centimeters to distend a puppy's lung to full potential. This distention of the lung is determined by the first-gasp. The pup has no other chance. That's why doctors slap babies on the butt, to startle them and create a great first-gasp.

Nine. Also, if a pup's born feet first, which means he was in the birth canal too long, or his birth is accompanied with a green discharge, then this pup will be a poor breather. That green color appears because the placenta has started to separate. Whenever the placenta separates the oxygen exchange between dam and pup is reduced. Now, when the placenta separates sufficiently enough, say 10 to 12 per cent of the area comes loose, the pup will take his first gasp. And if he gasps inside the birth canal then he's going to inhale fluid.

Also, being born feet first, which means the pup's been in the birth canal too long, the pup will gasp prematurely and inhale fluid in a contaminated environment.

Ten. To clear a pup's throat of mucous, hold him before you with both hands, tail pointing toward your chest, and swing him out and down in a great arc, throwing the mucous out of his throat (see photos). Open pup's mouth with a finger, or two fingers, and keep throwing him down so the mucous can be hurled out and away.

Eleven. A pup's body temperature the first two weeks should be 94–97 degrees, second to fourth week 97–99 degrees, fourth week on, 100–101 degrees. These temperatures are recorded with a rectal thermometer.

Now, a pup can generate sufficient body heat to endure a temperature seven degrees below normal. That is, a two-week old pup, that must have a body temperature of 94 degrees, can survive when his body temperature falls to 87 degrees. Remember this when you try to save a pup that's been pushed out of the litter by the dam. For this is precisely why she pushed him out: his body temperature dropped too low and she decided to sacrifice him in order to save the rest of the litter. How is she to know his ailment isn't contagious? Anyway, this is a present-day theory held by several scientists.

Twelve. But more important to us is the fact that when Pup gets chilled his digestive tract becomes paralyzed. Any food the pup takes just lays in his stomach: never digested. And this pup will usually die

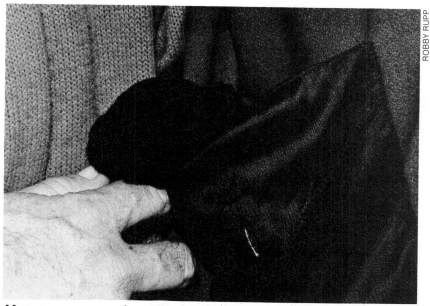

Men can warm a pup by putting him in inside coat pocket and going about their work; women can stuff pup in bra.

within 23 hours. Why 23 hours? Because all the pup's energy storehouse happens to be in his heart and liver at birth and that supply is consumed in 23 hours when there's no food supplement.

Thirteen. So the critical thing to do with a chilled pup is warm him up slowly. Why slowly? Well the first tissue to warm is the outer skin, then the subcutaneous tissues, and the moment these cells start to warm up they need more oxygen.

But what's happening? The cold puppy's respiratory rate has dropped from about 30 to 4 and his heart rate, which would usually be 220 under normal circumstances, has now dropped to 60.

The pup's still cold in the center and that's the delivery rate he's got going for him: his delivery rate for supplying oxygen.

So warm this pup up on the outside, the cells need more oxygen, they don't get it, so the cells die and there's hemorrhaging. This in turn kills the pup—because you tried to warm him too fast.

The best way to warm a pup is to place him in an inside coat pocket,

Two Lab pups: one five weeks, the other one week. The growth rate is phenomenal.

in your bra, or some place right next to your bare skin. Then go on about your work. Your body heat will gradually warm the pup, plus, your activity will jiggle the pup about and keep congestion from settling on a lower side.

When Pup's temperature reaches 94 degrees his breathing rate and his heart rate will return to normal, plus, he'll have the capability to suck a nipple. Return him to his mother and she'll accept him back in the litter and let him nurse.

Incidentally, you'll note a dam try to save a pup before she culls him. She licks him to raise his body temperature with her warm tongue, plus, the friction of the tongue jiggles and turns the pup's body to avoid congestion.

Also, this chilled pup can be helped by feeding him glucose. Pups are born with a little glucose but when that's used up they become low blood sugar.

Now, the colder a pup is the longer he can survive because his metabolism is low and he isn't burning energy very quickly. But if we warm him up we need to give him some energy producer. Thus, glucose.

Glucose can be used in the pup's body without any metabolism. All the pup has to do is absorb it. But table sugar? That's sucrose and has to be broken down—which takes energy and time. If you don't have glucose then use honey. If no honey then use Karo syrup. If no Karo then use sugar. Any supplement will be useful in getting Pup's blood sugar high enough so he will have the energy he needs to fight for his life.

Fourteen. A healthy, vigorous pup will double his birth weight by the time he's nine-days old. So weight gain can serve as your monitor to learn how well your litter is progressing.

Fifteen. And one final thing. A pup's body weight is 82 per cent water whereas a dog's is only 69 per cent. The pup requires 75 cubic centimeters of water per pound per day while a dog needs only 23 cubic centimeters. So Pups have a tremendous need for water: pound for pound, three times as great a need as an adult dog. Keep the water bowl full.

Sixteen. And last of all. If your bitch is undershot or overshot she can easily rupture a pup's belly button when severing the umbilical cord. Help her. Cut it yourself and tie if necessary. An excited bitch can also do harm to a pup when attempting to sever a cord: stay by and calm her, help her. Do the job for her if she proves too unstable.

So we've got Pup housed and cared for and we've got the tykes saved as best we can—there's still one thing we need to do before closing this book. We've got to learn first aid to assist Pup if he's hurt afield. Grab your swabs and stethoscope and let's get started.

18/First Aid

There's going to come days for you the way they've come for me. Like that time outside Kansas City—

I was campaigning a retriever who'd won two seconds in the open back to back. A first place would make his field championship and qualify him for the national open. The last series of the first day we were leading the pack when my contender stepped on a thorn, slightly puncturing a pad. I slapped some gunk on it, decided it wasn't serious enough for a vet, retired to my motel, got up the next morning to win my open—

I had a three-legged dog. We came in fifth. And you know? That dog never did win a first place. He had his day, every dog does, but I let him down.

So I went to a vet and talked him into staying after hours at his clinic teaching me first aid. That was 13 years ago and I became a tape and gauze nut. I was doctoring so many dogs in the field I should have been picked up for practicing veterinary medicine without a license. The dispensary in my kennel truck should have been on Noah's ark.

Between where I was pre-Kansas City, and what I became, there's a happy balance that should be you. So let's look at those injuries that may befall your dog afield and build ourselves a first aid kit, acquire ourselves a first aid knowledge.

I tell you the following in conjunction with Dr. Dick Royse, the man who helped us with chapter four, The Fit Pup; the man who stayed late those many years ago—and taught me.

Doc says, "There's no substitute for professional medical care, but every dog owner should know the basics of first aid for the sporting dog afield. Everyone, sometime, will have an ill or injured dog 50 to 100 miles from a vet. What eventually happens to that dog depends on what happens to him first. That's what it's all about, *first* aid."

Lacerations

Imperative! Stop the bleeding. Cut an 18-inch length of gauze and fold to two-inch square. Place as pressure bandage directly on wound. Hold firm. Bleeding stop? Fine. If you want to stay afield, remove compress, flush wound with distilled water, apply antiseptic, and fresh two-inch compress. Now wrap with gauze, ideally lapping 45 degrees to lay of bandage. Keep criss-crossing gauze, making a mummy-wrap. Don't cover gauze with tape, we want air to get to the wound. Secure gauze by catching hair with adhesive tape at edge of bandage.

But you say Pup has a cut pad and you want to keep hunting? Okay. Cover bandage completely with tape. Secure bandage by catching hair of Pup's leg. Pull old sweat sock over bandage and secure with tape to hair.

A rubber boot would be good protection for Pup at this time but it's usually too small to cover a fat bandage.

But what if the bleeding doesn't stop? Our compression bandage just won't stop the flow. As a last resort apply a tourniquet. And only as a last resort. Tourniquets can be more dangerous than the wound. For tourniquet material use a piece of rubber surgical hose, some two-inch gauze, Pup's leash, anything to apply pressure and twist in hand.

Imperative! Tourniquets should be applied just tight enough to control bleeding. No more. Tourniquet should be loosened every 15 to 20 minutes for about five minutes. Repeat sequence till Pup makes it to a vet. For that's where you and Pup are going. This wound is too major for field treatment. The same applies to any large-area wound.

Large-area wounds are treated differently than simple lacerations. For one thing, you don't apply water nor antiseptic. Not even if there's dirt in the wound. Antiseptics on a large wound may inhibit healing.

442

Too many antiseptics contain chemicals that are great for cleaning out bacteria, but most powders have talc as the vehicle to carry the medicine. Talcum inhibits healing.

Also, too many antiseptics destroy good bacteria as well as bad. You need to keep the anti-bodies alive to help heal Pup.

However, some vets recommend a small bottle of sterile, distilled water be carried to flush such wounds. It's your option—and your vet's preference.

And what about infection? Little concern. Takes about 24 hours for infection to become active and by that time Pup will be in a vet's care.

In administering first aid to lacerations there's several things you must remember. Never put cotton on a wound. The fibers stick. Also, remove a totally taped bandage as soon as possible. Let air in. Change bandage every day if Pup's kennel run is wet.

Also, never apply a bandage too tight. You'll stop blood circulation. Apply gauze firmly, but don't pull so the fabric stretches. When finished wrapping, you should be able to force your index finger under the bandage with minimal resistance.

On large-area wounds you may have to treat for shock—see below—and then move out fast.

And remember, a reflexive dog bite is an instinctual reaction to pain. And a reflexive bite makes a mean dog bite seem gentle as a bride's caress. To avoid being bitten, the dog must be immobilized, his muzzle closed.

Immobilizing and Muzzling

Precautions to be taken before attempting to administer first aid to a dog in pain include:

One, approach Pup from the rear and toss a blanket over him. Possibly he'll half-self-wrap and you can finish bundling. The blanket warms Pup to mitigate against shock and assists in his immobilization so he'll not further self-injure through panic-stricken-struggle.

Two, avoid reflexive dog bite by applying a muzzle. Take in each hand one end of a piece of rubber surgical hose, stand behind and above Pup, toss a loop of hose out over Pup's nose, let it swing under his chin, throw a half hitch in the hose, tighten. Pull half hitch as snug as you want. No way can you cut off Pup's breathing.

Three, if Pup's blanketed and muzzled, but still struggling, he must

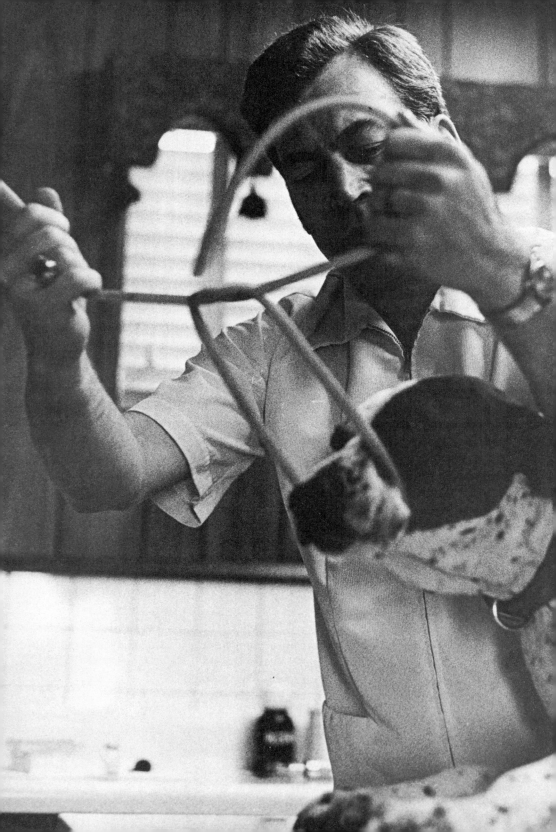

Doc Royse muzzles pointer with piece of surgical hose.

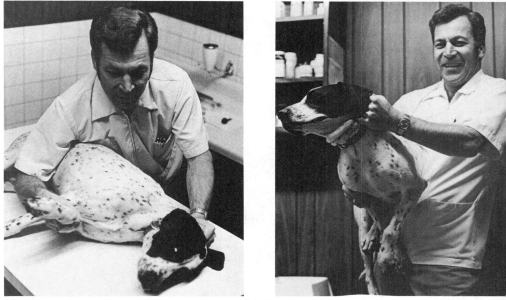

It's easy to immobilize and lift prone dog on high table . . .

be totally immobilized. Staying to the rear, drop to your knees, place Pup on his side with legs extended (see photos). Now lean forward and pin Pup's buttocks to the ground with your shoulder. Extend your arm forward to criss-cross and clamp Pup's front legs. Use your free hand to clutch several folds of skin at the scruff of Pup's neck. You've got him. You're not hurting him. Pup can't hurt himself. And he can't hurt you.

Four, to lift and carry Pup you must assure him a sense of balance. From the moment you start to pick him up, support him all the way. Don't let him feel he's going to fall: he'll panic and struggle. Release your hold on Pup's front legs—see three above—and slide hand back to the center of his chest. Bring that arm securely about his rib cage and over his rump. Pup's rear torso is wedged in your arm pit. The near-hand holding the scruff of Pup's neck is slid to side, adjacent to Pup's ear, so Pup can't turn his head and bite. Several folds of skin are taken in hand. You've got control. Now lift. Pup shouldn't feel he's going to fall. He's not able to kick. Neither can he leap forward. And he can't bite.

. . . but you've got to grunt and huff to raise him from field's floor.

Five, to walk Pup away, slide the far hand from his chest to grasp his far shoulder. Control is accomplished. Walk Pup to your pickup and drive to the nearest vet.

Punctures

Puncture wounds are treated the same as lacerations. But there is one exception. The foreign object that punctured Pup—piece of wire, glass, thorn, nail, fish hook—may still be in him. And it stands to reason so long as the foreign object remains, when Pup moves the wound may be aggravated.

So there's two things to do: one, try to remove the foreign object, but only if it comes easily. And I mean easily. Never use force. Or two, immobilize and muzzle Pup—if this is necessary—keep him quiet, and head for town.

Lab pup with fish hook puncture. Trainer had to enter pond and cut dog loose, carry him to truck, stand him on hood, snip hook, pull shank through hole, medicate. When accidents happen afield they happen lightning fast. Be ready.

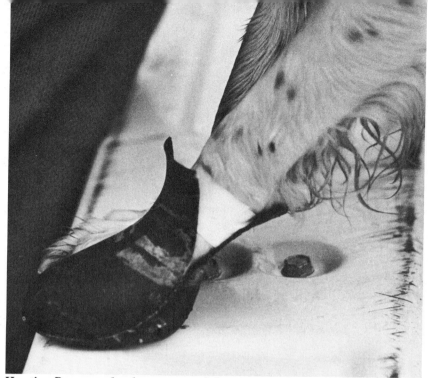

Hunting Pup on upland game several days in a row?

If the object stuck in Pup can be easily removed—let's say this is a minor wound—then pull it out and stop the resultant bleeding. Should you want to stay afield and keep hunting, then apply a bandage. But note: puncture wounds can be deceptive. How deep did Pup get stuck? So deep his wound may eventually appear to heal on the outside but infect within? If so, even though the foreign object comes freely to finger-pull, Pup should be retired for the day.

You'll generally find that punctured pads will cause Pup to lame-up the next day. And speaking of pads— Each of us must winterize our dogs. That includes roading, which gets Pup in shape but also toughens up his feet. Plus, there are skin-tougheners you can buy and apply. Doctor Royse's favorite is Coppertox, a product used to toughen horse's hooves.

Furthermore, rubber boots are recommended in briar and cactus country. Also, anyplace there's lots of rock. A rock can literally sheer a dog's pad right off his foot.

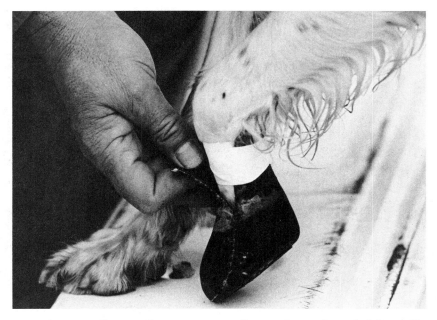

Then don't tape boots to fur, tape to tape. Bottom layer of tape is left on till hunt's completed for the week.

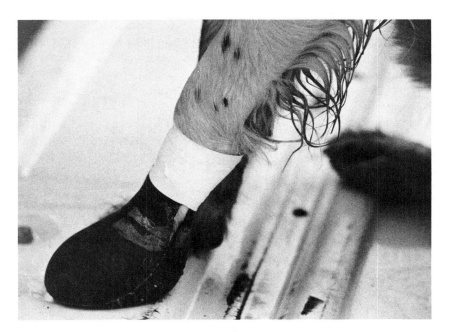

Fractures

Easy does it. Handle Pup gently. Keep him quiet. A struggling Pup can aggravate injury. Do not attempt to manipulate an injured limb— or feel about the torso, neck, or head.

Under no circumstances try to apply a splint. To attempt this you run a good chance of lacerating muscle tissue or severing an artery or vein with razor sharp bone splinters.

In case of suspected spinal injury slide Pup on a flat surface to be used as a stretcher and head for professional care. I once ripped the door off an abandoned ice box to use for this purpose.

And don't assume Pup's without fracture just because he's walking or running. Not three months ago I saw a house dog get hit by a car, breaking the pelvis in three places, yet, this little tyke ran home, entered the house and I'm told she crawled under a bed where she usually slept.

If you suspect fracture, treat for shock and head for professional care.

Shock

Shock is a canine corpsman's primary concern. Shock may occur with any serious injury. Symptoms are a docile Pup, depressed, semi-conscious or unconscious, possibly rapid panting, fixed stare to the eye.

Wrap Pup in a blanket and keep him warm, keep him quiet. In most cases of shock a dog experiences rapid drop in body heat. This must be brought back to normal—fast.

Approach Pup from behind and toss a blanket over him. Possibly he'll half-self-wrap and you can finish bundling. The blanket will warm Pup and also assist in immobilization.

Generally, if Pup's hurt bad enough to go into shock, he'll probably need a vet's care.

Heat Stroke

Signs of heat stroke can be rapid, heavy panting; raspy breathing; and with acute oxygen deprivation, Pup can literally collapse.

You must lower Pup's body temperature and do it fast. Even control-dump him in a cold stream. Remember, Pup's underbelly is comparable to a human's wrists. That's where the largest supply of superficial blood vessels is closest to the skin. This is where you concentrate your coolant. Should you have ice in a chest, wrap some in a cloth and apply to the base of Pup's skull for reasons discussed below. Or as a substitute for ice you can carry a bag of Kwik-Kold: the instant ice pack that's activated by striking the bag of white granules.

If Pup can drink, give small amounts of ice cold water at frequent intervals. Too much water, however, and Pup may vomit.

You've got to work fast with heat stroke. A dog's normal body temperature is 101.5. Heat stroke can send this temperature soaring. When body temperature rises it causes tremendous congestion which impedes circulation to the brain and this creates undue pressure, which in turn, may damage brain cells. That's why we apply ice to base of Pup's skull.

Incidentally, heat stroke may occur in the car as well as the field. A closed car under a summer sun can reach temperatures of 130 degrees in most temperate climates and 180—anyway it feels that hot—in the desert. When transporting Pup make sure he's got good ventilation, especially when your rig is stopped.

Frostbite

The natural inclination in treating frostbite is to do the wrong thing. Your impulse is to rub the affected areas; ears, tail, feet. Don't. If you rub extremely cold or frozen tissue you can easily fracture small capillaries in the peripheral blood circulation. When this happens it takes a long time for Pup's body to re-establish circulation in the affected area.

So, here's what you do. Soak a compress in warm water and apply moist heat to the affected area. Never apply a dressing. This, too, can damage peripheral circulation.

You can get warm water out of your car's radiator or use coffee from your thermos. And remember, frostbite is a subtle thing. There's usually no pain or discomfort suffered by Pup while his extremities are being frozen. It's your responsibility to be aware of critically cold temperature and not expose Pup too long at any one time.

But there is this; when it comes to heat or cold, Pup can take a heap of blizzard compared to but a bit of heatwave.

Poisons

Symptoms take two forms: one, incoordination, extensive nervousness to point of seizure and convulsion, and two, profuse vomiting and/or diarrhea.

A poisoned dog must vomit. This can be induced by giving one tablespoon of peroxide orally, or lacking this, then place one teaspoonful of salt on the rear of Pup's tongue. Save the vomitus and give to the vet for analysis.

Also, if Pup goes into seizure or convulsion you must protect him from self-injury. Wrap him in a blanket.

Toxic Exposure

If Pup contacts toxic or corrosive material—insecticides, crude pits in oil fields, acids, lyes—wash the skin with great amounts of water. Really flush him. And as with a poisoned dog, you must be prepared to wrap Pup in a blanket to avoid self-injury that may come from seizure or convulsions. Also, as you delivered the vomitus to the vet, you must also take the caustic agent for analysis.

Eye Injuries

It's difficult to evaluate eye injuries. They're usually more serious than they appear. You should do nothing more than flush the eye with common boric acid eye wash—if you do this much—and head for a vet.

In case of a seed or insect in Pup's eye, try to wipe it out—gently—with a tissue. Also, your vet can supply an eye lubricant I feel imperative for the field. Lubricant makes the eye tear excessively, constantly washing out foreign matter.

Spider Bite

Hard to detect in the field, for a hunting dog will usually ignore a spider bite. Yet, anywhere from three to seven days later Pup can likely show an area of dead tissue between the size of a dime and a quarter. The area will turn black, infect, and literally fall out. Don't attempt home treatment. Get Pup to a vet.

Snake Bite

Mandatory! Ignore the dog and kill the snake. Determine if it's poisonous. If you can't find the snake then look at the bite. Non-poisonous bites generally have a U-configuration and are multi-toothed. Such bites appear as superficial scratches and cause little pain. Cleanse the area well with an antiseptic and seek further treatment.

However, a poisonous snake usually leaves two fang marks. And, the victim may exhibit instantaneous, severe pain in the bite area. Depending on the potency of the venom—big snakes insert big doses, unless they've just killed, and some snakes are more poisonous than others—the dog may become incoordinate, vomit, convulse, or go into coma. If you don't get the dog to a vet within four hours the outlook for recovery is poor.

There's little you can do in the field for a poisonous snake bite. Get the snake. Keep the dog quiet. Permit no exercise which will stimulate venom's flow. Don't ever cut and suck: shades of winning the west.

Contain the venom by applying a flat constricting band—your belt's fine—between the location of the bite and the heart. Impede the flow of venom but don't block off arterial circulation: you are not applying a tourniquet.

A constricting band is properly adjusted if a finger can be inserted with minimal force. The band should be left intact until definite treatement is provided, or a maximum of two hours.

Now, here's the usual situation with a poisonous snake bite. You're hunting 200 miles from a metropolitan area. You take the bitten dog to a rural vet for treatment but the vet's a large animal doctor. He can treat Pup but he doesn't stock anti-venom. Yet, you do. That's right, you carry anti-venom to give to the vet to give to Pup.

Medical science is constantly improving anti-venom. Present shelf life is 12 to 18 months. That's under refrigeration. Yet, your car can get mighty hot. So carry anti-venom in a plastic bag within your ice chest, or in the tire well. Anywhere to keep the temperature as low as possible. When not afield, refrigerate anti-venom and buy a new kit often. Your vet can advise you.

And yes, once again you'll need to treat Pup for shock. Get him wrapped in a blanket.

One final thing, whether or not you apply ice to Pup's snake bite is up to you and your vet. It has been noticed, however, that iced appendages on humans suffering poisonous snake bites results in more amputations than for patients who don't use ice.

Accidental Gun Shot

Important! How far away was Pup when hit? This determines extent of tissue damage, how much shock to expect, how deep the pellets penetrated. If you accidentally shoot Pup close enough to knock him down you're going to be in trouble with a tremendous amount of shock. So, back to the blanket. Wrap Pup, keep him warm, get medical help as fast as possible.

However, let's say you just sprinkle Pup so he yipes, there's a few blood specks. You're probably not going to have any immediate problems. Cleanse area with antiseptic and either keep on hunting or head for a vet. It's up to you.

But if Pup's hit hard, and he comes through shock, he's going to be so muscle-sore he can hardly walk. This can be expected with any dog shot 40 yards or less.

So, if Pup's dusted with shot, treat in field. If he's knocked down, treat for shock and head for town.

Bee Sting

A bumble bee can knock Pup down. A flight of honey bees can drive him nearly mad. Make a baking soda paste and pile on one-half inch thick to affected area. Cover with damp compress and hold for 15 minutes. Follow this with an ice pack. The same treatment applies for wasp stings.

Burns

Move fast. For localized burns—say Pup touched the car's hot exhaust—apply ice, snow, your handkerchief saturated with water from a winter stream.

Yet, a large-area burn will cause shock. Now you've got to make a decision on priorities. Should you cool the wound or get the dog wrapped in a blanket? Large burns trigger Pup's body to consume great amounts of liquids. If Pup is not immobilized he will aggravate dehydration. Make your decision and proceed accordingly.

Incidentally, never apply ointment to a burn. That's just something Doc has to remove so he can proceed with treatment.

Choking

If you suspect something's lodged in Pup's throat, and you can handle his jaws so you don't get bitten, then open his mouth and pull the tongue out as far as possible. Now, can Pup inhale air? If he can't,

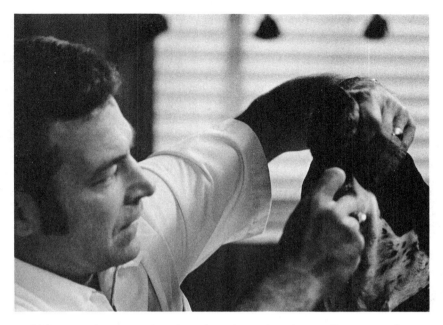

Fold lips into dog's mouth to keep from being bit, then pulling out and laying tongue to side, dog can't close mouth.

pick him up by his hind legs, hanging him head down, and give him a sharp slap either high across the back of his shoulders or across the front of his chest.

If a small object's lodged in the trachea it may jar out, or you may stimulate coughing which can blow it free.

Remember, never stick your fingers down Pup's throat. He may reflex-bite, and/or you might lodge the object even deeper.

To pull Pup's tongue from his mouth, compress the hinge of the jaw to force the mouth open, then continue to squeeze your thumb and forefinger on opposite sides of Pup's jaws, pressing the flesh of Pup's cheeks between his teeth. Now you can reach the tongue. Once the tongue's pulled out and laid to side, Pup can't bite.

Foreign Object In Ear

Hard to treat in the field. If there's anything in the ear deep enough to cause discomfort—Pup's shaking his head or scootching the side of his head along the grass or scratching at the ear with a paw—you probably won't be able to see it.

You may remove anything from Pup's ear you can reach with your fingers. For example, you might see a stalk of tickle grass in there. Pull it out. But, nothing smaller than your finger should ever be inserted.

Electrocution

Drag Pup from energy source with loop made of leash, belt, check cord—anything not wet and not a natural conductor.

Now you may be confronted with three simultaneous emergencies. One, respiratory failure. Induce breathing by artificial respiration. Lay Pup on his side, legs extended, place one or both hands flat in the middle of his rib cage three inches behind his shoulder, press firmly, listen to air expire, release abruptly. Repeat sequence 20 times a minute.

If Pup has stopped breathing you've got five minutes to get him started. After that time irreversible brain damage may already have occurred.

Two, Pup has been shocked. He's in shock. Treat for shock.

Three, treat for possible burns.

Drowning

Hard to drown a dog, except when a raccoon is taking a hound under. But strange things do happen: such as car accidents where Pup goes under water trapped in his crate. Your only assistance will be artificial respiration. See technique explained for electrocution.

Skunk Spray

Wash Pup in tomato juice if you want—if you honor this old wives' remedy. But I don't include tomato juice in our first aid kit. Skunk spray, far as I'm concerned, can only be alleviated by time. Tomato baths produce minimal benefit, plus, did you ever drive home with a gun dog soaked in tomato juice and skunk spray—him shaking all over the place?

Skunk spray does not affect a dog's scenting capability. Go ahead with your hunt. And yes, your dog got his rabies shot when you took him to the vet for his pre-hunting season check up. Right?

If Pup's sprayed in the face he'll usually head for water, then roll in dirt. Let him. This self-treatment seems to cut offensive odor about 40 percent. If you can't stand this 60 percent that remains there's one thing you can do. Build a fire, make lots of smoke, and short-tie Pup downwind. For some reason, smoke does clear the air.

Dog Fight

Injuries resulting from a dog fight can include broken bones, pulled teeth, dislodged eye balls, punctures, and lacerations. Be prepared to treat for shock. A dog fight can be your total calamity. Avoid them at all costs.

First Aid Kit

Our first aid kit contains 17 items called for above: 13 in the kit, four either on your person or carried in the car, plus whatever other items your own vet recommends.

Gauze bandage rolls, 2- to 4-inch width
Adhesive roll, 2-inch width
¼-inch rubber surgical tubing, 24-inches long
Blanket
Kwik-Kold instant ice pack

457

Boric acid eye wash
Antiseptic
Snake anti-venom
Baking soda
Old sweat sock
Bottle of sterile, distilled water
Salt or hydrogen peroxide
Eye lubricant
And, outside the kit, ice, hot coffee, tissue, and the belt from your pants.

The kit can be arranged in a cigar box, the cut-away bottom of a bleach bottle with plastic film cover secured by rubber band, a small fishing tackle box, a discarded brief case, whathaveyou?

This kit is generally adequate for retrievers, considering all they traditionally do in the field. But should you hunt your retrievers as you would a pointer or springer then it will also be necessary you carry two additional tools: one, a pair of bolt cutters to cut Pup out of a wire fence should he get hung up while leaping it, and two, a set of toenail clippers in case Pup splits or throws a nail.

Conditioning

Ever notice, it's the athlete out of shape that usually gets hurt. Part of Pup's health care includes good conditioning. As Doc Royse says, "Most of us are very conscious of keeping our car tuned periodically. We expect performance at its best. Try applying the same principal to your gun dog and you'll be pleasantly surprised.

"A visit to your vet 30 days before hunting season will pay dividends. That hunting companion of yours deserves a complete physical examination, parasite check, heartworm check, vaccinations, etc. Then, once it's established he's okay to hunt, give him a break, don't break him.

"Work him every day, extending the duration of each work period until he's in shape. This will prevent a lot of sore muscles, possible seizure, sore feet, and styleless performance.

"And when season's over, are you going to put your dog in the kennel and forget him till next year? Once again he deserves diagnosis and tune up. He just spent several months in the field, working hard, enduring all kinds of weather, tearing through cover like a Sherman tank.

It's difficult keeping dogs in shape on the road.

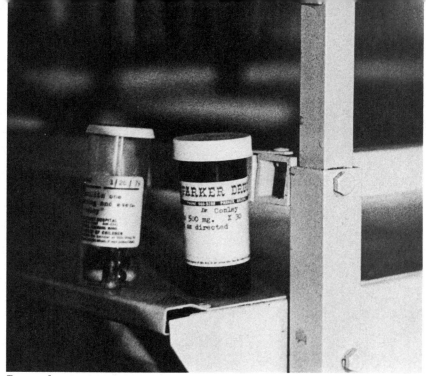

Remember to give prescription medicine to ailing pups.

Fill 1/4 oz. gelatin capsules with honey: give to Pup and take one yourself when energy starts to drain.

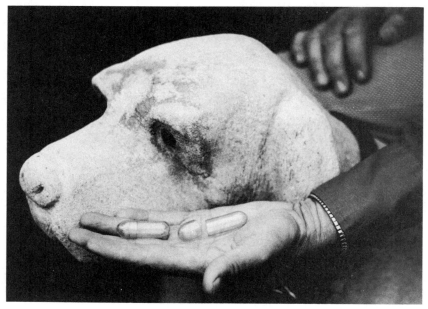

460

"It's just possible he may have picked up parasites, grass or awns in the ears, thorns in the feet— Let your vet check him out. But be sure he's in as good a shape after season as he was before. I can assure you—like that well-tuned car—you'll get a lot more mileage from him with such care."

Doc Royse and I may have touched upon your needs, your eventualities, your capabilities. Maybe not— Your own vet knows what's best for your dog in your country. Go talk to him. Get his advice. Pup needs that knowledge applied through you.

Now, let's go hunting.

19/Hunting Pup

"This is something that couldn't be done for a British writer," Don Revett, the decoyman of Nacton, tells me, "For it would bring the one thing that would destroy the decoy . . . people!"

I smile at Revett and tell him, "That's always the way journalists are received in Great Britain. Like the Queen's staff— They said the anti-blood sports would find fault if anything were disclosed about her gun dogs."

Revett asks, "Then you didn't get the Queen's story?"

"Oh I got it," I tell him.

"Then you must know someone high up," he reasons.

"Only God," I reply. And Revett smiles at me.

We continue walking up the path through the dark woods and I can hear the birds sing high in the trees, but not like American birds, instead, like music boxes, and I can feel the damp chill of this place on the front of my upper-legs and I can smell the national smell of England: mildew.

Occasionally the sun stabs through the heavy foliage to light the coat of Heidi, ". . . a brown, mongrelly dog ,,," as Revett describes her, and her coat gleams copper. She's a feisty, pinch-nosed, fluff of a thing. Bright and mischievous in the face. "From the dog catcher," according to Revett, "where all decoy dogs come from."

The Gazebo

I'm trying to catch sight of—to identify—the singing birds in the tall tree crowns, when I feel Revett's palm touch my chest. "Shhhh," he whispers. "See that gazebo up there? That's where we go. To the lookout. We'll see how the pond lays. For we have five pipes and from the lookout we can choose which one will give us the greater catch."

It's dark in the gazebo and the glass portholes are crinkled so when I try to focus my telephoto through them I get smudged ducks.

"Here, I'll help you," says Revett, removing a piece of wood from the wall, "that glass is 150 years old. Made by hand so it's not perfect."

I take pride in the glass, reasoning, if it were made by hand it has to be perfect.

Revett tells me, "I go now. Heidi and I will decoy the ducks. See those European widgeons ... and the mallards ... and the pintail ... right in front of the decoy pipe?"

I nod.

"Well, even though that pipe is slightly frontwinded ... and that's bad ... and even though that sunlight peers through now and again ... we'll use that one so you can get pictures. We'll see."

"Good luck," I tell him.

"Don't put your lens through that hole," he warns in parting, "Anything will spook these ducks."

Later I see man and dog—he's called the piper, and Heidi's the piper's dog—appear midst the screens along the south edge of the decoy pipe. What a complicated affair it all is. And so big. This has surprised me most—the decoy being so big. Maybe 20 feet high at the mouth, and just as wide, then tapering to one foot high at the tail. And the length of the thing? Sixty yards or so. And it's made of bent steel and woven rope netting.

I recall how long I've wanted to be here. Remember the first time I read the term "decoy" as being Dutch in origin. That was in Joel Barber's book, *Wild Fowl Decoys*. And Barber revealed the term "decoy" came from "Ende-Kooy," meaning duck-cage or trap. And he explained ducks were enticed up the decoy by working dogs. Yet— Everyone I knew was saying at the time, and still do, "Keep that dog down, it'll spook the ducks." And I was puzzled. How could a dog both gather ducks, yet spook them away?"

464

Near- and far-side decoys visible from gazebo: piper will work decoy that's backwinded.

So I vowed to one day see it all for myself. And I came none too soon. For this is the last working decoy—out of 400 in the 18th and 19th centuries—to still be worked in England. And Heidi is the last decoy dog.

No longer are ducks harvested for market with the decoy, which was the case till 1966, but now, instead of having their necks wrung, they have their legs ringed. That's what the British call banding. They "ring" em.

And this Nacton decoy, located on the southeast coast of England, presently operated by the Wildfowl Trust (comparable to our Audubon Society), was the most successful decoy of them all. Operated for over 100 years, it was. And until Revett took over, it had been worked the previous 55 years by Tom Baker, Revett's father-in-law. And Baker took 200,000 ducks from here—with a dog.

Market harvest was never outlawed in Great Britain. It's still legal: but no longer profitable. That's why the decoymen stopped. Just not enough birds. And it should be noted in passing, Great Britain feels the game belongs to the land owner. That he will be the best game warden.

So there is no "federal" warden, and each land owner does as he sees fit. Tom Baker worked for the owner of this estate. Baker caught ducks as a job, just as another man would milk cows, gather eggs, or fall timber. And all Tom's ducks were logged in the estate ledgers. That's why we have such an accurate tally: even to species taken. That's why Baker's 200,000 ducks are fact.

The Decoy

This decoy resembles a Calabash pipe laid on its side. You know? Made from a gourd, like Sherlock Holmes' great pipes. And the Calabash has a large opening, a bend in the middle, and a small end—just like this decoy.

Along the working side of the decoy, erected on the bank, is a series of woven grass screens.

First off, just next to the water's edge, are 12 dog screens, all laid in line, but standing at angle to each other. Like slats in a venetian blind. The dog is run about these screens to appear before the first one, disappear, then appear before the second, and so on.

Don Revett casts Heidi about breastwork screen to dislodge resting ducks.

Behind the dog screens is the running screen. When the ducks are enticed to the bend in the pipe, the decoyman heels his dog and runs back to the large opening at the entrance, waves a handkerchief and flushes the decoyed ducks up the tapering tail of the pipe to the waiting trap. Then the decoyman runs back, still behind the running screen— for there are trailing ducks still in the pipe the piper does not want to see him—and drops a guillotine door to trap the decoyed ducks.

If the decoyman merely ran behind the dog screens, the ducks in the pipe would see him pass each opening—and flush. Also, we now learn why the pipe is bent. One, so the incoming ducks can't see they're headed into a trap, and two, so the piper may drop the guillotine door without ducks still in the pipe, or on the pond, seeing what happens.

Now there's one more screen on the working side. That's the breastwork screen. You see the whole two-acre pond has been purposely built and cultivated so steep banks and foliage surround the perimeter—everywhere except right next to the pipe's entrance. So the ducks climb up on this cleared, low bank and sun themselves. Both the

Heidi lures ducks up pipe. Revett casts her about dog screens —monitoring her harvest by peeking through woven reeds. Heidi exits and enters by hopping beams: which means she appears and disappears in a flash. For some reason, this fascinates ducks.

population of wild ducks, plus the 100 tame call-mallards. The call-mallards give the place a lived-in appearance, plus tranquility.

When there's a commotion in the pipe, the wild ducks still on the pond look to see the call-mallards at peace in the pipe. They're in the pipe for that's where they are fed. Seeing the call-mallards at repose, the wild ducks relax.

So the piper's procedure is this:

He puts his dog about the breastwork screen to flush the idling ducks into the water, just before the pipe's mouth. Then the decoyman starts running the dog about the screens, which entices the startled and angered ducks up the pipe. Revett explains, "The startled ducks are generally the ones to swim up the pipe; the ones to decoy. Having been flushed they seem to take the greater umbrage at being disturbed and they are quite eager to follow the dog. And I suppose, also, the fact there are ducks flushing off that landing draws attention to the rest of the pond that a dog is present."

To finish explaining the construction of the decoy— There's one more screen to the other side of the water inlet. It serves as a blind to keep ducks on the pond from seeing what happens to their brethren who swim up the pipe.

Now, why does all this work? How does the dog lure ducks? NO ONE KNOWS. I repeat, NO ONE KNOWS. Not even Tom Baker who took 200,000 ducks from the decoy. Nor Peter Scott, world-famed ornithologist who founded the Wildfowl Trust and leased the Nacton decoy. But everyone has a theory.

Popular in Great Britain is the supposition the ducks, feeling there's safety in numbers, mob the dog. But I can't accept this. Crows mob an owl, e.g., but it's a noisy affair. Yet, ducks approach the decoy dog in silence.

I offer instead the simple fact that ducks, having found a pond they like, decide to stay—even though they spy a predator. Their solution is: just keep an eye on the rascal. He can't do any harm if all the ducks know where he is. Then when the dog is no longer seen? Out of sight, out of mind!

Heidi runs one screen after another, receiving a treat at the end of each cast. Ducks follow her progress up the pipe.

When ducks are halfway up pipe, Revette heels Heidi and runs back to entrance where he flashes handkerchief spooking ducks to fly into trap.

Hunting

And what does the decoy teach us about duck hunting? Plenty.

Tom Baker and Don Revett tell us, ''Never go around ducks unless you carry an ember of peat. You must have a smoke screen or the ducks'll smell you and leave.''

Tom further offers, ''Never speak while working ducks. A man's voice will lift them off the pond. For a duck to hear you is worse than his seeing you.'' This is why Heidi, and all decoy dogs, work only by hand signals. Plus, they learn the sequence. Dogs, as we now know, are very loyal to sequence. When Baker first trapped ducks for the Trust to ring and release them, his old market dog went nuts, trying to leap in the air and catch them. ''You just don't throw em away,'' was the dog's frantic observation, ''You break their necks.''

Tom Baker and Don Revett also agree: one, ''Ducks will not swim across a shadow laying on the water. They stop before it, just like it were a wall. So never build your duck blind where it will cast a shadow on the water ... or so there's timber behind the blind that will cast a

Revett drops guillotine door, traps captured ducks, transfers them to gunnysack and short-ties Heidi who likes to play with her catch.

shadow." This is why, they say, you shouldn't hunt ducks on a sunlit day: shadows.

Two, "Ducks will decoy to most any animal in the pipe." Tom Baker reveals, "I've seen em decoy to rabbits playing on the bank beside the inlet." And Revett tells me, "The other day I went down and the pipe was loaded with ducks. I was astounded. Then I noticed, there was a coypu playing in the water (a coypu is a large rodent, similar to the nutria in Louisiana). Only the coypu's head showed above the water," continues Revett, "but when he swam he left a wake, and all the ducks followed him."

I ask the two of them, "Why is it a piper always chooses a red dog? To resemble a fox?"

And they tell me, "Oh yes. But it needn't be a red dog. That's the tradition. But then, who's to say all ducks have seen a fox to begin with? And then there's the other thing ... we've seen ducks decoy to a black cat walking the side of the pipe."

Then Revett discloses, "At Slimbridge, the Trust's headquarters, they have a pipe but no dog. You know what they use to decoy ducks? They stick a stuffed fox on a pole between the dog screens. And it works. Just as waving a gunnysack works."

And Baker cautions, "Never work against the wind. That's the thing. Always build your decoy so the wind is either quartering or blowing down the back of your neck. Any other way ... to have the wind blowing in your face ... you'll not take a duck.

"And never let yourself be seen by the ducks, to be sure, but the dog— He can be seen all you want. Just make sure you keep him moving. And moving slowly. He can't stop and look at the ducks. It makes them nervous. He must be moving along and ignoring them. Then they'll follow."

This prompts Revett to remember. "It's any sudden move that lifts the ducks from the pond. A splash. That'll do it. We've all seen that ... like with a fish.

Hunting is what it's all about: an afternoon on creek of tinkling water and golden leaves . . .

"Take the coypu. As soon as the coypu shows itself the ducks go to it . . . they swim towards it. But then, if he goes and dives, or makes a sudden maneuver, they all flush away from him.

"Same as they will for a dog. So long as the dog moves slowly and quietly and shows no aggression of any sort, the ducks are quite happy. They'll follow it. But if the dog stops working and turns toward the ducks, and looks at them, they immediately stop and get very nervous . . . and sometimes flush away, or swim away from the dog."

Pup At the Duck Blind

Revett and Heidi trapped 12 ducks at Nacton the day I was there, but I left with knowledge tapped off 200 years of duck and duck dog experience. And if you think I didn't stay long, there's a reason. Only in very special circumstances, in connection with the Trust's research program, is anyone permitted to visit the decoy. The Trust made a great exception in my case and I thank them. But even my one-day presence at the pond disturbed the ducks. It was time to go.

Besides, I had what I'd come for: the harpoon to kill a myth. I

Hunting Pup Afield

Use Pup as you like when hunting upland game birds. In this book we've seen retrievers used to point, flush, and retrieve.

My primary concern for Pup afield is covered in our chapter on first aid. Don't let him get exhausted, become too thirsty, or get foreign matter lodged in feet, coat, or eyes. Check him often.

And remember, so many pheasant habitats are dusty, brittle, and dry. Pup can lose his nose to dust. Honor that.

Honor, too, ultragreen foliage, such as alfalfa, that can deny Pup's nose.

But Pup will please you, no matter how you use him. And he'll show nose you can't imagine. Like Keg of Black Powder, diving in snow banks to flush buried pheasants. Or Rene, leaping into a stream and diving under to retrieve a rock I'd plunked there. Or Poodie, my house dog, who trailed me to the elevator in a hospital the other day—jumped out of the car, serpentined through a block of parked cars, entered the pneumatic doors, managed the hallways, and stationed herself at the door to the lift. That's nose.

In it all, my wish for you, is happy hunting!

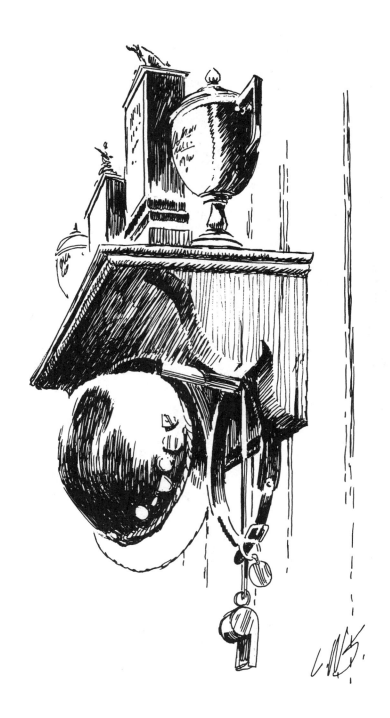

20/Trialing Pup

It's quiet now. Night has tucked the wind to sleep. That prairie wind— So insistent on having its own way. Slapping back limbs, scraping out dirt, so's not to trip its coming and going.

I'm glad it has had enough go its way to leave off for the day. Now I can hear God's murmuring life. The flutter of chimney swifts behind the kitchen stove. The zing of window screens when the June bugs bounce back. The great horned owl south of the pond dam with his nightly inquiry, "Who cooks for you?"

I hold to these soft treasures. As Robert Frost, America's rustic wordsmith, held to the crow in *Dust of Snow*. Frost penned, "The way a crow shook down on me the dust of snow from a hemlock tree has given my heart a change of mood and saved some part of a day I had rued."

Our days, I fear, are rued because of the rude. Like now. I must plug into the nation's paranoia. I must turn on the TV. TV's and telephones can be rude. But that's another matter. Tonight the President relates our energy crisis.

So the chimney swift's flutter and the June bug's zinging and the owl's soft hoots must give way to statements of peril.

Before the tube I slouch and attend. The President smiles and talks and I am passive. Then he says these words, "Reward those who conserve, penalize those who waste," and I leap in cheer.

That's it. That's what I've said all along. And now we have a leader who's got his head on straight. For if he's a man of his word(s) then what's good for gasoline has to be good for gadwalls. If the credo applies to fuel it must apply to fowl.

And I shout, "Hurray," in joy of sanity, man, nature, and dog.

For I've said all along, and say here again, any man who goes to wetlands with a trained retriever deserves a bonus of birds. And the President must agree. "Reward those who conserve," are his words.

And he must also concur, those who go for ducks without this 40-yard arm—that's what a trained retriever is, a canine device whereby man can reach out 40 yards and pick up a bird—should be penalized for wasting. Though retrievers are also used for upland game that's not my concern: some upland game we can raise in a pen and release. Suffice to say, I'll leave it to the governmentalists to work out the details. Praise be, the President's given the assignment. Or at least the spiritual leadership.

Yet I know. I'm off on a lark. What's good for propane won't apply to pintail. It's motorists, not mallards, we want to perpetuate.

But I was going there for a minute, wasn't I? I saw every wildfowler with a retriever at side, training this canine conservationist to heel, sit, stay, fetch, back, get over, come in. I envisioned every bird shot plopping in the pot. Instead of floating days later against the shoreline, belly up, where the snapping turtles snatch at its back and the crows peck at its gut.

American Kennel Club

And in that giddy moment when I thought man could be true to nature as well as a gasoline pump, could apply common sense to the marsh as well as the motor car, could grant man a bonus for bringing every bird to hand with a trained dog, could penalize, or at least embarrass, every man who'd go for birds ill-conceived and ill-prepared minus the services of a retriever—I thought how AKC has shown the way. Has already established the tests and testing procedure, the judges and the judging to determine criteria for bonus dogs.

AKC did this for retrievers with the field trial. Duplication of a sportsman's day afield. The shooting and casting-for and harvesting upland game and waterfowl. The making certain no matter the clime of day nor lay of land whatever's shot is fetched.

If America just had that alone it would up it's bird harvest 40 per cent. No, that isn't a government figure. That's my figure. Compiled from years of trying to get to a duck blind at a public marsh and having to verbally force my retrievers each step of the way for, if not, they would bring me my limit of ducks from yesterday's deadfall and I'd have to go home with this gathering of someone's neglect.

AKC does not envision its service to man as bird conservationist. Instead, AKC is chartered as a registrar and credentials trustee of pure-bred dogs. But, through field trials sanctioned and licensed by AKC upon the petition of interested sportsmen, AKC has entered the field trial business. And the result of this is gamebird conservation.

Granted, AKC oversees many breed trials: Brittany, Beagle, Basset, Pointer, Setter, various continental breeds, etc., but AKC's service to bird as well as dog is singularly pronounced in the retriever program. It stands to reason, a retriever retrieves. What's knocked down he picks up. No bird is lost. Whereas, other breeds are cast to seek, the retriever is cast to fetch.

Without field trials, Americans could never have known just how well a distant falling bird could be discovered and brought to hand. Never could they have envisioned the miracle work of retrieving dogs without AKC testing.

Field Trials

So, field trials are not a game people play. Field trials are work people perform who respect God's gift of bird so much they don't want to lose a feather.

Field trials are one of the few legacies left where man understands God's plan and plans his life to fit it. That's remarkable in an age converted to man-made-man, where nature is wired to a toggle switch.

The field trial man accepts Genesis: no, that's not a new rocket program. The field trial man accepts the teaching he was given dominion over the bird, the bird was given as man's sustenance, and the dog was given to get the two together.

A field trial is that place, that process, where good retrievers are made great. Not in a year. Not in a generation. But in lifetimes of breeding, training, studying, handling, and vying to produce that superlative animal that never lets man down by never failing to fetch a bird up.

Field trials are where dogs and men get happy. Never talk to a field trial man about the cruelty of working dogs. Yes, I know— Retrievers

America's seasoned retriever judge, Dale Lundstrom (1), and national open winner, John Honore, stand tightlipped in appraisal of passersby on way to run the derby. August Belmont rubs neck in concern of upcoming test while retriever glances about, nonchalant.

are ordered to elbow up on ice flows, charge through dusty rowcrops in a high sun, snake through bramble, mincefoot over jagged points of beaver-sharpened sticks in a log jam. But look at the tail— Count the beats. Look at the grin behind the bird stuffed in that dog's face. Look at those cocked ears. Hear the whine on line, "Let me at it ..." If man no longer understands his place in the universe, don't let him assume all God's creatures have become equally confused and trivial.

Field trials are where Nodrog Penny, one of the two most inspirational retriever bitches I was ever privileged to witness, breaks ice to fetch a trio of birds then hops in a station wagon to suckle her litter. Where the gritty Chesapeake, Dilwyne Montauk Pilot, enters Great South Bay for a swimaway duck and doesn't get back for two series. Where 11-year old River Oaks Corky—for the first time in his life—breaks on two birds in two opens because his master and mistress have permitted another retriever in the house. Breaking is a puppy-fault, but

Field trials are good times:

A gals' talkfest . . .

500-point Corky conceived this way to register his disappointment at this breaking of the faith.

Field trials are sacrifice. Each to his own brim. To August Belmont, the patient years of working through the AKC chairs—as his father before him—to serve dogdom within four walls when his life is afield. A million dollar grant by John Olin for creation of an Orthopedic Foundation for Animals to combat hip dysplasia. The 150 weeks (that's three years of a man's life) given by Dale Lundstrom in judging assignments. The plus-two years given by John McAssey. Bill Connor, the epitome of bachelor neglect, one red sock and one blue, cooking 200 hamburgers at Pueblo to pick up the banquet tab and underwrite the club. Owning a hot dog, too hot to keep kenneled, and knowing you'll never have the finances and time to campaign him as he deserves so you're Stan Gacek, printer, and you sell the best dog you'll ever know—for you'll not stand between him and his destiny. Or you're Pete Jones, seasoned amateur, and others like him who go out of their way to welcome the newcomer, make him feel welcome, explain the game, help him win, and ask him back.

484

... the trophys and trappings of trying, a festooned straw pooch at open house, and a tailgate offering for hungry passersby.

Field trials are hilarity. The bellowing incredulity of a John Love when he discovers the Dallas blind planter has built an open fire and is roasting pheasant. No wonder the dogs keep sucking over there. World renowned attorney, Oscar Brewer, and industrialist, Bing Grunwald, tooling to Omaha from a field trial in separate cars when arrested for allegedly speeding. Oscar dazzling the local justice of the peace with dog work in the courtroom—so's to derail the judge's mind from fines and think of the accused as humanists due to their love of animals, especially since they didn't have a penny between them—then the judge concluding, "Guilty." Dave Elliot driving two black Labs, sitting in the backseat of Jay Carlisle's Dusenberg, to the first field trial in America—who'd ever seen a black dog?—and the filling station attendant asking, "Where you taking those dogs?" Answer, "To a trial." Pause, "What are the dogs charged with?"

Field trials are heartbreak. School teacher Jim Culbertson with brilliant Keg of Black Powder qualified for the only national the man could ever afford to campaign up to—finding on the second day of the running his diminutive performer has come into season. Dr. Gene Starkloff seeing his dogs coast down the bank in the car—to drown in the training pond. Mahlon Wallace, Jr., unable to leave his car, watching at a distance through the windshield, as Baird's Centerville Sam wins the 1973 national open under the capable handling of Tom Sorenson. Missing the brusk banter of Ted Fajen because his throat possibly hurts and no longer does he shout at me in jest, "Whatever possessed you to call a dog PeePee?" for I was running one named Pepe.

Field trials are seeing nature for the first time—especially concrete cave dwellers. Studying the way the wind blows, the lay of the land, the run of the pond's waves. Realizing it makes a difference whether an animal has a right- or left-hand lead.

Field trials are a reaffirmation of the old barn raising spirit. For the have-nots budgeting the five-spot it takes to join their local club. And tossing birds at trials. Toting gunnysacks of decoys. Rowing the boat. Building a plank bridge. Posting the traffic signs. And turning their back when the girl with her first derby entry goes out in the first series and holds her dog in the front seat of a pickup and cries into his neck-fur for an hour.

Field trials are driving 1,000 miles on a weekend with one pup to compete in a field of 100. Making bird boys of wife and toddlers. Having high hopes and little payback. Except— Except for standing there with clammy palms, daring not even to pray the dog won't bend

486

It's a long line of spectators at this national amateur running in Wisconsin. And a large field of helpers at a Florida national open. Field trials call for sacrifice, dedication, and a willingness to share.

This is where it all ends: Field Trial Hall of Fame. Bing Grunwald (checkered blazer) attends charter meeting at author's request to represent the retriever world. Bill Brown, publisher, American Field *(center of photo with hands flat to coat), is lifeblood of the hall. Delmar Smith (fifth from right) serves as Hall's first executive director.*

to the bank, that he'll hold his line through the hourglass of land and launch on to sea to fetch the bird floating on a shingle, held fast by a clothespin.

Field trials are accepting the responsibility of a living creature. Rubbing the coat for ticks and gagging with disgust when you find one big as hominy. Designing kennel runs so the tail's wag won't de-fur the tip. Trying to keep cool water in a desert, running water in Alaska. Helping the dam in delivery. Waiting for the white-faced elder with the arthritic limp. Convincing the pup, box turtles are not what you want in hand. Poking feces with a stick looking for worms. Lowering the car windows so there's circulation.

Field trials are knowing dogs. Studying pedigrees. Saving pennies to get a pup from that once in a lifetime mating. Traveling abroad and planning your itinerary to visit all the heralded kennels. Always keeping your eye out in a barnyard for a dog that shows potential, or noting the country beside the interstate for a likely training pond. Always listening another man out when he's talking dog.

Field trials are beauty. Where wind and water and web-footed dogs are wed to purpose. Where dogs make people good, more than the other way around. Where the rules of the game are fair and impartial and may the best dog win. Where the luck of the draw teaches us something of life. Where second best never wins first. Where to be first mantles one with humility, not conceit. Where success does not thrust forth the trophy but sets the challenge.

Field trials are where no two dogs show equal, but all men come out that way.

Field trials are the proving ground dedicated to enhancing fur and conserving feather.

To Bed and Dream

So, Mr. President, I know you were thinking of off-shore oil, not off-shore ducks, when you gave your reward and penalize statement. But if you ever have a shift in priorities, I know an outfit that determines whether dogs are bonus or not.

But I can see the evening is late— Need to turn the dogs out to tinkle. Can't hear the owl. He's swooping somewhere for dinner. And the chimney swifts have gone to sleep. The June bugs? They lie on their backs on the concrete patio and whir in fizzle.

To bed and dream. Of ducks up north building their nests. Of the President in Washington solving our mess. Of dogs and man and bird— And the old Labs will sigh at my footboard, for they dream, too. Grand dreams like I just had where man could be natural and sensible, maybe for the first time. And we could put a program into our marshes, instead of protests. And those who conserve really could be rewarded. A dream where dogs finally have their day.

Index

Photos by Bill Tarrant with special credit to Dorothy Carter, Bill Connor, Bob Feffer, Jack Hays, Joan Ludwig, Harry Morgan, Jack Nelson, Robby Rupp, and Delmar Smith.